TRIALS OF 1971
BANGLADESH GENOCIDE

Through a Legal Lens

TUREEN AFROZ

PARTRIDGE

To order additional copies of this book, contact
Toll Free 800 101 2657 (Singapore)
Toll Free 1 800 81 7340 (Malaysia)
orders.singapore@partridgepublishing.com

www.partridgepublishing.com/singapore

CONTENTS

Dedication

This book is dedicated to

the three million martyrs of

the 1971 Liberation War of Bangladesh.

Acknowledgement

This book is based on research conducted on the International Crimes Tribunal (ICT-BD) trials of genocide that happened during the 1971 Liberation War of Bangladesh. This work would not have been possible without the partial financial support of the Centre for Genocide Studies (CGS), University of Dhaka. This book contains a modified version of my PhD research work on criminal justice.

I would like to express my profound feeling of gratitude to my reverend supervisors *Prof. Dr. Jerry E. Carlson*, Professor, Department of Law, American Independent University, California, USA and *Prof. Dr. Zahidul Islam*, Professor, Department of Anthropology, University of Dhaka for their sincere cooperation, proper guidance and constant trust upon my capability to carry on this research.

I am grateful to all of those with whom I have had the pleasure to work with. Specifically, I would like to express my special thanks of gratitude to *Md. Pizuar Hossain*, Lecturer, Department of Law, East West University, Bangladesh for his tremendous assistance in discussing the relevant issues, and providing critical comments that greatly improved the quality of this research work. I have been immensely benefitted by the last moment proof-reading by the young researcher *Ms. Esrat Jahan Siddiki*.

I express my sincere gratitude to various national and international scholars, academics, activists, and practitioners who offered their valuable comments and critics during many national and international conferences in which I presented various parts of my research work included in this book. Some of them also provided me one-to-one guidance to fine-tune many of the arguments presented in this book. I would like to explicitly mention some of their names, such as (in alphabetical order) *Dr. Adam Jones*, Professor of Political Science, University of British Columbia (Canada); *Judge Agnieszka Klonowiecka-Milart* of the Extraordinary Chambers in the Courts of Cambodia (Cambodia); *Dr. Alexander Hinton*, Director of the Centre for the Study of Genocide and Human Rights, Professor of Anthropology, and UNESCO Chair in Genocide Prevention at Rutgers University, Newark (USA); *Dr. Anuradha Rai*, Assistant Professor of the Amity University (India); *Dr. Daniel Feierstein*, President of the International Association of Genocide Scholars, Director of the Centre of Genocide Studies at the National University of Tres de Febrero in Buenos Aires, Argentina, Professor of the University of Buenos Aires and National University of Tres de Febrero (Argentina); *Judge Daniel Horacio Obligado*, a Member of the Argentinean Tribunal (Argentina); *Dr. Delwar Hossain*, Professor of the International Relations, University of Dhaka (Bangladesh); *Ms. Elizabeth Silkes*, Director, International Coalition of Sites of Conscience (USA); *Judge Fowzul Azim*, Chief Research Officer, Law Commission (Bangladesh); *Dr. Helen Jarvis*, Advisor to the Royal Government of Cambodia (Cambodia); *Mr. Helmut Scholz*, a Member of the European Union Parliament (Germany); *Mr. Hiranmoy Karlekar*, Consultant Editor of *The Pioneer* and former Editor of *Hindustan Times* (India); *Dr. Imtiaz Ahmed*, Professor of the International Relations, University of Dhaka (Bangladesh); *Dr. Irene Victoria Massimino*, Professor, University of Lomas de Zamora (Argentina); *Dr. Jayanta Kumar Ray*, National Research Professor, Government of India (India); *Mr. Julian Francis*, Social Worker (Uk); *Dr. Katharina Hoffmann*, Member of the Working

Group Migration – Gender – Politics at Carl Von Ossietzky University Oldenburg (Germany); *Birprotik Kazi Sazzad Ali Zahir,* Lieutenant Col., (Retd.), (Bangladesh); *Mr. Man Sokkoeun,* Human Rights Activist (Cambodia); *Mr. Manosh Ghosh,* Journalist (India); *Dr. Md. Rahmat Ullah,* Professor, Department of Law, University of Dhaka (Bangladesh); *Dr. Mesbah Kamal,* Professor of History, Dhaka University (Bangladesh); *Mr.Michel Gottret,* Special Adviser to the Task Force for Dealing with the Past (Switzerland); *Ms. Mina Watanabe,* Secretary General of the Women's Active Museum on War and Peace (Tokyo); *Mr. Mofidul Haque,* Trustee of the Liberation War Museum (Bangladesh); *Mr. Mohssen Arishie,* Managing Editor, Egyptian Gazette (Egypt); *Dr. Muntassir Mamoon,* historian and Bangabandhu Professor, University of Dhaka (Bangladesh); *Mr. Niran Anketell,* Attorney at Law and Director, South Asian Centre for Legal Studies, Colombo (Sri Lanka); *Mr. Paulo Casaca,* Founder and Executive Director, South Asia Democratic Forum and a former member of the European Parliament (Belgium); *Mr Shahriar Kabir,* Writer, Journalist and Human Rights Activist (Bangladesh); *Mr. Sheikh Hafizur Rahman,* Associate Professor, Department of Law, University of Dhaka (Bangladesh); *Mr. Thomas A. Dine,* Faculty Member, Prague Leadership Institute (Czech Republic); and *Dr. Trudy Huskamp Peterson,* Archival Consultant and Certified Archivist (USA).

Further, I want to thank my colleagues *Prosecutor Zead-al-Malum, Prosecutor Sultan Mahmud,* and *Prosecutor Barrister Tapas Kanti Baul* of the Office of the Chief Prosecutor, ICT-BD who allowed me to quote their remarks in this book. I would also like to thank *Mr. Md. Abdul Hannan Khan,* Coordinator and *Mr. M. Sanaul Huq,* Co-Coordinator of the Investigation Agency of the ICT-BD who provided valuable insights to carry on this research.

Finally, I express my deepest gratitude and admiration towards *Prof. Dr. Mohammed Salim Bhuyan,* Vice President, American

Independent University, California, USA for his constant and valuable encouragement to accomplish this difficult task amidst my extra-ordinarily busy professional life.

Above all, I want to thank my only child, *Tejoshwee Tureen (Shumedha)*, who has been my inspiration to carry on this research work for the future generation of the world.

Tureen Afroz

Chapter 1

Introduction

1.1 Introduction

During the Liberation War of 1971 in Bangladesh, the Pakistani Army and their local collaborators launched several systematic and planned attacks against the pro-liberation Bengali people.[1] Specifically, the attack was initiated on the night of 25 March, 1971 by launching the 'Operation Searchlight'.[2] The Liberation War of 1971 continued for long 9 months when the brave hearted people showed their sacrifices for Bangladesh disregarding the arduous and torturous journey of achieving the victory.[3] Many men, women, and children were indiscriminately killed, many women were reportedly raped, properties of the people were robbed as well as destroyed, and so on.[4] As a matter of fact,

---

[1] *The Chief Prosecutor vs. Mir Quasem Ali*, ICT-BD Case No. 03 of 2013 [ICT-BD 2] at page 7 at para 11.

[2] *Id.*

[3] *The Chief Prosecutor vs. Professor Ghulam Azam*, ICT-BD Case No. 06 of 2011 [ICT-BD 1] at page 8 at para 11.

[4] *Abdul Quader Molla vs. The Government of the People's Republic*

compared to other historically inhuman incidents such as bombing throughout the cities of Hiroshima and Nagasaki; death in the gas chamber by the millions; the horrors of the concentration camps, and the war in Vietnam etc.,[5] the atrocities of 1971 which were committed by the Pakistani Army and their auxiliary forces as well as collaborators were the most heinous one.

Taking into account the nature and patterns, the inhuman attacks launched by the perpetrators in 1971 can be viewed as the worst genocide in the history that took away several lives of innocent people. The massacres conducted with deliberate plans and targets which allegedly amount to the "crime of genocide" because the plans were essentially designed to disarm and liquidate Bengali policemen, soldiers and military officers; to arrest, kill and round up professionals, intellectuals, and students. As far as the target groups are concerned, primarily the national group along with both the religious and political groups have been targeted specifically the Bengali military men of the East Bengal Regiment, the East Pakistan Rifles, police and para-military Ansars; the Hindus; the Awami Leaguers; the college and university students; and the Bengali intellectuals.[6]

In short, the non-exhaustive list of the crimes committed against the Bengali people of Bangladesh by the perpetrators include widespread atrocities; tortures; inhuman, humiliating, degrading, and cruel treatment; hostage taking; disappearances; executions

---

of Bangladesh, represented by the Chief Prosecutor, International Crimes Tribunal, Dhaka, Bangladesh, Criminal Appeal Nos. 24-25 of 2013 at page 4.

[5] *The Chief Prosecutor vs. Muhammad Kamaruzzaman*, ICT-BD Case No. 03 of 2012 [ICT-BD 2] at page 15 at para 7.

[6] Anthony Mascarenhas, *The Rape of Bangla-Desh* (Delhi: Vikas Publications, 1972) at pages 116-17.

without trials; and use of rape as war weapon.[7] Approximately, 30 lacs people were killed, 2-4 lacs women were raped, about 1 crore people were deported to India as refugees, million others were internally displaced, and properties were destroyed.[8]

It has already been portrayed that not only the Pakistani Army but also their local auxiliary para-militia forces, and local collaborators perpetrated international crimes in horrendous magnitude in 1971.[9] As a first initiative of bringing the local perpetrators under trial, the *Bangladesh Collaborators (Special Tribunals) Order*, 1972[10] was enacted which was, nonetheless, repealed on 31 December, 1975.[11] Subsequently, the *International Crimes (Tribunals) Act, 1973 (ICTA)* was enacted which came into force on 20 July, 1973 even though no Tribunal was set up at that time.

Later on, the International Crimes Tribunal -1 (ICT-1) and the International Crimes Tribunal-2 (ICT-2) were formed on 25 March, 2010 and 22 March, 2012 respectively. The Tribunals have jurisdiction to conduct trials relating to the detention, prosecution and punishment of the persons responsible for

---

[7]   Wardatul Akman, "Atrocities against Humanity during the Liberation War in Bangladesh," (2002) 4 *Journal of Genocide Research* at pages 543-59; Yasmin Saika, "Beyond the Archive of Silence: Narratives of Violence of the 1971 Liberation War of Bangladesh," (2004) 58 *History Workshop Journal* at pages 275-87.

[8]   Archer K. Blood, *The Cruel Birth of Bangladesh: Memories of an American Diplomat* (Dhaka: UPL, 2002); Ashfaque Hossain and Umme Wara, "The United Nations and the International Crimes (Tribunal) Act 1973 of Bangladesh," (2014) *Journal of the 1st Winter School* (Center for the Study of Genocide and Justice), Liberation War Museum at page 11.

[9]   *Quader Molla, op. cit. no. 4.*

[10]   *President's Order No. 8 of 1972.*

[11]   The *Bangladesh Collaborators (Special Tribunals) (Repeal) Ordinance*, 1975, Article 2.

committing the crime of genocide, crimes against humanity, war crimes etc. between 25 March and 16 December, 1971 in the territory of Bangladesh. This book, however, focuses on the "crime of genocide" committed by the perpetrators and the trials of the same by the International Crimes Tribunal of Bangladesh (ICT-BD).

1.2 Research Objective

After about 40 years of the Liberation War of Bangladesh, some of the war criminals who are responsible for committing the crimes of genocide have been given punishment by the ICT-BD following the trial processes. It has been proved before the ICT-BD that the perpetrators were liable for committing or aiding/abetting/contributing/facilitating/conspiring to commit the offence of genocide during the War of Liberation in 1971. Many victims and witnesses, both eye witnesses and part-eye witnesses, of such grave offences provided their testimonies before the ICT-BD based on which, *inter alia*, the perpetrators were convicted and sentenced. In this research, the main objective, thus, is to explore the trials of genocide from the Bangladesh perspectives. Not only that, this research aims to explore certain new and unique trends and rationales of the ICT-BD genocide trials concentrating on the first 20 cases of the same.

1.3 Research Question

The ICT-1 decided 19 cases and the ICT-2 decided 11 cases so far in which most of the charges were brought on the 'crimes against humanity' and a few charges were brought on the 'crime of genocide'. However, the overall experience of the genocide trials of the ICT-BD is still unexplored. To explore this issue, it is essential to find the reasons as to why only a very few charges on the "crime of genocide" were brought and proved during the trial process of the ICT-BD. Along with, what are the up-to-date trends of the trials of genocide of the ICT-BD have yet to bring into spotlight. Curiously, what are the rationales behind such trends need to be highlighted in connection with the challenges that the prosecution faced, if at all and the observations of the ICT-BD regarding the genocide trials.

For this purpose, this research would endeavour to come back with the view-points of the historical perspectives of Bangladesh genocide, remarkable features of the *ICTA*, analysis of the first 20 cases pointing out the total number of genocide charges brought in each concerned case, brief accounts of the accused persons, and deliberations of the ICT-BD focusing on the genocide charges only. Henceforth, this research is significant because even after the decisions of the 30 cases of the ICT-BD, no authoritative research work on the overall experience of the genocide trials of Bangladesh has been done yet.

1.4 Research Methodology

The methodology employed in this research work includes both the qualitative and quantitative approaches on the "genocide trials" and their "trends" and "rationales" from the ICT-BD perspectives. The theoretical approach gives an overview of the historical backdrops of the 1971 Liberation War of Bangladesh focusing on the incidents, and authoritative comments and findings of the crime of genocide committed by the Pakistani Army, their auxiliary forces, and local collaborators; fundamental features of the *ICTA i.e.* conducting trials in absentia, the right to bail, right to appeal, right to invoke review proceedings, and to apply for clemency to the President of Bangladesh; understanding the crime of genocide and its genocidal group and intent requirements along with the methods of committing the same.

For this purpose, this research is based on an analytical approach and a critical appraisal on the first 20 cases of the ICT-BD: (1) *the Chief Prosecutor vs. Moulana Abdul Kalam Azad*, ICT-BD Case No. 05 of 2012; (2) *the Chief Prosecutor vs. Abdul Quader Molla*, ICT-BD Case No. 02 of 2012; (3) *the Chief Prosecutor vs. Delowar Hossain Sayeedi*, ICT-BD Case No. 01 of 2011; (4) *the Chief Prosecutor vs. Muhammad Kamaruzzaman*, ICT-BD Case No. 03 of 2012; (5) *the Chief Prosecutor vs. Professor Ghulam Azam*, ICT-BD Case No. 06 of 2011; (6) *the Chief Prosecutor vs. Ali Ahsan Muhammad Mujahid*, ICT-BD Case No. 04 of 2012; (7) *the Chief Prosecutor vs. Salauddin Quader Chowdhury*, ICT-BD Case No. 02 of 2011; (8) *the Chief Prosecutor vs. Md. Abdul Alim @ M. A. Alim*, ICT-BD Case No. 01 of 2012; (9) *the Chief Prosecutor vs. Ashrafuzzaman Khan @ Naeb Ali Khan & Chowdhury Mueen Uddin*, ICT-BD Case No. 01 of 2013; (10) *the Chief Prosecutor vs. Motiur Rahman Nizami*, ICT-BD Case No. 03 of 2011; (11) *the Chief Prosecutor vs. Mir Quasem Ali*, ICT-BD Case No. 03 of 2013; (12) *the Chief Prosecutor vs. Zahid Hossain Khokon*, ICT-BD Case No. 04 of 2013; (13) *the Chief Prosecutor vs. Md. Mobarak Hossain @ Mobarak Ali*, ICT-BD Case No. 01 of 2013; (14) *the Chief Prosecutor vs. Syed Md. Qaiser*, ICT-BD Case No. 04 of 2013; (15) *the Chief Prosecutor vs. A. T. M. Azharul Islam*, ICT-BD Case No. 05 of 2013; (16) *the Chief Prosecutor vs. Moulana Abdus Sobhan*, ICT-BD Case No. 01 of 2014; (17) *the Chief Prosecutor vs. Md. Abdul Jabbar Engineer*, ICT-BD Case No. 01 of 2014; (18) *the Chief Prosecutor vs. Md. Mahidur Rahman & Md. Afsar Hossain @ Chutu*, ICT-BD Case No. 02 of 2014; (19) *the Chief Prosecutor vs. Syed Md. Hachhan alias Syed Md. Hasan alias Hachhen Ali*, ICT-BD Case No. 02 of 2014; and (20) *the Chief Prosecutor vs. Md. Forkan Mallik @ Forkan*, ICT-BD Case No. 03 of 2014.

Furthermore, the overall analysis will be contextualized based on many Statutes and judicial decisions of certain Courts/Tribunals *i.e.* ICT-BD, International Criminal Tribunal for the Former Yugoslavia (ICTY), International Criminal Tribunal for *Rwanda (ICTR), International Criminal Court (ICC), Special Court for Sierra Leone (SCSL), and the Nuremberg Military Tribunals (NMT) etc.. Again,* relevant reports, books, journal articles, and internet materials have been used and considered to discuss the core issues of this book.

1.5 Chapter Outline

This book incorporates 6 distinguished chapters on the introductory outlooks; the historical backgrounds of the 1971 Liberation War of Bangladesh; the features of the *ICTA*; trials under the *ICTA*; trends of the ICT-BD genocide trials; and the rationales behind the trends on genocide trials.

Chapter 1 discusses the introductory historical perspectives of Bangladesh genocide that took place during the 1971 Liberation War. It also includes the primary history of enacting both the *Bangladesh Collaborators (Special Tribunals) Order,* 1972 and the *ICTA* and constitution of the Tribunals. Significantly, this chapter describes the research objective, research question, research methodology, and overall observations and the outline of the chapters of this book itself.

Chapter 2 explains the historical aspects of the 1971 Liberation War in detail pondering on the various incidents of Bangladesh genocide. It has been found that the perpetrators targeted primarily the "national group" along with both the "religious" and "political groups" specifically the Bengali military men of the East Bengal Regiment, the East Pakistan Rifles, police and para-military Ansars; the Hindus; the Awami Leaguers; the college and university students; the Bengali intellectuals such as professors and teachers *etc.* The atrocities were initiated by executing the 'Operation Searchlight' on 25 March, 1971 night which ended with causing an estimated 30 lacs people's death, rape of 2 - 4 lacs Bengali women, about 1 crore people's deportation to India as refugees, internal displacements of million others, and destruction of many properties. This chapter also includes the initial emergence of the *Bangladesh Collaborators (Special Tribunals) Order*, 1972 and subsequently, the *ICTA* and constitution of the ICT-BD (ICT-1 and ICT-2) in 2010 and 2012 respectively. Not only that, this chapter talks about the trials under the *Bangladesh Collaborators (Special Tribunals) Order*, 1972 which explores that the process of such trials started from April 1972.[12] Most relevantly, the thorough Parliamentary debates of enacting the *ICTA* have been portrayed in this chapter. Lastly, a brief of the ICT-BD trials of the first 20 cases have been given at the end of the chapter which have been broadly described in the chapter 4 of this book.

Chapter 3 mainly concentrates on ongoing debate concerning whether ICT-BD trials meet the international standard or not. It explores the features of this law to respond to such concern. For this purpose, this chapter focuses on the fundamentally significant features of the *ICTA* addressing the issues of internalization of international law; supremacy of the 1973 *Act*; formation of a domestic tribunal to conduct trials of the accused of the offences of genocide, crimes against humanity, war crimes, and other crimes concerning violation of international law. After that, one

---

[12] Wali-ur-Rahman, "Background Notes on Adoption of 1973 International Crimes (Tribunal) Act, 1973," (2014) *Journal of the 1st Winter School* (Center for the Study of Genocide and Justice), Liberation War Museum at page 106; Caitlin Reiger, "Fighting Past Impunity in Bangladesh: A National Tribunal for the Crimes of 1971" International Centre for Transnational Justice, Briefing Paper, July 2010 at pages 2-3.

of the major features *i.e.* sentences provided under the 1973 *Act* has been discussed in detail focusing on the circumstances in which the death sentence should be given to the convicts. Further, this chapter also focuses on the ambits of the definition of genocide in detail and the provision of conducting trials in *absentia* together with the rights of the accused including the right to bail, right to appeal, right to invoke review proceedings, and to apply for Presidential pardon. It must, essentially, be stated that all the above mentioned features of the 1973 *Act* have been discussed drawing the concerned international perspectives of the international criminal law.

Chapter 4 briefly discusses the first 20 cases emphasizing on the charges brought against the convicts and the sentences awarded to them by the respective Tribunal. This chapter finds that the prosecution brought specific and direct genocide charges in 10 cases out of 20 cases of the ICT-BD and succeeded in proving its charge only in 7 cases. There were 200 charges in total brought in these concerned 20 cases in which conviction took place in 130 charges. Among all, there were 35 charges brought in relation to genocide while 12 charges have been managed to prove before the Tribunal by the prosecution.

Chapter 5 endeavours to find the "trends" of the trials of the ICT-BD focusing on the charges in relation to genocide. Generally, trend analysis, involves the practice of gathering information with a view to attempting to spot a pattern or trend based on the same. For this purpose, this chapter focuses on the first 20 cases of the ICT-BD which are listed in research methodology part. The thorough study of these cases mainly shows 6 separate trends in this chapter including *i.e.* "Lesser Number of Genocide Charges", "Less Number of Genocide Charges Compared to Incidents of Mass Killing", "Categories of Genocide Charged", "Group Identification", "Conviction Rate of Genocide Charges", and "Punishment for Genocide Charges".

Chapter 6 refers to the trends explored in chapter 5 that the prosecution brought lesser number of genocide charges; and less number of genocide charges compared to the "mass killing" incidents. Again, the prosecution considered only "killing" as the method of committing the crime of genocide while in certain charges the prosecution faced legal challenges to establish group identification requirement. Moreover, the overall conviction rate of genocide charges and the punishments awarded for the same have been explored. After identifying those trends of the genocide charges of the relevant cases, five rationales behind such trends have been explored with the critical appraisals of the prosecution and the ICT-BD.

1.6 Conclusion

To sum up, it can be said that after the Liberation War of 1971, the people of Bangladesh finally achieved the victory on 16 December, 1971. However, the perpetrators committed many atrocious and dreadful crimes during the 9-month long wartime. However, the *ICTA* includes mainly the crimes of genocide, crimes against humanity, and war crimes to try such perpetrators who are responsible for committing the same during that period of time. The trials of some of the perpetrators have been conducted and convicted accordingly by the ICT-BD following the required procedures. The crimes for which the perpetrators have been tried are mainly the "crimes against humanity" and the "crime of genocide". Therefore, this book focuses on the comprehensive research of the trials of genocide in the ICT-BD from the 1971 Bangladesh genocide experiences. In doing so, this book explored some trends and rationales of the ICT-BD genocide trials which are significant *per se*.

Chapter 2

Historical Background of Bangladesh Genocide and ICT-BD Trials

2.1 Introduction

'[During the Liberation War of Bangladesh] [a] young freedom fighter was arrested by the Pakistani army in Rohanpur area of Rajshahi in June 1971. Despite terrible torture, he refused to disclose any information. A Pakistani major finally held a stengun to his chest and said, answer my question or I'll kill you right now. The fearless young freedom fighter bent down and kissed the ground of his motherland for the last time, stood up straight and said, I'm ready to die. My blood will free this country.'[1]

---

[1] *The Chief Prosecutor vs. Syed Md. Qaiser,* ICT-BD Case No. 04 of 2013 [ICT-BD 2] at page 6 at para 17; See also, Siddiq Salik, *Witness to Surrender* (Karachi: The University Press Limited (1st ed.), 1997) at page 104.

Many of such atrocious incidents took place in Bangladesh as a part of organized or systematic and planned attack by the Pakistani militaries in 1971.[2] The contemporary world has witnessed many grave crimes against humanity such as bombing throughout the cities of Hiroshima and Nagasaki; death in the gas chamber by the millions; the horrors of the concentration camps, and the war in Vietnam etc.[3] However, the brutal attack on the people of Bangladesh by the Pakistani army is the most heinous one that happened as an outcome of central planning and conspiracy hatched at *Larkana* and reinforced at *Rawalpindi* by General Yahya Khan and other Generals.[4] The attack was initiated on the night of 25 March, 1971 in which the main targets were mostly the civilians of Bangladesh and the Bengali paramilitary forces *i.e.* East Pakistan Rifles and Police on the basis of their ethnic identity.[5]

From 1947 to 1971, the people of the then East Pakistan (now Bangladesh) have observed several incidents while almost all of the time; they were deprived of their rights.[6] However, more particularly, in the long 9 months War of Liberation in 1971, the road to achieve freedom for the people of Bangladesh was arduous and torturous, smeared with blood, toil and sacrifices but the brave hearted people of Bangladesh showed to the entire world that true patriotism and sacrifices for the motherland can protect its self-worth.[7] Perhaps no nation paid as dearly as the

---

[2] *The Chief Prosecutor vs. Mir Quasem Ali,* ICT-BD Case No. 03 of 2013 [ICT-BD 2] at page 7 at para 11.

[3] *The Chief Prosecutor vs. Muhammad Kamaruzzaman,* ICT-BD Case No. 03 of 2012 [ICT-BD 2] at page 15 at para 7.

[4] S. A. Karim, "Triumph and Tragedy," (2009) *The University Press Limited* at pages 172-176.

[5] *Id.*

[6] See below Part 2.2 and accompanying texts.

[7] *The Chief Prosecutor vs. Professor Ghulam Azam,* ICT-BD Case No.

people of Bangladesh did for their freedom.[8] Many men were killed, women were raped; in a word, the people of Bangladesh had been robbed of everything they owned except their spirit of making their country as free from every kind of exploitation of the West Pakistani Authorities.[9]

It must be mentioned here that the inhuman attack of 1971 can be regarded as, *inter alia*, the worst genocide in the history that took away several lives of innocent people.[10] It is claimed that the indiscriminate killings of innocent and unarmed civilians with the planned and deliberately pursued intention of exterminating the people of Bangladesh were the common scenarios of that period.[11] In general, widespread atrocities; tortures; inhuman, humiliating, degrading, and cruel treatment; hostage taking; disappearances; executions without trials; and systematic rape were mostly committed by the West Pakistani militaries and the local collaborators.[12]

---

06 of 2011 [ICT-BD 1] at page 8 at para 11.

[8]   *Id.*

[9]   *Abdul Quader Molla vs. The Government of the People's Republic of Bangladesh, represented by the Chief Prosecutor, International Crimes Tribunal, Dhaka, Bangladesh*, Criminal Appeal Nos. 24-25 of 2013 at page 4.

[10]   See below Part 2.2 and accompanying texts.

[11]   *Ibid.*

[12]   Wardatul Akman, "Atrocities against Humanity during the Liberation War in Bangladesh," (2002) 4 *Journal of Genocide Research* at pages 543-59; Yasmin Saika, "Beyond the Archive of Silence: Narratives of Violence of the 1971 Liberation War of Bangladesh," (2004) 58 *History Workshop Journal* at pages 275-87; Raunaq Jahan, *Eyewitness Accounts: Genocide in Bangladesh* (New York: Garland Publishing, 1997) at pages 26-41.

In the war of 1971, Pakistani troops, their local auxiliary para-militia forces, and local collaborators perpetrated international crimes in horrendous magnitude.[13] For the purpose of bringing the local collaborators under trial, the ICT-1 and subsequently, the ICT-2 had been formed under the purview of the *ICTA*.[14] Through the passage of time, this matter had solicited both national and international attention that created a standard example of justice to the people.

2.2 The Liberation War of 1971: Perspectives of Bangladesh Genocide

In 1971, Bangladesh was born as an independent State following its Liberation War against the then West Pakistan (now Pakistan). Nevertheless, from the year of 1947 when the division of India into two countries such as India and Pakistan took place, the people of Bangladesh started to be aware of establishing their own identity.[15] The two-nation theory was the basis of the said partition which gave birth to two new States, one a secular State named India, and the other the Islamic Republic of Pakistan.[16] Essentially, this theory concluded to the creation of Pakistan that was comprised of two geographically and culturally separate zones to the East and the West of India.[17] The western zone was eventually named as West Pakistan and the eastern zone was named as East Pakistan, which is now Bangladesh.[18]

---

[13]   *Quader Molla, op. cit. no.* 9.

[14]   Available at <http://ict-bd.org/ict1/>.

[15]   *The Chief Prosecutor vs. Zahid Hossain Khokon @ M. A. Zahid @ Khokon Matubbar @ Khokon*, ICT-BD Case No. 04 of 2013 [ICT-BD 1] at page 2 at para 2.

[16]   *Muhammad Kamaruzzaman, op. cit. no.* 3 at page 5 at para 2.

[17]   *Id.*

[18]   *Professor Ghulam Azam, op. cit. no.* 7 at page 5 at para 5.

After the creation of Pakistan, the Pakistan Government eventually started to adopt and execute certain discriminatory policies backed by its bureaucracy and Army to rule over the people of East Pakistan which caused a great disparity in every field including education, welfare, health, armed services, civil bureaucracy, economic and social developments.[19] One of such discriminatory and undemocratic policies of the Government of Pakistan was the 1952's endeavor to impose 'Urdu' as the only State language of Pakistan while Bangla was the language of the majority population there.[20]As a consequence, the people of the then East Pakistan started movement for getting Bangla language recognized as their State language when many people of Bangladesh sacrificed their lives for the aforesaid purpose.[21] From that period, the concerned people of the then East Pakistan began thinking of their own liberation and started a political movement for getting provincial autonomy for the East Pakistan.[22] In other words, the language movement of 1952 ultimately turned into the movement for greater autonomy and self-determination and finally, independence of Bangladesh.[23]

---

[19] *The Chief Prosecutor vs. Delowar Hossain Sayeedi*, ICT-BD Case No. 01 of 2011 [ICT-BD 1] at page 4 at para 7.

[20] *The Chief Prosecutor vs. Salauddin Quader Chowdhury*, ICT-BD Case No. 02 of 2011 [ICT-BD 1] at page 5 at para 7.

[21] *Muhammad Kamaruzzaman, op. cit. no.* 3 at page 5 at para 8; *The Chief Prosecutor vs. Moulana Abdul Kalam Azad*, ICT-BD Case No. 05 of 2012 [ICT-BD 2] at page 3 at para 7; *The Chief Prosecutor vs. Ali Ahsan Muhammad Mujahid*, ICT-BD Case No. 04 of 2012 [ICT-BD 2] at page 4 at para 7; *The Chief Prosecutor vs Md. Abdul Alim @ M. A. Alim*, ICT-BD Case No. 01 of 2012 [ICT-BD 2] at page 5 at para 8; *The Chief Prosecutor vs. Md. Mobarak Hossain @ Mobarak Ali*, ICT-BD Case No. 01 of 2013 [ICT-BD 1] at page 2 at para 3; *Delowar Hossain Sayeedi, op. cit. no.* 19 at page 4 at para 7.

[22] *Professor Ghulam Azam, op. cit. no.* 7 at page 6 at para 6.

[23] *Muhammad Kamaruzzaman, op. cit. no.* 3 at page 5 at para 8; *Abdul Kalam Azad, op. cit. no.* 21 at page 3 at para 7; *Ali Ahsan Muhammad*

In the general election of 1970, the Awami League under the leadership of Bangabandhu Sheikh Mujibur Rahman became the majority party of Pakistan by winning 167 seats out of 300 seats of the National Assembly of Pakistan.[24] Even after this landslide victory in the said election, Pakistan government did not hand over the power to the leader of the majority party as democratic norms required.[25] Instead, on 22 February, 1971 the Generals in West Pakistan took a decision to crush the Awami League and its supporters.[26] As a consequence, a movement started in the territory of the then East Pakistan and Bangabandhu Sheikh Mujibur Rahman, in his historic speech of 7 March, 1971, called on the Bangalee nation to struggle for liberation if people's verdict is not respected.[27]

Subsequently, General Yahya Khan at the February conference declared "Kill three million of them and the rest will eat out of our hands" which is regarded as a campaign of genocide.[28] Accordingly, on the night of 25 March, 1971 the Pakistani armies launched the 'Operation Searchlight' that was essentially designed to disarm and liquidate Bengali policemen, soldiers and military officers; to arrest, kill and round up professionals,

---

Mujahid, op. cit. no. 21 at page 4 at para 7; *Md. Abdul Alim, op. cit. no.* 21 at page 5 at para 8; *Mobarak Hossain, op. cit. no.* 21 at page 2 at para 3; *Delowar Hossain Sayeedi, op. cit. no.* 19 at page 4 at para 7.

[24] *Professor Ghulam Azam, op. cit.no.* 7 at page 6 at para 6.

[25] *The Chief Prosecutor vs. Syed Md. Hachhan alias Syed Md. Hasan alias Hachhen Ali,* ICT-BD Case No. 02 of 2014 [ICT-BD 1] at page 12 at para 23.

[26] *Professor Ghulam Azam, op. cit. no.* 7 at page 6 at para 7.

[27] *Id.*

[28] Robert Payne, *Massacre: The Tragedy at Bangla-Desh and the Phenomenon of Mass Slaughter throughout History* (Macmillan Company (1st ed.), 1973) at page 50.

intellectuals, and students.[29] Following the onslaught of the 'Operation Searchlight' by the Pakistani militaries, Bangabandhu declared independence of Bangladesh in the early hour of 26 March, 1971 immediately before he was arrested by the Pakistani authorities.[30]

The people of Bangladesh finally achieved the victory on 16 December, 1971.[31] Massive grave and recurrent horrific atrocities directing the Bengali civilians in the territory of Bangladesh by the Pakistani armies and the local collaborators could not thrive to foil the highest sacrifice of the nation.[32] It was estimated that during the Liberation War of Bangladesh, 30 lakh people were killed, 2 – 4 lakh women were raped, about 1 crore people were deported to India as refugees, million others were internally displaced, and properties were destroyed in an unprecedented manner in all over Bangladesh by the Pakistani armies along with the local collaborators.[33]

---

[29]   Siddiq Salik, *op. cit. no.*1 at 145.

[30]   *Muhammad Kamaruzzaman, op. cit. no. 3* at page 5 at para 9; *Abdul Kalam Azad, op. cit. no. 21* at page 4 at para 8; *Ali Ahsan Muhammad Mujahid, op. cit.no. 21* at pages 4-5 at para 8; *Md. Abdul Alim, op. cit. no. 21* at page 5 at para 9; *Mobarak Hossain, op. cit.no. 21* at page 2 at para 4; *Delowar Hossain Sayeedi, op. cit. no.19* at page 5 at para 8; *Professor Ghulam Azam, op. cit no. 7.*

[31]   *The Chief Prosecutor vs. Moulana Abdus Sobhan,* ICT-BD Case No. 01 of 2014 [ICT-BD 2] at page 6 at para 18.

[32]   *Id.*

[33]   *Professor Ghulam Azam, op. cit. no. 7* at page 7 at para 9; *Muhammad Kamaruzzaman, op. cit. no. 3* at page 4 at para 6; *Abdul Kalam Azad, op. cit. no. 21* at page 2 at para 3; *Ali Ahsan Muhammad Mujahid, op. cit. no. 21* at page 4 at para 5; *Md. Abdul Alim, op. cit. no. 21* at page 4 at para 6; *Mobarak Hossain, op. cit. no. 21* at page 3 at para 5; *Delowar Hossain Sayeedi, op. cit. no. 19* at page 4 at para 15; Mr. Williams A. Boe, the then Secretary General of the Norwegian Refugee Council who flew in Calcutta from Delhi, told newsman at

In major aspects, the genocide of Bangladesh bears comparison with the most savage atrocities on the modern record such as the genocide of *Christians in the Ottoman Empire during the First World War, Japanese rampages in China,* and *the Nazi genocides in Eastern Europe during the Second World War.*[34] The gravity and systematic character of the massacre were nothing short of breathtaking.[35] It can be quoted from a report titled *'A Country Full of Corpses'* published in SUMMA Magazine, Caracas, October, 1971 that:

> 'The extermination of the Jewish people by the Nazi regime, the atomic crime of Hiroshima and Nagasaki, the massacre of Biafra, the napalm of Vietnam, all the great genocides of humanity have found a new equivalent: East Pakistan. Despite the world press having supplied a clear exposition of facts, the people do not appear

---

Dum Dum airport on 10 October 1971 that *at the influx of over nine million evacuees into India could be said to be 'the biggest tragedy since World War II.',* Ministry of External Affairs, New Delhi, *Bangladesh Documents Vol. II* at page 200; Archer K. Blood, *The Cruel Birth of Bangladesh: Memories of an American Diplomat* (Dhaka: University Press Limited, 2002); Dr. Ashfaque Hossain and Umme Wara, "The United Nations and the International Crimes (Tribunal) Act 1973 of Bangladesh," (2014) *Journal of the 1st Winter School* (Center for the Study of Genocide and Justice), Liberation War Museum at page 11; Raunaq Jahan, *op. cit. no.* 12 at page 291; and Barrister Tureen Afroz, 'Thrish lokkho Shohider Shongkhayatotto', The Bangladesh Protidin, Saturday, 2 January, 2016 <http://www.bd-pratidin.com/first-page/2016/01/02/118433>.

[34] Adam Jones, "The Bangladesh Genocide Comparative Perspective," (2014) *Journal of the 1st Winter School* (Center for the Study of Genocide and Justice), Liberation War Museum at page 11.

[35] *Id.*

to have raised that at this moment—and again in Asia—millions and millions of human beings face destruction of their life and mother land ... A pathetic view of the tragedy is given to us by the fact that in a single night in the city of Dacca were killed 50,000 persons by the invading army. Between 26th March—the date of invasion— and this moment, the dead reach more than a million, and every day 30,000 persons leave East Pakistan and take refuge in Indian territory.'[36]

Moreover, former Chief Justice Surendra Kumar Sinha has observed in his judgment rendered in the case of *Abdul Quader Molla*[37] that:

'What has happened in Bangladesh is nothing short of genocide. If what Hitler did in Germany and Poland was an example of racial genocide, if the tragedy of Jallianwala Bagh was an example of colonial genocide by the use of armed might, what happened in Bangladesh was no less a case of cultural and political genocide on a scale unknown to history. The whole of Bangladesh became truly a Jallianwala Bagh, hallowed and sanctified by the blood of patriotic martyrs and innocent defenceless people; whose only fault was that they were somewhat different than those who came to rule them from Pakistan. If Bangladesh has survived the onslaught and has

---

[36] *Bangladesh Documents-Volume II* at page 76 as referred in *Muhammad Kamaruzzaman, op. cit. no.* 3 at page 7 at para 15; *Ali Ahsan Muhammad Mujahid, op. cit. no.* 21 at page 6 at para 13; *Md. Abdul Alim, op. cit. no.* 21 at page 12 at para 6.

[37] *Abdul Quader Molla, op. cit. no.* 9 at page 4.

been able to confine more than three divisions of Pakistan's Army to cantonments and towns, it is because the people of Bangladesh, who laid down their lives at the altar of freedom to pay the price of liberty in the coin of blood and sufferings and did not permit the Pakistani troops to clamp colonial rule on the 75 million people of Bangladesh.'[38]

In a very broader context, the targeted groups of Bangladesh genocide were mostly the Bengali military men of the East Bengal Regiment, the East Pakistan Rifles, police and para-military Ansars; the Hindus; the Awami Leaguers; the college and university students; the Bengali intellectuals such as professors and teachers whenever damned by the army as "militant".[39] Based on the class of the targeted people, the genocidal strategies employed in Bangladesh in 1971 can be categorized into a few thoughts. For illustration:

Firstly, the targeting of nationalist intellectuals, academics and students, cultural figures, media workers, and even sports figures is a time honoured feature of genocide which is called as *Eliticide* throughout modern history.[40] The 'Operation Searchlight' of 25 March, 1971 consisted essentially of a devastating attack on these groups, designed to kill Bengali nationalism at a single stroke. A well-known researcher on genocide, R.J. Rummel, points out:

'In East Pakistan [General Agha Mohammed Yahya Khan and his top generals] also planned to murder its Bengali intellectual, cultural,

---

[38] *Ibid*, at page 42.

[39] Anthony Mascarenhas, *The Rape of Bangla-Desh* (Delhi: Vikas Publications, 1972) at pages 116-17.

[40] Adam Jones, *op. cit. no.* 34 at pages 13-14.

and political elite. They also planned to indiscriminately murder hundreds of thousands of its Hindus and drive the rest into India. And they planned to destroy its economic base to insure that it would be subordinate to West Pakistan for at least a generation to come."[41]

Next, it has been found out by a comparative genocide studies that when the men, women, and boys are most likely to be targeted in genocide especially in its early stages, it is known as *Gendercide*.[42] In Bangladesh genocide, females, younger men, and adolescent boys, of whatever social class, were equally targets.[43] According to Rounaq Jahan, "All through the liberation war, able-bodied young men were suspected of being actual or potential freedom fighters. Thousands were arrested, tortured, and killed. Eventually cities and towns became bereft of young males who either took refuge in India or joined the liberation war." Especially 'during the first phase' of the genocide, he has written, "young able-bodied males were the victims of indiscriminate killings."[44] Likewise, R. J. Rummel states that:

> 'The Pakistan army [sought] out those especially likely to join the resistance -- young boys. Sweeps were conducted of young men who were never seen again. Bodies of youths would be found in fields, floating down rivers, or near army camps. As can be imagined, this terrorized all young men and their families within reach of the army. Most

---

[41]   Rudolph J. Rummel, *Statistics of Democide: Genocide and Mass Murder Since 1900* (Munster: LIT Verlag Minister, 1998) at chapter 15.

[42]   Adam Jones, *op. cit. no.* 34 at pages 13-14.

[43]   *Muhammad Kamaruzzaman, op. cit. no.* 3 at page 34 at para 95.

[44]   Raunaq Jahan, *op. cit. no.* 12 at page 298.

between the ages of fifteen and twenty-five began to flee from one village to another and toward India. Many of those reluctant to leave their homes were forced to flee by mothers and sisters concerned for their safety.'[45]

Moreover, the targeting of Bengali women for mass rape, repeatedly followed by murder as a further expression of gendered hatred and desire to cover up the crime.[46] In regards of the brutality on the women by Pakistani Army in 1971, Susan Brownmiller pointed out that:

> '... 200,000, 300,000 or possibly 400,000 women (three sets of statistics have been variously quoted) were raped. Eighty percent of the raped women were Moslems, reflecting the population of Bangladesh, but Hindu and Christian women were not exempt. ... Hit-and-run rape of large numbers of Bengali women was brutally simple in terms of logistics as the Pakistani regulars swept through and occupied the tiny, populous land ...'[47]

In addition to that, reporter Aubrey Menen told about one such assault which targeted a recently married woman at that time: 'Two [Pakistani soldiers] went into the room that had been built for the bridal couple. The others stayed behind with the family, one of them covering them with his gun. They heard a barked order, and the bridegroom's voice protesting. Then there was

---

[45] Rudolph J. Rummel, *Death by Government* (New Brunsweek: Transaction Publishers, 1994) at page 329.

[46] Susan Brownmiller, *Against Our Will: Men, Women and Rape* (New York: Simon & Schuster, 1975) at page 81.

[47] *Id.*

silence until the bride screamed. Then there was silence again, except for some muffled cries that soon subsided. In a few minutes one of the soldiers came out, his uniform in disarray. He grinned to his companions. Another soldier took his place in the extra room. And so on, until all the six had raped the belle of the village. Then all six left, hurriedly. The father found his daughter lying on the string cot unconscious and bleeding. Her husband was crouched on the floor, kneeling over his vomit."[48]

Finally, the political leaders especially the Awami Leaguers, all office bearers, and volunteers down to the lowest link in the chain of command were one of the targeted groups which are classified as *Politicide*.[49] In Bangladesh genocide, there is no doubt that through the 'Operation Searchlight', the Pakistani armies attempted to eliminate all actual and even potential supporters of the Awami League and Mukti Bahini.[50]

In order to achieve the independence of Bangladesh, the Bangalee people of all spheres whole heartedly supported and participated in the Liberation War of 1971.[51] Nonetheless, a few numbers of Bangalees, Biharis, other pro-Pakistanis, and members of a number of different religion-based political parties such as *Jamat-E-Islami (JEI)* and its student wing *Islami Chatra Sangha (ICS)* joined and/or collaborated with the Pakistan militaries to oppose the creation of free-Bangladesh.[52] A huge number of auxiliary forces[53]; for instance, the Razakars, the Al-Badar, the

---

[48]   *Ibid*, at page 82.

[49]   Anthony Mascarenhas, *op. cit. no.* 39.

[50]   Adam Jones, *op. cit. no.* 34 at pages 13-14

[51]   *Ali Ahsan Muhammad Mujahid, op. cit. no.* 21 at page 5 at para 11.

[52]   *Id.*

[53]   Section 2(a) of the *ICTA*, 1973 defines that "auxiliary forces" includes forces placed under the control of the Armed Forces for operational, administrative, static and other purposes.

Al-Shams, the Peace Committee etc. have been formed by the Pakistan government and the militaries.[54] The main activities of the said forces were to identify and eliminate pro-liberation people; minority religious groups particularly the Hindus; political groups especially the Awami League; Bangalee intellectuals; and unarmed civilian population of Bangladesh.[55] Their intention was to stamp out the Bengali National Liberation Movement, and to mash the national feelings and aspirations of the Bangalee nation.[56] In this respect, former Chief Justice Surendra Kumar Sinha recounts the following observation:

> 'The birth of Bangladesh has been preceded by injustice; false promise and economic and social abuses us pending the session of the elected National Assembly of 1970 *sine die* followed by the persecution of the legally elected people entitled to form the Government and frame the Constitution, by resorting to commit mass killing, rape and arson by an illegal regime headed by a usurper. These atrocities were perpetrated by the Pakistan's occupation army with their cohorts, i.e., the Rajakar, Al-Badr, Al-shams and various other local killing squads in 1971. Although the killing of unarmed civilians during late March seemed abrupt and sporadic, it soon became a planned act of violence with operation 'Search Light' enforced at midnight, on 25th March, 1971

---

[54] *Md. Abdul Alim, op. cit. no.* 21 at page 5 at para 10.

[55] *Syed Md. Hachhan, op. cit. no.* 25 at page 102 at para 202.

[56] *Muhammad Kamaruzzaman, op. cit. no.* 3 at page 12 at para 6; *Ali Ahsan Muhammad Mujahid, op. cit. no.* 21 at page 5 at para 9; *Md. Abdul Alim, op. cit. no.* 21 at page 5 at para 10.

as part of the central planning and conspiracy hatched at Larkana.'[57]

Concerning the strength of locally formed *para militia* and other forces intending to provide collaboration with the Pakistani occupation army in 1971, Jagjit Singh Aurora very lucidly points out that:

> 'During the liberation war in Bangladesh, there were about eighty thousand Pakistani soldiers, twenty five thousand militia, twenty five thousand civilian forces, and fifty thousand Razakars, Al-Badr, and Al-Shams members. On the other side there were about one hundred and seventy five thousand freedom fighters. Near the end of the war another two hundred and fifty thousand Indian soldiers joined the freedom fighters. At the end of the war after the surrender, about ninety one thousand Pakistani prisoners were transported to India.'[58]

Indeed, the killing of the people of Bangladesh in 1971 can be considered as one of the dreadful and pre-planned genocides where in one hand, many people sacrificed their lives for achieving independence of Bangladesh, and on the other hand, a small number of people actively opposed the Liberation War. In the following discussion, certain laws and matters concerning the trials of those perpetrators such as Razakars, Al-Badr, and Al-Shams members etc. have been focused on.

---

[57] *Mir Quasem Ali, op. cit. no.* 2 at page 6 at para 8; See also, S. A. Karim, *op. cit. no.* 4; *Abdul Quader Molla, op. cit. no.* 9.

[58] *Syed Md. Qaiser, op. cit. no.* 1 at page 7 at para 20; *Figures from the Fall of Dacca by Jagjit Singh Aurora in the Illustrated Weekly of India,* 23 December, 1973.

2.3 The *Bangladesh Collaborators (Special Tribunals) Order*, 1972

It has been stated in the previous discussion that certain people individually or as members of organizations collaborated the Pakistani armed forces, and aided as well as abetted the said forces in committing genocide, crimes against humanity and atrocities against men, women, children, and against the person, property, and honour of the civilian population of Bangladesh in 1971.[59] Certainly, they have acted in the interest of Pakistan armies, helped expanding their illegal occupation, waged war, and abetted in waging war against Bangladesh.[60] Hence, in order to ensure punishment to the collaborators effectively and adequately complying with the due process of law, the *Bangladesh Collaborators (Special Tribunals) Order*,1972[61] was enacted. However, this *Order* of 1972 was repealed on 31 December, 1975 by the enactment of the *Bangladesh Collaborators (Special Tribunals) (Repeal) Ordinance, 1975.*[62]

Soon after Sheikh Mujibur Rahman was released from Pakistan jail and his arrival in Dhaka on 10 January, 1972,[63] this *Order* was promulgated on 24 January, 1972 that came into force at once and deemed to have taken effect on the 26 day of March, 1971.[64] The pro-Pakistani people of East Pakistan including the

---

[59] The *Bangladesh Collaborators (Special Tribunals) Order*, 1972, the Preamble.

[60] See above Part 2.2 and accompanying texts.

[61] *President's Order No. 8 of 1972.*

[62] The *Bangladesh Collaborators (Special Tribunals) (Repeal) Ordinance,* 1975, Article 2.

[63] "Father of the Nation: Bangabandhu Sheikh Mujibur Rahman," High Commission for Bangladesh, London <http://www.bhclondon.org.uk/Father%20of%20the%20Nation.html>.

[64] The *Bangladesh Collaborators (Special Tribunals) Order*, 1972,

26

Razakars, Al-Badr and *Al-Shams* forces and the members of Peace Committees were formally declared as collaborators under this *Order*.[65] In this *Order*, a collaborator was defined as a person who was found (i) to have helped, cooperated with or supported the Pakistan army in maintaining their unlawful occupation in Bangladesh; (ii) to have offered substantial cooperation to the Pakistan army directly or indirectly or to have helped the occupation army through speeches or statements, agreements and activities; (iii) to have fought or have attempted to fight against Bangladesh; (iv) to have given any statement or have participated in any campaign in favour of the Pakistan army, and to have been a member of any delegation or a committee of that army, and to have participated in the by-elections held in 1971.[66]

Essentially, four amendments had been brought into this *Order* while its first amendment introduced certain major provisions.[67] Besides, certain minor amendments have been brought under subsequent amendments in the dates of 6 February 1972;[68] 1 June 1972;[69] and 29 August 1972[70] accordingly.

Article 1(3).

[65] *Ibid*, the Preamble.

[66] *Ibid*, Article 2(b).

[67] Please follow the discussion on the *Bangladesh Collaborators (Special Tribunals) Order*, 1972 in Part 2.4 and accompanying texts.

[68] The *Bangladesh Collaborators (Special Tribunals) (Amendment) Order*, 1972 of 6 February, 1972.

[69] The *Bangladesh Collaborators (Special Tribunals) (Amendment) Order*, 1972 of 1 June, 1972.

[70] The *Bangladesh Collaborators (Special Tribunals) (Amendment) Order*, 1972 of 29 August, 1972.

2.4 Trial under the *Bangladesh Collaborators (Special Tribunals) Order,* 1972

After the enactment of the *Order* of 1972, several accused of different crimes were arrested since January 1972.[71] Proceedings have been initiated against the accused from April 1972.[72] By September 1972, nearly 41000 collaborators were arrested while charges were brought against 37,471 collaborators against whom there were specific allegations.[73] Till 31 October 1973, 2884 cases were resolved by the 73 Collaborators Tribunals and 752 were convicted.[74] During the trial, on April 17, 1973 the Government issued a press release as regards war criminals for the first time.[75] In the press release, 195 persons were termed as war criminals.[76]

---

[71] Chintito, "Justice Delayed is Never Justice Denied," 9(12) *The Daily Star Weekend Magazine* (19 March 2010) <http://www.thedailystar. net/magazine/2010/03/03/chintito.htm>.

[72] *Id.*

[73] Wali-ur-Rahman, "Background Notes on Adoption of 1973 International Crimes (Tribunal) Act, 1973," (2014) *Journal of the 1st Winter School* (Center for the Study of Genocide and Justice), Liberation War Museum at page 106; Bangabandhu's General Amnesty Declaration: Documentary Evidences and Relevant Stories, <http://www.ebangladesh.com/2010/07/24/ bangabandhus-general-amnesty-declaration/>.

[74] *Ibid*; Humayun Reza, 'War Crimes and Genocide in 1971: The Reality of the Trial' - a paper presented at the International Conference on Genocide, Truth and Justice, Dhaka, 1-2 March 2008; Conference Proceeding 2008 at page 55; Caitlin Reiger, "Fighting Past Impunity in Bangladesh: A National Tribunal for the Crimes of 1971" International Centre for Transnational Justice, Briefing Paper, July 2010 at pages 2-3; Nazrul Islam, "Pro-liberation Forces' Unity can Defeat War Criminals," *The Daily Star* (12 November 2007) <http:// www.thedailystar.net/story.php?nid=11199>.

[75] *Id.*

[76] Wali-ur-Rahman, *op. cit. no.* 73; See also M. A. Hasan, "War Crime

To quote from the August 2004 report of the Redress Trust (London): 'In Bangladesh, there was apparent political will to prosecute and punish those accused of perpetration of crimes relating to the 1971 events. The then government of Sheikh Mujibur Rahman decided to try those members of the Pakistani army who had surrendered, reportedly more than 95,000 in total, on charges of international crimes. Following an investigation, a decision was made to put on trial 195 'major war criminals' against whom strong evidence was said to be available.'[77]

In regards of the above noted 195 persons, Clause 13 of the *Tripartite Agreement between India, Pakistan, and Bangladesh* signed in New Delhi on 9 April, 1974 mentions as follows: 'The question of 195 Pakistani prisoners of war was discussed by the three Ministers, in the context of the earnest desire of the Governments for reconciliation, peace and friendship in the sub-continent. The Foreign Minister of Bangladesh stated that the excesses and manifold crimes committed by these prisoners of war constituted, according to the relevant provisions of the U.N. General Assembly Resolutions and International Law, war crimes, crimes against humanity and genocide, and that there was universal consensus that persons charged with such crimes as the 195 Pakistani prisoners of war should be held to account and subjected to the due process of law. The Minister of State for Defence and Foreign Affairs of the Government of Pakistan said that his Government condemned and deeply regretted any crimes that may have been committed.'

Moreover, in general, Clause 14 of the *Agreement* depicts that: 'In this connection the three Ministers noted that the matter

---

Trials: Our Failure and Future," *The Daily Star* (14 December 2007) <http://archive.thedailystar.net/newDesign/news-details.php?nid=15341>.

[77] August 2004 report of the Redress Trust (London).

should be viewed in the context of the determination of the three countries to continue resolutely to work for reconciliation. The Ministers further noted that following recognition, the Prime Minister of Pakistan had declared that he would visit Bangladesh in response to the invitation of the Prime Minister of Bangladesh and appealed to the people of Bangladesh to forgive and forget the mistakes of the past, in order to promote reconciliation. Similarly, the Prime Minister of Bangladesh had declared with regard to the atrocities and destruction committed in Bangladesh in 1971 that he wanted the people to forget the past and to make a fresh start, stating that the people of Bangladesh knew how to forgive.'

Sheikh Mujibur Rahman declared a "General Amnesty"[78] to the suspected war criminals of 1971.[79] Nevertheless, those who had committed criminal offences like murder, rape, arson etc. were not included in the said amnesty.[80] The Press Note on "General Amnesty" has been portrayed verbatim in the following:

This amnesty let to the release of 2600 local arrestees, however, the remaining 1100 were in custody and facing trials.[81] As a matter of fact, the trial process of the alleged local perpetrators

---

[78] On 30 November, 1973 Bangabandhu declared the General Amnesty.

[79] Md. Sayedur Rahman, Md. Tanziul Islam, and Abu Reza Md. Towfiqul Islam, "Evaluation of Charismatic Leader of Bangabandhu Sheikh Mujibur Rahman," 2014 (4) *International Journal of Scientific and Research Publications* 1, 5.

[80] *Id.*

[81] A Government gazette notification of 30 November 1973 shows that none of the war criminals had been pardoned; Suzannah Linton, "Completing the Circle: Accountability for the Crimes of the 1971 Bangladesh War of Liberation" (2010) 21 *Criminal Law Forum*, at page 205; See above parts 2.3 and 2.4, and accompanied texts.

came to a standstill after the assassination of the then President Sheikh Mujibur Rahman and the fall of his government in a military coup on 15 August, 1975.[82] The military oligarchy assumed power and repealed the *Order* of 1972 on 31 December, 1975 by the enactment of the *Bangladesh Collaborators (Special Tribunals) (Repeal) Ordinance, 1975*.[83] Eventually, all 1100 alleged local collaborators and war criminals were released from custody, handed back confiscated citizenship, rehabilitated them in key government positions and politics, and allowed the banned *Jamat-e-Islam* to register and function as a political party.[84]

However, remarkably, though the trials of the collaborators were abandoned, Article 47(3) of the *Constitution of Bangladesh*[85] and the *ICTA* itself which offer the trial of war criminals including the "auxiliary forces" for committing genocide, crimes against humanity, war crimes, and other crimes under international law had not been annulled by any government and are still applicable. The following discussion explains the essence of the Article 47(3) of the *Constitution* and historical backdrop of *ICTA* of 1973.

---

[82] S Ahamed, "Trials and Error," *BD News* (5 June 2010) at page 13 <http://opinion.bdnews24.com/2010/06/05/trials-and-error/>, 5 June 2010; See also Justice Mohammad Gholam Rabbani, "The International Crimes (Tribunals) Act, 1973," Genocide, War Crimes & Crimes Against Humanity in Bangladesh, Trial under *International Crimes (Tribunals) Act*, 1973, Forum for Secular Bangladesh and Trial of War Criminal of 1971 at page 5.

[83] See above Part 2.3 and accompanying texts.

[84] Caitlin Reiger, *op. cit. no. 74*.

[85] The *Constitution of the People's Republic of Bangladesh*, 1972.

2.5 The *International Crimes (Tribunals) Act, 1973* (*ICTA, 1973*)

On 15 July, 1973 the *Constitution of Bangladesh* was amended for the first time under the *Constitution (First Amendment) Act, 1973* so that the process of war crimes' trials could be eased. Article 47 (3) of the *Constitution*, added under the said first amendment reads as follows:

> '(3) Notwithstanding anything contained in this Constitution, no law nor any provision thereof providing for detention, prosecution or punishment of any person, who is a member of any armed or defence or auxiliary forces or who is a prisoner of war, for genocide, crimes against humanity or war crimes and other crimes under international law shall be deemed void or unlawful, on the ground that such law or provision of any such law is inconsistent with, or repugnant to, any of the provision of this Constitution.'

On 20 July, 1973 the *ICTA* of 1973 was enacted with an aim to establish special International Crimes Tribunals "to provide for the detention, prosecution and punishment of persons for genocide, crimes against humanity, war crimes and other crimes under international law".[86] The alleged local perpetrators and collaborators who are now convicted and on trials under the *ICTA* of 1973 were not tried and punished before under the *Order of 1972*.[87] The *ICTA* of 1973 came 'into force at once' at its enactment

---

[86] The *International Crimes (Tribunals) Act (No. XIX)*, 1973, the Preamble.

[87] M. Rafiqul Islam, "Adoption of the *International Crimes (Tribunals) Act*, 1973: Its History and Application, Non-retroactivity and Amendments," (2014) *Journal of the 1st Winter School* (Center for

and covers the entire territory of Bangladesh.[88] The provisions of this *Act* shall have effect over other laws even if any contrary provision exists in any other law for the time being in force.[89]

Along with the Government of the newly formed Bangladesh, the formation of this *Act* involved the International Commission of Jurists in Geneva.[90] Ian MacDormatt, the then Chairperson of the International Commission of Jurists and Professor Jescheck, of the Max Plank Institute of International Criminal Law in Freibourg, Baden Baden, Germany, contributed to the contents of the *Act*.[91]

Law Minister Sree Monoronjon Dhar proposed for the *International Crimes (Tribunals) Bill,* 1973 on 19 July, 1973.[92] Before passing the *Act*, debates had been made among the Parliamentarians regarding the proposed Bill.[93] Sree Manobendra Narayan Larma proposed that before passing the Bill, it should be handed over to a selection committee, who would submit a report regarding it within 22 July, 1973.[94] After that, Mr. Moynuddin Manik (Rajshahi) proposed that the Bill should be circulated for public opinion before passing it in the Parliament within 25 July, 1973 while Mr. Abdus Sattar (Tangail) proposed 24 July, 1973 for

---

the Study of Genocide and Justice), Liberation War Museum at page 72.

[88] *Ibid,* at pages 71-72; Section 1(3) of the *ICTA,* 1973.

[89] *Ibid,* Section 26.

[90] Wali-ur-Rahman, "A Brief History of the Farming of the *International Crimes (Tribunals) Act,* 1973," (Dhaka, 2009) at pages 37-38.

[91] *Id.*

[92] *Shangshad Bitorko Khondo 2,* Shonkhya 37 at pages 2344-2373.

[93] *Id.*

[94] *Id.*

the same purpose.[95] In this respect, Mr. Dhar said that asking for motion or public opinion of the Bill would mean the non-acceptance of passing the proposed Bill in the Parliament, thus, concerned Parliamentarians should explain their reasons before the house. Mr. Moynuddin expressed that the number 195 in comparison with 93 thousand was not satisfactory at all and the proposed Bill was not an appropriate one to try the Pakistani Military who brutally tortured the people of Bangladesh.[96] Since this Bill was a long awaited process of justice for the common people of Bangladesh, it was better to circulate for public opinion before passing it in the Parliament.[97] Subsequently, Mr. Sattar addressed that the *Constitution* had been amended on 15 July, 1973 for the purpose of this Bill as through establishing a Tribunal in Bangladesh.[98]

Later on, Mr. Serajul Huq took the floor and put his comments before the House.[99] He mentioned that it was a glorious moment because such a law was going to be enacted for the first time in the history of mankind and this Bill was introduced not because Bangladesh wanted revenge on the perpetrators but for clearing the conscience of humanity, not because the perpetrators devastated our land but because this country had responsibility towards the suffering of humanity where the entire world was looking to Bangladesh for this.[100] He discussed some aspects of the proposed Bill like he mentioned that this law was not for those 195 persons who were prisoners of war, but for our own

---

[95] *Id.*

[96] *Id.*

[97] *Id.*

[98] *Id.*

[99] *Id.*

[100] *Id.*

armed forces and our own people.[101] For this reason, it could not be criticized that the law was being made only for the prisoners of war.[102] It was important to let the world know that Bangladesh had put same standard and scale for own armed forces and for others.[103] Secondly, the Bill had followed the principles enunciated in other trials of Nuremberg, Yamachita and Tokyo trials.[104] Even it had gone one step further than other trials by inserting a provision to appeal for the convicted persons.[105] Besides, the Bill had given all the rights than an accused was entitled to get in international jurisprudence and international conception of criminal law, thus, the "Summum Bonum" of the law was justice for all and at all cost.[106] Lastly, Mr. Huq concluded expecting that the Bill would be passed in the Parliament without any hindrance.[107]

After that, the then Law Minister took the floor and gave his final submission and mentioned that the Bill had been drafted after proper scrutiny and discussion by the national and international experts where they found that the perpetrators had violated Articles 2, 3, 5, 7, 9, 17, 18 and 19 of the *Universal Declaration of Human Rights (UDHR)*, 1948 which was considered as a customary international law.[108] They had also violated Articles 6, 7, 16 and 18 of the *International Covenant on Civil and Political Rights (ICCPR)*, 1966.[109] He also mentioned that the systematic

---

[101] *Id.*

[102] *Id.*

[103] *Id.*

[104] *Id.*

[105] *Id.*

[106] *Id.*

[107] *Id.*

[108] *Id.*

[109] *Id.*

destruction of life and property, the killing, arbitrary detention and torture of members of Awami League and other political parties or students, intellectuals and of the Hindus for no other reason except they belonged to that group were clear violations of the above mentioned principles.[110] The Pakistani authorities also violated the principle of non-discrimination through their activities.[111] Furthermore, common Article 3 of the *Geneva Convention*, 1949 which talked about the protection of the prisoners of war was violated by them too in spite of being a signatory party to the Convention.[112] Moreover, Bangladesh had accepted the *Genocide Convention*, 1948 which created a liability upon Bangladesh to try and punish those persons who had broken the principles of the *Geneva Convention*.[113] In addition to that, the 21st session of *Human Rights Convention* recommended establishment of principles and punishment of such crimes.[114]

Lastly, Mr. Dhar said that the Bill had to be passed in the Parliament today but his friends had proposed three proposals, two were circulation motions and one was related to the selection committee.[115] Though he had faith on them that being a patriot person, they would retract their proposals or the honorable Parliament should reject those improper proposals.[116] After his speech, the honorable Speaker asked opinion of Mr. Moynuddin Ahmed, Sree Manobendra Narayan Larma and Md. Abdus Sattar whether to press their previous proposals or not.[117] Mr.

---

[110] *Id.*

[111] *Id.*

[112] *Id.*

[113] *Id.*

[114] *Id.*

[115] *Id.*

[116] *Id.*

[117] *Id.*

Moynuddin Ahmed was not present at the session then but other two Parliamentarians withdrew their proposals respectively.[118] After the entire Parliamentary debates, the Bill was enacted by the Parliament and the assent of the President was received on 19 July, 1973.[119]

So far the *Act* has been amended for two times *i.e.* on 14 July, 2009 and 17 February, 2013.[120] It is important to note here that the 2013 amendments have been given retrospective effect from 14 July 2009, by bringing the judgment and sentence in the *Quader Molla case*[121] within the purview of the amended provisions.[122] The amendment of 2009 inserted the terms "individual or group of individuals," to expand the Tribunal's jurisdiction beyond members of "armed, defense or auxiliary forces."[123] Similarly, the words "or organization," have been inserted after "group of individuals," by the amendment of 2013.[124]

---

[118]   *Id.*

[119]   *Id.*

[120]   *Muhammad Kamaruzzaman, op. cit. no.* 3 at page 3 at para 3; *Abdul Kalam Azad, op. cit. no.* 21 at page 6 at para 13; *Ali Ahsan Muhammad Mujahid, op. cit. no.* 21 at page 3 at para 3; *Md. Abdul Alim, op. cit. no.* 21 at page 3 at para 3; *See also, International Crimes (Tribunals) (Amendment) Act,* 2009 (Act No. LV of 2009); Bangladesh Gazette, Additional Issue, Law No. 55 of 14 July 2009 (2009 Amendment); *International Crimes (Tribunals) (Amendment) Act,* 2013 (Act No III of 2013) (2013 amendment).

[121]   *Quader Molla, op. cit. no.* 9.

[122]   "Memory and Justice," *The Daily Star* (15 November 2013) <http://www.thedailystar.net/memory-and-justice-3100>.

[123]   Section 3(1), the *International Crimes (Tribunals) Act,* 1973, as amended in 2009.

[124]   Section 3(1), the *International Crimes (Tribunals) Act,* 1973, as amended in 2013.

The *Act* manifested that the 'Crimes against Humanity'[125], 'Crimes against Peace'[126], 'Genocide'[127], 'War Crimes'[128] are crimes within the jurisdiction of the Tribunal constituted under

---

[125] 'Crimes against Humanity: namely, murder, extermination, enslavement, deportation, imprisonment, abduction, confinement, torture, rape or other inhumane acts committed against any civilian population or persecutions on political, racial, ethnic or religious grounds, whether or not in violation of the domestic law of the country where perpetrated.'

[126] 'Crimes against Peace: namely, planning, preparation, initiation or waging of a war of aggression or a war in violation of international treaties, agreements or assurances.'

[127] 'Genocide: meaning and including any of the following acts committed with intent to destroy, in whole or in part, a national, ethnic, racial, religious or political group, such as:
(i) killing members of the group;
(ii) causing serious bodily or mental harm to members of the group;
(iii) deliberately inflicting on the group conditions of life calculated to bring about its physical destruction in whole or in part;
(iv) imposing measures intended to prevent Births within the group;
(v) forcibly transferring children of the group to another group.'

[128] 'War Crimes: namely, violation of laws or customs of war which include but are not limited to murder, ill-treatment or deportation to slave labour or for any other purpose of civilian population in the territory of Bangladesh; murder or ill-treatment of prisoners of war or persons on the seas, killing of hostages and detenues, plunder of public or private property, wanton destruction of cities, towns or villages, or devastation not justified by military necessity;
(e) violation of any humanitarian rules applicable in armed conflicts laid down in the Geneva Conventions of 1949;
(f) any other crimes under international law;
(g) attempt, abetment or conspiracy to commit any such crimes;
(h) complicity in or failure to prevent commission of any such crimes.'

the *Act* for which there shall be individual responsibility.[129] It has been appeared from section 3(1) of the *ICTA* that even any person (individual), if he is *prima facie* found accountable either under section 4(1)[130] or 4(2)[131] of the *ICTA* for the perpetration of offence(s), can be brought into justice under the *Act*.[132]

Furthermore, it has been entailed in this *Act* that the official position of the accused shall not free an accused from responsibility for any crime.[133] However, if is it found that the accused acted pursuant to his/her domestic law or to order of his Government or of a superior, the Tribunal may mitigate his/her punishment if justice so requires.[134] In regards of power of the Tribunals, the *Act* depicts, *inter alia*, that a Tribunal may punish any person, who obstructs or abuses its process or disobeys any of its orders or directions, or does anything which tends to prejudice the case of a party before it, or tends to bring it or any of its members into hatred or contempt, or does anything which

---

[129] *The International Crimes (Tribunal) Act*, 1973, Section 3.

[130] *Ibid*, Section 4(1) reads as follows:
'(1) When any crime as specified in section 3 is committed by several persons, each of such person is liable for that crime in the same manner as if it were done by him alone.'

[131] Section 4(2) reads as follows:
'(2) Any commander or superior officer who orders, permits, acquiesces or participates in the commission of any of the crimes specified in section 3 or is connected with any plans and activities involving the commission of such crimes or who fails or omits to discharge his duty to maintain discipline, or to control or supervise the actions of the persons under his command or his subordinates, whereby such persons or subordinates or any of them commit any such crimes, or who fails to take necessary measures to prevent the commission of such crimes, is guilty of such crimes.'

[132] *Moulana Abdus Sobhan, op. cit. no.* 31 at page 3 at para 7.

[133] *The International Crimes (Tribunal) Act*, 1973, Section 5(1).

[134] *Ibid*, Section 5(2).

constitutes contempt of the Tribunal.[135] The *Act* recognizes the rights of the accused during trial including the right to give any explanation relevant to the charge made against him, the right to conduct his own defense before the Tribunal or to have the assistance of counsel, the right to present evidence at the trial in support of his defense, and to cross-examine any witness called by the prosecution.[136] It recognizes that upon conviction the competent Tribunal shall give the reasons on which the decision of particular case is based while the Tribunal is authorized to award sentence of death or such other punishment proportionate to the gravity of the crime as appears to the Tribunal to be just and proper.[137]

As far as appeal is concerned, Section 21 was amended by the *International Crimes (Tribunals) (Amendment) Act,* 2013[138] adding the possibility of appeal against an "order of sentence" to be filed by the complainant, the informant, and the Government, whereas previously the Government could only file an appeal against an "order of acquittal".[139] Additionally, where under the original *Act* a period of 60 days was allowed for the filing of a case, the amendment limits that period to 30 days after the date of conviction, sentence or acquittal.[140] The amendment also imposes an entirely new duty on the Appellate Division, requiring

---

[135] *The International Crimes (Tribunal) Act,* 1973, Section 11(4); The punishment of such offences is simple imprisonment which may extend to one year, or with fine which may extend to Taka five thousand, or with both.

[136] *Ibid*, Section 17.

[137] *Ibid*, Section 20.

[138] Act No. III of 2013.

[139] *Ibid*, Section 21(2).

[140] *Ibid*, Section 21(3).

them to dispose of any appeal within a maximum of 60 (sixty) days from the date of its filing.[141]

This *Act* provides indemnity to the Government or any person for anything, in good faith, done or purporting to have been done under this *Act*.[142] It is important to mention that the *ICTA* entails the provisions in relation to constitution of the Tribunals,[143] Prosecutors,[144] investigation,[145] commencement of the proceedings,[146] procedure of trial,[147] *trial in absentia*,[148] powers of the Tribunal,[149] power to transfer cases,[150] provision for defense counsel,[151] restriction of adjournment,[152] statement or confession of accused persons,[153] pardon of an approver,[154] charge framing,[155] no excuse from answering any question,[156]

---

[141] *Ibid*, Section 21(4).

[142] *Ibid*, Section 25.

[143] *Ibid*, Section 6.

[144] *Ibid*, Section 7.

[145] *Ibid*, Section 8.

[146] *Ibid*, Section 9.

[147] *Ibid*, Section 10.

[148] *Ibid*, Section 10A.

[149] *Ibid*, Section 11.

[150] *Ibid*, Section 11A.

[151] *Ibid*, Section 12.

[152] *Ibid*, Section 13.

[153] *Ibid*, Section 14.

[154] *Ibid*, Section 15.

[155] *Ibid*, Section 16.

[156] *Ibid*, Section 18.

rules of evidence,[157] rules of procedure,[158] certain laws not to apply,[159] and bar of jurisdiction.[160]

It is important to address here that a question may arise as to the relevance of the *doctrine of double jeopardy* in respect of trials of war criminals under the *ICTA, 1973*. In this regards, the issue of double jeopardy had been raised in the case of the *Chief Prosecutor vs. Moulana Abdul Kalam Azad*[161] that whether the accused could have been prosecuted and tried under the *Collaborators Order, 1972* and if prosecuted present prosecution for same offences is barred by the *doctrine of double jeopardy* or not? It has been stipulated in this particular case that in order to determine as to whether the trial under the *Act* of 1973 is said to be barred by the *doctrine of double jeopardy*, it is to be tested whether two criminal offences are the same for the purposes of double jeopardy jurisprudence.[162] Lord Morris explained that:

> 'What has to be considered is whether the crime or offence charged in the later indictment is the same or is in effect or is substantially the same as the crime charged (or in respect of which there could have been a conviction) in a former indictment and that it is immaterial that the facts under examination or the witnesses being called

---

[157] *Ibid*, Section 19.

[158] *Ibid*, Section 22.

[159] *Ibid*, Section 23.

[160] *Ibid*, Section 24.

[161] ICT-BD Case No. 05 of 2012 [ICT-BD 1].

[162] *Ibid*, at page 25 at paras 66-67; See also, Article 35(2) of the *Constitution of Bangladesh*.

in the later proceedings are the same as those on some earlier proceedings.'[163]

It has been stated in this case that 'the *Collaborators Order, 1972* was a different legislation aiming to prosecute the persons responsible for the offences enumerated in the schedule thereof. It will appear that the offences punishable under the Penal Code were scheduled in the *Collaborators Order 1972*. While the 1973 *Act* was enacted to prosecute and try the crimes against humanity, genocide and other system crimes committed in violation of customary international law. There is no scope to characterize the offences underlying in the *Collaborators Order 1972* to be the same offences as specified in the *Act* of 1973.'[164] Moreover, in the case of *the Chief Prosecutor vs. Md. Mahidur Rahman & Md. Afsar Hossain @ Chutu,*[165] it has been stipulated by the Tribunal that 'mere lodgment of the above mentioned case [the case filed under the *Collaborators Order* 1972] does not readily lead us to conclude that the accused persons were eventually convicted or acquitted, on full trial and the said case involved the event of criminal acts for which now they again stand trial under the *Act* of 1973.'[166] Hence, it can be said that *albeit* the question of *double jeopardy* comes into being in case of trials under the *ICTA* of 1973, the trials would not be barred by the said doctrine as the characters of the offences entailed in the *Collaborators Order 1972* are different from the offences as indicated in the *ICTA* of 1973.

---

[163] *Ibid*, at page 25 at para 67; See also, *Connelly vs. Director of Public Prosecutions* [1964] A.C. 1254 at 1306 [H.L.(E.)].

[164] *Ibid*, at pages 25-26 at para 69.

[165] ICT-BD Case No. 02 of 2014.

[166] *Ibid*, at page 22 at para 72.

2.6 Constitution of the Tribunals

Even though the *ICTA* came into force on 20 July, 1973, no Tribunal was set up and no trial took place under the *Act* until the government established the ICT-1 on 25 March, 2010.[167] The Tribunal was established by the sovereign parliament of Bangladesh as a domestic judicial forum for the purpose of holding trials relating to the detention, prosecution and punishment of persons responsible for genocide, crimes against humanity, war crimes, and crimes committed in the territory of Bangladesh, in violation of customary international law, particularly between the period of 25 March and 16 December, 1971.[168] It is essential to mention here that the government is empowered to set up one or more Tribunals each consisting of a Chairman and not less than two and not more than four other Members under section 6 of the *Act*.

Further, the government, by Official Gazette notification, established another Tribunal *i.e.* ICT-2 on 22 March, 2012 which is governed by the *ICTA* of 1973 and by the *Rules of Procedure* of

---

[167] *Mobarak Hossain, op. cit. no.* 21; *Syed Md. Hachhan, op. cit. no.* 25; *The Chief Prosecutor vs. A. T. M. Azharul Islam,* ICT-BD Case No. 05 of 2013 [ICT-BD 1]; *The Chief Prosecutor vs. Sheikh Sirajul Haque alias Siraj Master, Khan Akram Hossain, and Abdul Latif Talukder [now dead],* ICT-BD Case No. 03 of 2014 [ICT-BD 1]; *Zahid Hossain Khokon, op. cit. no.* 15, *The Chief Prosecutor vs. Md. Abdul Jabbar Engineer,* ICT-BD Case No. 01 of 2014 [ICT-BD 1]; Dr Ashfaque Hossain and Umme Wara, *op. cit. no.* 33 at page 124.

[168] The Tribunal constituted under the Act shall have the power to try and punish any individual or group of individuals or organizations, or any member of any armed, defense or auxiliary forces irrespective of his nationality, who commits or has committed, in the territory of Bangladesh, whether before or after commencement of this *Act*, any crimes mentioned in sub section [2] of section 3 of the *Act*.

2012.[169] Each of the Tribunal consists of three Judges of whom one is Chairman and two are members.[170] The government constituted a Prosecution team headed by a 'Chief prosecutor' under section 7 of the *Act* and the Investigation Agency under section 8 of the *Act*.[171] Moreover, the registry is composed of Registrar, Deputy Registrar and personnel.[172]

Both the Tribunals established under the *ICTA, 1973* were in operation with the same jurisdiction mentioned in section 3 of the *ICTA, 1973*. However, since 15 September, 2015 only the ICT-1 has been functioning on being reconstituted while the ICT-2 remains non-functioning.[173]

2.7 Conclusion

Unquestionably, many atrocious and dreadful crimes had been committed during the nine months long war of liberation in 1971 which resulted in the birth of Bangladesh, an independent State, and the long cherished motherland of the Bengali nation. The world has observed that untold atrocious resistance on part of thousands of Pakistani militaries and local collaborators could not impede the nation's valiant journey to freedom. The nation shall remain ever indebted to those best sons and daughters of the soil who paid supreme sacrifices for an indelible motherland – Bangladesh.[174] The nation always pays tribute and homage to the blood of millions of patriotic martyrs and innocent defenseless

---

[169]   *Op. cit. no. 14.*

[170]   *Id.*

[171]   *Id.*

[172]   *Id.*

[173]   Available at <http://www.ict-bd.org/ict2/>.

[174]   *Moulana Abdus Sobhan, op. cit. no.* 31 at page 6 at para 18.

people.[175] Even though Bangladesh paid a heavy price for its birth as an independent nation, the people who committed the acts of mass murder were not punished before 2010. However, the popular demand of the people has been fulfilled by trying the actual war criminals.

---

[175] *Id.*

Chapter 3

Salient Features of the International Crimes (Tribunals) Act, 1973

3.1 Introduction

The previous chapter shows that both the ICT-1 and ICT-2 have so far decided 30 cases under the *ICTA*, 1973. However, it is to be pondered here that there is an ongoing debate concerning whether this particular law meets the international standard or not. Therefore, it is very important to explore the features of this law to respond to such concern. For this purpose, this chapter focuses on the fundamentally significant features of the 1973 *Act* addressing the issues of internalization of international law; supremacy of the 1973 *Act*; formation of a domestic tribunal to conduct trials of the accused of the offences of genocide, crimes against humanity, war crimes, and other crimes concerning violation of international law. After that, one of the major features *i.e.* sentences provided under the 1973 *Act* has been discussed in detail focusing on the circumstances in which the death sentence should be given to the convicts. Further, this chapter also ponders on the ambits of the definition of genocide and the provision of conducting trials in *absentia*, together with the rights of the accused including the right of bail, right to appeal, right to invoke review proceedings, and to apply for Presidential pardon. It must, essentially, be stated that all the above mentioned features of the 1973 *Act* have been discussed drawing the concerned international perspectives of the international criminal law.

3.2 Internalization of the International Law

After the World War II, Adolf Eichmann[1] was tried under the *Nazis and Nazi Collaborators (Punishment) Law*, which was adopted by the Knesseth on August, 1950.[2] Section 1 of this *Act* depicts that any person who has "done, during the period of the Nazi regime, in an enemy country, an act constituting a crime against the Jewish people" or an "act constituting a crime against humanity" or "an act constituting a war crime" is liable to the death penalty. This law was a creation of their national jurisprudence to try the concerned accused of international crimes corresponding to the said provision.[3] Likewise, the 1973 *Act* of Bangladesh, in a way, internalized the international legal rules and principles along with customary international law.[4] The ambits and limits of the crimes mentioned in this law are being gathered from

---

[1] *Attorney General vs. Adolf Eichmann*, Criminal Case No. 40/61 (11 December 1961) <http://www.internationalcrimesdatabase.org/Case/192/Eichmann/> accessed on 22 August 2016.

[2] Hans W. Baade, "The Eichmann Trial: Some Legal Aspects," (1961) *Duke Law Journal* at page 401.

[3] Michael J. Bazyler and Julia Y. Scheppach, "The Strange and Curious History of the Law Used to Prosecute Adolf Eichmann," (2012) 34 *Loyola of Los Angeles International and Comparative Law Review* at page 423.

[4] Please look at the features of this law in the subsequent part of this chapter.

the principles of international humanitarian laws. This was not unusual for a country of which the constitution clearly states to do so. For example, the Article 25 of the *Constitution of the People's Republic of Bangladesh*, 1972 touches upon the aspect of 'Promotion of international peace, security and solidarity' which reads as follows:

> 'The State shall base its international relations on the principles of respect for national sovereignty and equality, non-interference in the internal affairs of other countries, peaceful settlement of international disputes, and respect for international law and the principles enunciated in the United Nations Charter, and on the basis of those principle shall-

(a) Strive for the renunciation of the use of force in international relations and for general and complete disarmament;

(b) uphold the right of every people freely to determine and build up its own social, economic and political system by ways and means of its own free choice; and

(c) support oppressed peoples throughout the world waging a just struggle against imperialism, colonialism or racialism.'[5]

Under the purview of this provision, Bangladesh as a sovereign nation is entitled to internalize international law as well as invoke its own domestic law to conduct any trial. Moreover, if there is no ambiguity or insufficiency in any such law, the Courts may not draw upon the principles incorporated in the international instruments.[6]

---

[5] The *Constitution of Bangladesh*, Article 25.

[6] Mahmudul Islam, *Constitutional Law of Bangladesh* (Dhaka: Mullick

3.3 Supremacy of 1973 *Act* over the Constitution

According to Article 7 of the *Constitution of Bangladesh*, the Constitution itself is supreme law in the land of Bangladesh and any other law which is inconsistent with this Constitution would be void to the extent of the inconsistency. This provision reads as follows: 'This Constitution is, as the solemn expression of the will of the people, the supreme law of the Republic, and if any other law is inconsistent with this Constitution and other law shall, to the extent of the inconsistency, be void.'[7]

Therefore, it is clear that this Article explicitly encompasses supremacy of the constitutional law of Bangladesh. Besides, as per Article 26 of the *Constitution of Bangladesh*, any law which is inconsistent with any of the fundamental rights ensured under the Constitution itself would be void to the extent of its inconsistence. This Article reads as follows:

> '(1) All existing law inconsistent with the provisions of this Part shall, to the extent of such inconsistency, become void on the commencement of this Constitution.
>
> (2) The State shall not make any law inconsistent with any provisions of this Part, and any law so made shall, to the extent of such inconsistency, be void.

Brothers (3rd ed.), 2012); *H. M. Ershad vs. Bangladesh,* (2001) BLD (AD) 69, 70; *Bangladesh National Women Lawyers Association vs. Ministry of Home Affairs,* (2009) 61 DLR 371.

[7]   The *Constitution of Bangladesh,* Article 7(2).

(3) Nothing in this article shall apply to any amendment of this Constitution made under article 142.'

However, the *Constitution (First Amendment) Act,* 1973 expressly included in Article 47(3) that any law providing for the detention and trial of war criminals would be kept out of the purview of the provisions of Part III of the *Constitution of Bangladesh i.e.* Fundamental Rights. This provision reads as follows:

'Notwithstanding anything contained in this Constitution, no law nor any provision thereof providing for detention, prosecution or punishment of any person, who is a member of any armed or defence or auxiliary forces or any individual, group of individuals or organization or who is a prisoner of war, for genocide, crimes against humanity or war crimes and other crimes under international law shall be deemed void or unlawful or ever to have become void or unlawful, on the ground that such law or provision of any such law is inconsistent with, or repugnant to, any of the provisions of this Constitution.'[8]

Further, Article 47(A) reads as follows:

'(1) The rights guaranteed under article 31, clauses (1) and (3) of article 35 and article 44 shall not apply to any person to whom a law specified in clause (3) of article 47 applies.

(2) Notwithstanding anything contained in this Constitution, no person to whom a law specified

---

[8]   *Ibid,* Article 47(3).

in clause (3) of article 47 applies shall have the right to move the Supreme Court for any of the remedies under this Constitution.'[9]

Now, if we look at both Articles 7 and 26 of the Constitution, we would realize that the Constitution itself has compromised with its supremacy by creating Article 47 to ensure trials of the individuals or group of individuals or organization responsible for genocide, crimes against humanity, war crimes, and other crimes under international law. The 1973 *Act* has been protected in respect of detention, prosecution and punishment of any person, who is a member of any armed or defence or auxiliary forces or any individual, group of individuals or organization who is a prisoner of war for genocide, crimes against humanity, war crimes, and other crimes under international criminal law. Under the *Act*, such person cannot challenge the legality of the proceedings on any of the grounds contained in Articles 26, 27, 28, 31, 35 and 44 by resorting to Article 102 or other provisions of the Constitution. Sub-clause (2) of Article 47A debars an accused person who is being prosecuted or punished under the *Act* of 1973 to move the High Court Division (HCD) for any of the relief(s) available under the Constitution other than the one provided in the *Act*. Thus, it can be said that the Constitution has, undoubtedly, given protection to the 1973 *Act*; in other words, the provisions in relation to the said offences have been given supremacy over the Constitution itself.

3.4 Domestic Tribunal

There are, so far, 4 models of Tribunal to conduct trials of accused of the aforesaid offences namely: (1) the United Nations Sponsored Tribunal; (2) the Hybrid Tribunal; (3) the Pure

---

[9]   *Ibid*, Article 47A.

International Tribunal; and (4) the Domestic Tribunal. The UN Security Council, under its Chapter VII powers,[10] created the International Criminal Tribunal for the former Yugoslavia (ICTY)[11] in 1993 and the International Criminal Tribunal for Rwanda (ICTR)[12] in 1994. Subsequent to the establishment of the ICTY and ICTR, a demand was recognised for other tribunals to address serious crimes committed in other parts of the world.[13] The ICTY

---

[10] The *UN Charter* sets out in Chapter VII the UN's power to ensure the "maintenance of international peace and security". To ensure the "maintenance of international peace and security", after securing Security Council approval, the UN may take military and/or non-military action.

[11] In May 1993, the Tribunal was established by the United Nations in response to mass atrocities then taking place in Croatia and Bosnia and Herzegovina. Reports depicting horrendous crimes, in which thousands of civilians were being killed and wounded, tortured and sexually abused in detention camps and hundreds of thousands expelled from their homes, caused outrage across the world and spurred the UN Security Council to act. The ICTY was the first war crimes court created by the UN and the first international war crimes tribunal since the Nuremberg and Tokyo tribunals.

[12] The International Criminal Tribunal for Rwanda (ICTR) was established to "prosecute persons responsible for genocide and other serious violations of international humanitarian law committed in the territory of Rwanda and neighbouring States, between 1 January 1994 and 31 December 1994." The Tribunal is located in Arusha, Tanzania, and has offices in Kigali, Rwanda. Its Appeals Chamber is located in The Hague, Netherlands. The ICTR is the first ever international tribunal to deliver verdicts in relation to genocide, and the first to interpret the definition of genocide set forth in the 1948 Geneva Conventions which also defined rape in international criminal law and recognise rape as a means of perpetrating genocide for the first time.

[13] International Criminal Law & Practice Training Materials, International Criminal Law Services <http://wcjp.unicri.it/ deliverables/docs/Module_4_International_war_crimes_courts.

and ICTR were located far from the countries they served. Treaty based, hybrid courts with national and international elements were thus proposed to help create efficient, locally based courts to address serious international crimes.[14] Hybrid Tribunal essentially includes the Special Court for Sierra Leone (SCSL),[15] and the Extraordinary Chambers in the Courts of Cambodia (ECCC).[16] Pure international tribunal includes the International Military *Tribunal* at *Nuremberg*.[17] The Nuremberg trials were a series of 13 trials carried out in Nuremberg, Germany, between 1945 and 1949.[18] Finally, the "Domestic Tribunal" entails the tribunal formed under the *Nazis and Nazi Collaborators (Punishment) Law*, 1950, the Court of Bosnia and Herzegovina, and the War Crimes Division of the High Court of Uganda that

---

pdf> accessed on 23 August 2016.

[14]   *Ibid.*

[15]   The Special Court for Sierra Leone was set up in 2002 as the result of a request to the United Nations in 2000 by the Government of Sierra Leone for "a special court" to address serious crimes against civilians and UN peacekeepers committed during the country's decade-long (1991-2002) civil war.

[16]   It is a special Cambodian court which receives international assistance through the United Nations Assistance to the Khmer Rouge Trials (UNAKRT). The court is more commonly referred to by the more informal name the Khmer Rouge Tribunal or the Cambodia Tribunal. In 1997, the government requested the UN to assist in establishing a trial to prosecute the senior leaders of the Khmer Rouge. Therefore, in 2001, the Cambodian National Assembly passed a law and created this court to try serious crimes committed during the Khmer Rouge regime 1975-1979; See also, Sarah Williams, *Hybrid International Criminal Tribunals* [2014] DOI: 10.1093/OBO/9780199796953-0069.

[17]   Center on Law and Globalization <https://clg.portalxm.com/library/keytext.cfm?keytext_id=189>.

[18]   Nuremberg Trials <http://www.history.com/topics/world-war-ii/nuremberg-trials>.

have been created to try international crimes.[19] Similar to the last model of tribunals, the ICT-BD is a tribunal of domestic nature. Under Section 6 of the 1973 *Act*, the ICT-BDs were formed which are consisting of a Chairman, and minimum two and maximum four other members.[20] As regards appointment of Chairman or a member of a Tribunal, a person has to be a Judge, or qualified to be a Judge, or been a Judge, of the Supreme Court of Bangladesh.[21] It is important to mention here that 'the Tribunal shall be independent in the exercise of its judicial functions and shall ensure fair trial.'[22]

Section 6 of the 1973 *Act* reads as follows:

> '(1) For the purpose of section 3, the Government may, by notification in the official Gazette, set up one or more Tribunals, each consisting of a Chairman and not less than two and not more than four other members.
>
> (2) Any person who is a Judge, or is qualified to be a Judge, or has been a Judge, of the Supreme Court of Bangladesh, may be appointed as a Chairman or member of a Tribunal.
>
> (2A) The Tribunal shall be independent in the exercise of its judicial functions and shall ensure fair trial.
>
> (3) The permanent seat of a Tribunal shall be in Dhaka: Provided that a Tribunal may hold

---

[19]   Baade, *op. cit. no.* 2.

[20]   The *International Crimes (Tribunals) Act*, 1973, Section 6(1).

[21]   *Ibid*, Section 6(2).

[22]   *Ibid*, Section 6(2A).

its sittings at such other place or places as it deems fit.

(4) If any member of a Tribunal dies or is, due to illness or any other reason, unable to continue to perform his functions, the Government may, by notification in the official Gazette, declare the office of such member to be vacant and appoint thereto another person qualified to hold the office.

(5) If, in the course of a trial, any one of the members of a Tribunal is, for any reason, unable to attend any sitting thereof, the trial may continue before the other members.

(6) A Tribunal shall not, merely by reason of any change in its membership or the absence of any member thereof from any sitting, be bound to recall and re-hear any witness who has already given any evidence and may act on the evidence already given or produced before it.

(7) If, upon any matter requiring the decision of a Tribunal, there is a difference of opinion among its members, the opinion of the majority shall prevail and the decision of the Tribunal shall be expressed in terms of the views of the majority.

(8) Neither the constitution of a Tribunal nor the appointment of its Chairman or members shall be challenged by the prosecution or by the accused persons or their counsel.'[23]

---

[23]   *Ibid*, Section 6.

As per the prior discussion, Judges of the ICT-BD are appointed by the concerned Government, along with, the Prosecution, the Investigation Agency, while the total budget to conduct the entire trials are domestic *i.e.* Bangladeshi.

3.5 Definition of Genocide

Genocide was not a crime under the International Military Tribunal at Nuremberg while only "Crimes against Humanity" formed the basis for prosecuting the atrocities perpetrated by the Nazis against European Jews.[24] None of the Nazis tried at Nuremberg were found guilty of genocidal acts committed prior to 1 September, 1939, the day the war broke out.[25] However, the necessary link between genocide and war in international law was not tolerated for long. Genocide as an international crime had, therefore, been established under the *Convention on the Prevention and Punishment of the Crime of Genocide* (hereinafter referred as *Genocide Convention*), adopted by the General Assembly of the United Nations on 9 December, 1948.[26]Article II of this Convention stipulates that 'genocide means any of the following acts committed with intent to destroy, in whole or in part, a national, ethnical, racial, or religious group, as such : (a) killing members of the group; (b) causing serious bodily or mental harm to members of the group; (c) deliberately inflicting on the group conditions of life calculated to bring about its physical destruction in whole or in part; (d) imposing measures intended to prevent births within the group; (e) forcibly transferring children of the group to another group.' This definition is confined to four

---

[24] *Op. cit. no. 17.*

[25] *Ibid.*

[26] United Nations-Treaty Series (No. 1021)
<https://treaties.un.org/doc/publication/unts/volume%2078/volume-78-i-1021-english.pdf> accessed on 20 August 2016.

groups, which may be called *indelible* or *protected* groups, and five distinct methods of committing genocide. It is to be noted that intention to destroy the said group(s), wholly or partly, is a precondition for being the offence of genocide.

Subsequent to that, the genocide has been defined as an international crime in many statutes such as the ICTY Statute of 1993 (Article 4(2));[27] the ICTR Statute of 1994 (Article 2(2));[28] the ICC Statute of 1998 (Article 6(2)).[29] The definitions of

---

[27]   The *ICTY Statute*, Article 4(2) reads as follows:
'Genocide means any of the following acts committed with intent to destroy, in whole or in part, a national, ethnical, racial or religious group, as such: (a) killing members of the group; (b) causing serious bodily or mental harm to members of the group; (c) deliberately inflicting on the group conditions of life calculated to bring about its physical destruction in whole or in part; (d) imposing measures intended to prevent births within the group; (e) forcibly transferring children of the group to another group.'

[28]   Article 2(2) of the *ICTR Statute* reads as follows:
'Genocide means any of the following acts committed with intent to destroy, in whole or in part, a national, ethnical, racial or religious group, as such: a) Killing members of the group; b) Causing serious bodily or mental harm to members of the group; c) Deliberately inflicting on the group conditions of life calculated to bring about its physical destruction in whole or in part; d) Imposing measures intended to prevent births within the group; e) Forcibly transferring children of the group to another group.'

[29]   The *ICC Statute*, Article 6 reads as follows:
'For the purpose of this Statute, 'genocide' means any of the following acts committed with intent to destroy, in whole or in part, a national, ethnical, racial or religious group, as such: (a) Killing members of the group; (b) Causing serious bodily or mental harm to members of the group; (c) Deliberately inflicting on the group conditions of life calculated to bring about its physical destruction in whole or in part; (d) Imposing measures intended to prevent births within the group; (e) Forcibly transferring children of the

genocide in such statutes are quite analogous to the definition of genocide provided in the *Genocide Convention*. The 1973 *Act of Bangladesh* has also defined genocide under Section 3(2)(c) as an international crime corresponding to the definition of the *Genocide Convention* with the purpose of giving punishments to the perpetrators responsible for committing such a heinous crime. Section 3(2)(c) reads as follows:

> '(c) Genocide: meaning and including any of the following acts committed with intent to destroy, in whole or in part, a national, ethnic, racial, religious or political group, such as:

(i) killing members of the group;
(ii) causing serious bodily or mental harm to members of the group;
(iii) deliberately inflicting on the group conditions of life calculated to bring about its physical destruction in whole or in part;
(iv) imposing measures intended to prevent Births within the group;
(v) forcibly transferring children of the group to another group.'[30]

This definition includes, *inter alia*, political group as one of the protected groups which was not, however, included in the definition of other statutes mentioned in the above. As regards, the *Genocide Convention*, many observers have noted that there was an "under-the-table" compromise made during the Convention to exclude political groups.[31] This was done to secure

---

group to another group.'
[30]   The *International Crimes (Tribunals) Act*, 1973, Section 3(2)(c).
[31]   Kok-Thay Eng, Redefining Genocide
<http://www.genocidewatch.org/images/AboutGen_Redefining

ratification by member states that feared that their internal suppression of dissents might be subject to external interference under the Convention.[32] Anyway, it is highly contended that exclusion of political group from the *Genocide Convention* seems to be a failure of the Convention.[33]

3.6 Right of Bail

The 1973 *Act* exclusively recognizes the right of bail as enshrined under Rule 9(5) of the *Rules of Procedure* (read with Section 22[34] of the 1973 *Act*). This provision depicts that the Investigation Agency must conclude investigation of a particular case within one year of the arrest of the accused. However, if the Investigation Agency fails to accomplish investigation within the specified period, the accused may be released on bail after fulfilling certain conditions as imposed by Tribunal.[35] In exceptional circumstances, the Tribunal may extend the period of custody of the accused person as well as investigation for six months by showing reasons and recording the same in writing.[36] Apart from the provision of providing bail during investigation period, the Tribunal may release an accused on bail at any stage of the proceedings in the interest of justice under Rule 34(3) of the *Rules*

_Genocide.pdf> accessed on 20 August 2016.

[32] Frank Chalk & Kurt Jonassohn, *The History and Sociology of Genocide: Analysis and Case Studies* (New Haven and London: Yale University Press, 1990) at page 44.

[33] *Id.*

[34] The *International Crimes (Tribunals) Act*, 1973, Section 22 reads as follows:
'Subject to the provision of this Act, a Tribunal may regulate its own procedure.'

[35] The *Rules of Procedure*, Rule 9(5).

[36] *Id.*

of Procedure. However, the said bail must be granted following certain conditions while the Tribunal may modify any of such conditions on its own motion or on the prayer of either party.[37] It must be mentioned here that if the accused person violates any of the conditions as specified by the Tribunal, the accused person may be taken into custody by canceling his bail.[38]

As for instance of providing bail by the ICT-BD, the case concerning *Md. Abdul Alim @ M. A. Alim*[39] was the first case in which the concerned accused was granted bail.[40] On hearing both the sides, the Tribunal allowed the accused to remain at large on conditional bail by its order dated 31 March, 2011.[41] Since then, he was on conditional bail and made his appearance before the Tribunal as and when directed.[42] However, the Tribunal ordered directing the Investigation Agency to interrogate the accused at his home where he has been residing, considering his old age health complications instead of allowing the same to bring the accused to safe home as prayed by the Chief Prosecutor.[43] Another example is the case concerning Syed Md. Qaiser[44] in which the Tribunal released the accused person on conditional bail, taking his physical condition as well as old age complications into account.[45]

---

[37]   *Ibid*, Rule 34(3).

[38]   *Id.*

[39]   *The Chief Prosecutor vs. Md. Abdul Alim @ M. A. Alim*, ICT-BD Case No. 01 of 2012 [ICT-BD 2].

[40]   *Ibid*, at page 2 at para 1.

[41]   *Ibid*, at page 7 at para 15.

[42]   *Ibid*, at page 7 at para 15.

[43]   *Ibid*, at page 7 at para 16.

[44]   *The Chief Prosecutor vs. Syed Md. Qaiser*, ICT-BD Case No. 04 of 2013 [ICT-BD 2].

[45]   *Ibid*, at page 9 at para 26.

3.7 Trial in *Absentia*

It is crucial for the tribunals and courts to be truly effective and credible to investigate and prosecute the most serious crimes of international concern dealing with the problem of non-appearance of the accused. In this concern, the mechanism for trials in *absentia* could be the ultimate solution because when a trial in the absence of the accused is a legal possibility, there is no need to wait for the trial to proceed. To begin with, the *Nuremberg International Military Tribunal (IMT) Charter* (hereinafter referred as *Nuremberg Charter*) provided for trials in *absentia* in Article 12. It is mentioned that:

> 'The Tribunal shall have the right to take proceedings against a person charged with crimes set out in Article 6 of this Charter in his absence, if he has not been found or if the Tribunal, for any reason, finds it necessary, in the interests of justice, to conduct the hearing in his absence.'[46]

This possibility to convict a person charged with crimes set out in the Nuremberg IMT's jurisdiction was used only once before the Tribunal in the case of *Martin Bormann*.[47] The indictment against *Martin Bormann* was based on participation in a common plan or conspiracy, war crimes, and crimes against humanity, which are all included in Article 6 of the *Nuremberg Charter*.[48] *Martin*

---

[46]   Charter of the Nuremberg International Military Tribunal <http://www.yale.edu/lawweb/avalon/imt/proc/imtconst.htm#art12>.

[47]   Anne Klerks, Trials in Absentia in International (Criminal) Law, page 17 <http://arno.uvt.nl/show.cgi?fid=81103>.

[48]   Judgement of Bormann, <http://www.yale.edu/lawweb/avalon/imt/proc/judborma.htm>.

Bormann himself was not present at the trial. His counsel said that *Martin Bormann* was dead and that the Tribunal should not use Article 12 of the *Nuremberg Charter* to convict his client *in absentia*.[49] However, the Nuremberg IMT presumed him to be alive and decided to convict *Martin Bormann* in *absentia*.[50] Another question regarding trial in *absentia* came before the Nuremberg IMT *i.e. Gustav Krupp Von Bohlen und Halbach* case.[51] His counsel noted that his health did not permit him to attend the trial, and that a trial in his absence would not be desirable. However, *Gustav Krupp Von Bohlen und Halbach* was not convicted finally in *absentia*, because he was declared mentally incapable of standing trial.[52]

In case of ECCC, as stated in Article 33 of the *Law on the Establishment of the Extraordinary Chambers*, the jurisdiction of the Extraordinary Chambers shall be practised in accordance with the international standards of justice, fairness, and due process of law.[53] More specifically, this Article makes it clear that the chambers' exercise of jurisdiction shall be in accordance with Articles 14 and 15 of the *International Covenant on Civil and Political Rights* (ICCPR), 1966.[54] The right of the accused to

---

[49]   *Id.*

[50]   Bormann, *op. cit. no.* 48.

[51]   Klerks, *op. cit. no.* 47, page 18.

[52]   Nazi Conspiracy and Aggression – Chapter IV, <http://www.yale.edu/lawweb/avalon/imt/document/nca_vol1/chap_04.htm>.

[53]   Law on the Establishment of the Extraordinary Chambers, with inclusion of amendments as promulgated on 27 October 2004 (NS/RKM/1004/006), article 33 <http://www.eccc.gov.kh/english/cabinet/law/4/KR_Law_as_amended_27_Oct_2004_Eng.pd>.

[54]   Cambodia signed and ratified the ICCPR on 26 May 1992, which is directly enforceable in the domestic legal order (based on Article

be tried in his or her presence, based on Article 14(3)(d) of the ICCPR, is more explicitly stated in Article 35(d) of the *Law on the Establishment of the Extraordinary Chambers*. Moreover, Rule 81 of the *Internal Rules of Procedure of the Cambodian Extraordinary Chambers* states, "the right of the accused to be tried in his or her own presence".[55] Nevertheless, in this rule, some exceptions to this right are laid down. When after his or her initial appearance, and after having been duly summoned, the accused refuses or fails to attend the proceedings, the proceedings may continue in his or her absence.

The *Statute of the Special Court for Sierra Leone* (SCSL) depicts in Article 17(4)(d) that the accused has the right to be tried in his or her presence. However, Rule 60 of the *Rules of Procedure and Evidence* mentions two exceptions to this general rule. It makes clear in subsection (A) that an accused who has made his initial appearance, may be tried in his absence when i) "he has been afforded the right to appear at his own trial but he refuses to do so or ii) is at large and refuses to appear in court".[56] Based on Rule 60 (B), the accused may be represented by his or her own counsel or a counsel appointed by the Court. Moreover, as stated in Rule 60(B), the case may only proceed when the judge or Trial Chamber is satisfied, "that the accused has, expressly or impliedly, waived his or her right to be present". An example of the use of Rule 60(B) is the case of *Prosecutor of the Special*

31 of the 1993 *Constitution of Cambodia*).

[55] Extraordinary Chambers in the Courts of Cambodia, *Internal Rules* (Rev.1) as revised on 1 February 2008, Rule 8 <http://www.eccc.gov.kh/english/cabinet/fileUpload/27/Internal_Rules_Revision1_01-02-08_eng.pdf>.

[56] Special Court for Sierra Leone, *Rules of Procedure and Evidence* (amended on 19 November 2007), <http://www.sc-sl.org/Documents/rulesofprocedureandevidence.pdf>.

Court vs. Issa Sesay, Morris Kallon and Augustine Gbao[57] in which *Augustine Gbao* made his initial appearance before the Court on 16 April 2003.[58] However, on 7 July 2004, he refused to go to Court.[59] The Court was satisfied, in light of the foregoing findings, that *Augustine Gbao* had waived his right to be present at trial, and the trial proceeded in his absence. The defence team of *Augustine Gbao* continued to represent him, as allowed for under Rule 60(B) of the *Rules of Procedure and Evidence of the Special Court* for Sierra Leone.[60]

The most recent tribunal *i.e.* the *Special Tribunal for Lebanon* (STL) enshrines the possibility of holding trials in *absentia* as well. As stated by the Secretary General, the inclusion of a provision on trials in *absentia* would be crucial "to ensure that the legal process would not be unduly delayed because of the absence of the accused".[61] The possibility of holding trials *in absentia* does not mean that these kinds of trials are allowed for under all circumstances. Article 16(4)(d) of the Statute of the STL makes clear that subject to the provisions of Article 22 and Rules 105 and 106 of the *Rules of Procedure and Evidence*, the accused has the minimum guarantee to be tried is his or her presence. Following this, Article 22 of the Statute of the STL makes it clear that a trial

---

[57]   *The Prosecutor of the Special Court vs. Issa Sesay, Morris Kallon and Augustine Gbao*, (SCSL Trial Chamber), March 2, 2009.

[58]   Klerks, *op. cit. no. 47*, pages 54-55.

[59]   *Id.*

[60]   *The Prosecutor vs. Sesay, Kallon and Gbao* (SCSL-04-15-T), 'Ruling on the issue of Refusal of the Third Accused, Augustine Gbao, to Attend Hearing of the Special Court for Sierra Leone on 7 July 2004 and succeeding days', 7 July 2004, <http://www.sc-sl.org/Transcripts/RUF-070704.pdf>.

[61]   Report of the Secretary-General on the establishment of a special tribunal for Lebanon, UN Doc. S/2006/893, 15 November 2006, at paragraph 32.

proceeding in the absence of the accused shall only be conducted under strict conditions. For this purpose, the Article distinguishes three kinds of situations, namely when the accused:

(a) 'has expressly and in writing waived his or her right to be present;
(b) has not been handed over to the Tribunal by the State authorities concerned; and
(c) has absconded or otherwise cannot be found and all reasonable steps have been taken to secure his or her appearance before the Tribunal and to inform him or her of the charges confirmed by the Pre-Trial Judge.[62]

The holding of a trial in absence of the accused is, thus, limited to these three situations. When the hearings are conducted in the absence of the accused, the STL shall ensure that "the accused has been notified, or served with the indictment, or notice has otherwise been given of the indictment through publication in the media or communication to the State of residence or nationality".[63] Moreover, the STL must ensure that the accused has appointed a defence counsel of his or her own choosing which will be remunerated by the accused, or when it is proved that the accused cannot pay for the defence counsel, the defence counsel will be paid by the Tribunal.[64] Whenever the accused fails or refuses to designate a defence counsel, the counsel shall be assigned to him or her by the defence office of the STL.[65] It can be mentioned here that the STL is currently trying four accused persons (a fifth accused's case may be joined to the main case) in *absentia*, i.e. these persons have not been arrested, but the trial against them proceeds nonetheless. It is important to

---

[62]   Article 22 (1), Sub-articles (a), (b), and (c) of the *Statute of the STL*.

[63]   The *Statute of the STL*, Article 22(2)(a).

[64]   *Ibid*, Article 22(2)(b).

[65]   *Ibid*, Article 22(2)(c).

mention here that under Article 22(3) of the STL Statute, even if a trial in *absentia* has taken place against an accused, if he or she appears before the tribunal later and seeks permission for retrial, the same is often allowed, except where an absent defendant was represented at trial by counsel of his or her own choosing. It can be mentioned here that this is a unique phenomenon in international criminal law; none of the other tribunals have employed this procedure.

Moving on the context of Bangladesh, it is provided under Rule 22 of the *Rules of Procedure* that the Tribunal fixes a date for appearance of the accused after taking cognizance of an offence.[66] Again, Rule 31 (read with Rule 32[67]) of the *Rules of Procedure* directs that if the accused person cannot be produced before the Tribunal as specified under Rule 22, a notice must be given in two daily newspapers, one in English and another in Bangla, asking the accused to appear before the Tribunal on the date fixed. However, Section 9 of the 1973 *Act* states that 'where a proceeding is commenced under sub-section (1) of section 9, the tribunal, before fixing the date for the trial under sub-section

---

[66]   The *Rules of Procedure*, Rule 22 reads as follows:
'After taking cognizance of an offence the Tribunal shall fix a date for appearance if he is not already in custody of the accused and issue summons or warrant for appearance as it thinks proper.'
Read Rule 30 with Rule 22 of the same as given in the following:
'After congnizance of an offence is taken, the Tribunal shall issue processor warrant, as it thinks fit and proper, in accordance of rule 22.'

[67]   *Ibid*, Rule 32 reads as follows:
'If the accused, despite publication of notice in daily newspapers, fails to appear before the Tribunal on the date and time so specified therein, and the Tribunal has reason to believe that the accused has absconded or concealing himself so that he cannot be arrested and produced for trial and there is no immediate prospect for arresting him, the trial of such accused shall commence and be held in absentia.'

(2) of the said section, has reason to believe that the accused person has absconded or concealed himself so that he cannot be produced for trial, may hold the trial in his absence [*trial in absentia*] following the procedure as laid down in the *Rules of Procedure* made under Section 22 for such trial.' In this regard, Section 10A of the 1973 *Act*, read with Rule 43(1)[68] of the *Rules of Procedure*, depicts that the Tribunal may direct to engage a Counsel at the cost of the Government with a view to defending the accused person.[69]

3.8 Sentencing Considerations

As regards giving sentence, it is included in Section 20 of the 1973 *Act* that 'upon conviction of an accused person, the Tribunal shall award sentence of death or such other punishment proportionate to the gravity of the crime as appears to the Tribunal to be just and proper.'[70]Corresponding to this provision, the trial of the ICT-BD can be exemplified which had been initiated by establishing the International Crimes Tribunals with the purpose of holding

---

[68]   *Ibid*, Rule 43(1) reads as follows:
'Where an accused is not represented by any counseling the trial of a case, the Tribunal shall appoint a counsel to defend such an accused at the expense of the Government.'

[69]   The *International Crimes (Tribunals) Act*, 1973, Section 10A of the 1973 *Act*.

[70]   *Ibid*, Section 20(1) and (2); Section 20 reads as follows:
'(1) The Judgment of a Tribunal as to the guilt or the innocence of any accused person shall give the reasons on which it is based: Provided that each member of the Tribunal shall be competent to deliver a judgment of his own.
(2) Upon conviction of an accused person, the Tribunal shall award sentence of death or such other punishment proportionate to the gravity of the crime as appears to the Tribunal to be just and proper.'

trials relating to the detention, prosecution, and punishment of persons responsible for genocide, crimes against humanity, war crimes, and crimes committed in the territory of Bangladesh, in violation of customary international law, particularly between the period of 25 March and 16 December, 1971.[71] The inmates were responsible for indiscriminate killings of innocent and unarmed civilians with the planned and deliberately pursued intention of exterminating the people of Bangladesh.[72] They had substantially contributed to commit widespread atrocities; tortures; inhuman, humiliating, degrading, and cruel treatment; hostage taking; disappearances; executions without trials; and systematic rape in Bangladesh.[73] Hence, on the basis of the charges brought against the convicts especially in relation to the "Crimes against Humanity" and "Genocide", and gravity of the offences committed by them, they were provided death sentence to ensure justice to people of Bangladesh.

However, many opponents of death sentence claim that it should be abolished to ensure fundamental human rights to the accused. On the other hand, the proponents of death sentence argue that it has been established in many cases that death sentence should

---

[71]   The Tribunal constituted under the Act shall have the power to try and punish any individual or group of individuals or organizations, or any member of any armed, defense or auxiliary forces irrespective of his nationality, who commits or has committed, in the territory of Bangladesh, whether before or after commencement of this *Act*, any crimes mentioned in sub section [2] of section 3 of the *Act*.

[72]   *Ibid.*

[73]   Wardatul Akman, "Atrocities against Humanity during the Liberation War in Bangladesh," (2002) 4 *Journal of Genocide Research* at pages 54-59; Yasmin Saika, "Beyond the Archive of Silence: Narratives of Violence of the 1971 Liberation War of Bangladesh," (2004) 58 *History Workshop Journal* at pages 275-87; Raunaq Jahan, *Eyewitness Accounts: Genocide in Bangladesh* (New York: Garland Publishing, 1997) at pages 26-41.

not be absolutely abolished rather in the rarest of the rare cases it should prevail in the form as it is. Moreover, remembering the matters of public confidence and the doctrine of proportionality, the death sentence should not be abolished. The following discussion portrays the descriptions of the aforesaid reasons:

3.8.1 Rarest of the Rare Cases[74]

'[A] crime is an act that is deemed by law harmful not merely for the individual victim but for the society as a whole...'[75] On the other hand, punishments are given to the convicts to deter the people not to commit such abhorrent crime again. Likewise, death sentence is an exception in the matter of awarding punishment for murder.[76]

Generally, when a case is brought before the competent Court concerning a crime which shocks the "collective conscience of the society", then such case is regarded as the rarest of rare case.[77] The supporters of the death penalty argue that in such

---

[74] Lord Macaulay stated:
'First among the punishment provided for offences by this case stands death. No argument that has been brought to our notice has satisfied us that it would be desirable wholly to dispense with this punishment. But we are convinced that it ought to be very sparingly inflicted; and we propose to employ it only in cases where either murder or the highest offence against the state has been committed.'

[75] The statement has been given by Salmond.

[76] *Ambaram vs. State of M. P.*, AIR 1976 SC 2196.

[77] *Delhi Gang Rape Case* <http://www.ibnlive.com/news/india/full-text-4-638638.html>; Utkarsh Anand, How the Apex Court Defines 'Rarest of Rare', *The Indian Express* (Online), 12 February 2013 <http://archive.indianexpress.com/news/how-the-apex-court-defines-rarest-of-rare/1072728/>.

cases death sentence must be given to the guilty person. For illustration, in the case of *Bachan Singh vs. State of Punjab*,[78] the Indian Supreme Court held that death penalty has to be imposed in the rarest of the rare cases.[79] In order to determine as to whether a case will come under the ambit of the rarest of the rare cases, there are many factors that have to be considered. It is well established that *prima facie* "brutality" would obviously be an existing factor for such determination.[80]

However, in the case of *Mohammad Ajmal Amir Kasab vs. State of Moharastra*[81], popularly known as the *Bombay bomb attack case*, the Supreme Court of India reiterated the importance of death sentence and provided certain concrete factors those have to be taken into consideration to determine the rarest of the rare cases. The following discussion focuses on the factors in detail:

3.8.1.1 Method of Committing a Proven Offence

When any offence especially murder has been committed in 'an extremely brutal, grotesque, diabolical, revolting or dastardly manner so as to arouse intense and extreme indignation of the community', the case can come into the ambit of the rarest of the rare cases.[82] For illustration, 'when the victim is subjected to inhuman acts of torture or cruelty in order to bring about his or

---

[78]   (1980) 2 SCC 684 <http://www.deathpenaltyindia.com/landmarkcase/bachan-singh-vs-state-of-punjab/>; See also, *Shashi Nayar vs. Union of India*, AIR 1992 SC 395.

[79]   *Review Petition of Kamaruzzaman Case*, at page 21.

[80]   *Ibid*, at page 23; See also *Registrar General, High Court of Karnataka vs. Prakash Jadav*, 2006 *Criminal Law Journal* 3393 (3409).

[81]   Criminal Appeal No. 1899 – 1900 of 2011 <http://indiankanoon.org/doc/193792759/>.

[82]   *Kamaruzzaman, op. cit. no. 79*, at page 24.

her death', and 'when the body of the victim is cut into pieces or his body is dismembered in a fiendish manner.'[83]

3.8.1.2 Intention behind the Intention to Commit the Offence

If the motive of committing any concerned offence evinces total depravity and meanness to the humanity, it can also be a factor of determining the same.[84] As for example, '(a) a hired assassin commits murder for the sake of money or reward; (b) a cold-blooded murder is committed with a deliberate design in order to inherit property or to gain control over property of a ward or a person under the control of the murderer or *vis-à-vis* whom the murderer is in a dominating position or in a position of trust, or (c) a murder is committed in the course for betrayal of the motherland.'[85]

3.8.1.3 Nature of the Crime: Socially Abhorrent

When murder of a member or members of any targeted community 'is committed not for personal reasons but in circumstances which arouse social wrath', then the concerned case can be regarded as the rarest of the rare case.[86] For instance, 'committing crime in order to terrorize such persons and frighten them into fleeing from a place or in order to deprive them of, or make them surrender, lands or benefits conferred on them with a

---

[83] *Ibid*, at page 24.

[84] *Ibid*, at pages 24-25.

[85] *Id*.

[86] *Id*.

view to reversing past injustices and in order to restore the social balance.'[87]

3.8.1.4 Scale of Cruelty Committed against Human Being

Whether a case can be regarded as the rarest of the rare case, it depends on the gravity of the offence in relation to the concerned case.[88] For illustration, 'when multiple murders say of all or almost all the members of a family or a large number of persons of a particular caste, community, or locality, are committed.'[89]

3.8.1.5 Individuality of the Victims

'When the victim of murder is (a) an innocent child who could not have or has not provided even an excuse, much less a provocation, for murder; (b) a helpless woman or a person rendered helpless by old age or infirmity; (c) when the victim is a person *vis-à-vis* whom the murderer is in a position of domination or trust; and (d) when the victim is a public figure generally loved and respected by the community for the services rendered by him and the murder is committed for political or similar reasons other than personal reasons.'[90]

3.8.2 Public Confidence

The supporters of death penalty also argue that this punishment should not be abolished to uphold public confidence. Otherwise,

---

87   *Id.*

88   *Id.*

89   *Id.*

90   *Id.*

the main purpose of punishment *i.e.* to deter others not to commit the same crime again, will be of no value. In support of this argument, in the case of *Mahesh vs. State of MP*,[91] the Supreme Court refused to interfere with death sentence and stipulated:

> '[I]t will be a mockery of Justice to permit the accused to escape the extreme penalty of law when faced with such evidence and such cruel acts. To give lesser punishment to the accused would be to render the justicing [sic] system of the country suspect. The common man will lose faith in Courts. In such cases, he understands and appreciates the language of deterrence more than the reformative Jargon.'[92]

Moreover, in the case of *State of Karnataka vs. Krishna alias Raju*,[93] the Supreme Court stated that consideration of undue sympathy in cases of grave offences will lead to miscarriage of justice as well as weaken the confidence of the public to the effectiveness of the criminal justice system.[94]

3.8.3 Proportionality Doctrine

The earlier discussion also portrays that to determine punishment of any offence, the gravity of the offences has to be taken into consideration which is, in other words, regarded as following the proportionality doctrine. To put emphasis on the doctrine of proportionality, in the case of *Satwant Singh vs. State of*

---

[91]   AIR 1987 SC 1346.

[92]   *Kamaruzzaman, op. cit. no.* 79, at pages 26-27.

[93]   1987 1 SCC 538.

[94]   *Kamaruzzaman, op. cit. no.* 79, at page 27.

Punjab,[95] the Supreme Court of India depicted that 'the measure of punishment to be awarded upon conviction for an offence has to be commensurate with the nature and seriousness of the offence and that if the accused is unable to show that the sentence imposed upon him is not in any way excessive, the fact that a co-accused charged with abetment of the same offence, received a lighter sentence is not a relevant circumstances.'[96] In those cases, the Court(s) should also consider the circumstances under which the offences were committed, 'degree of deliberation shown by the offender, provocation, offenders' antecedents, and that while the sentence should be adequate to the offence, they should not be excessive either.'[97]

3.8.4 International Laws on Death Sentence

It has been found in many international laws which support death sentence as well. Article 6(5) of the *International Covenant on Civil and Political Rights, 1966* (ICCPR)[98] depicts that in case of the most serious offences, death sentence can be imposed on the convicts.[99] Moreover, in *United Nations Human Rights Committee, General Comment 6, Article 6 (Sixteenth session, 1982)*, it has been iterated that 'State parties are not obliged to abolish the death penalty totally they are obliged to limit its use and, in particular, to abolish it for other than the "most serious

---

95   AIR 1960 SC 266.

96   *Kamaruzzaman, op. cit. no.* 79, at pages 28-29.

97   *Ibid*, at page 29; *Adamji Umer Dolal vs. State of Bombay*, AIR 1952 SC 14; *Roghunath vs. Paria*, AIR 1967 Goa 95; *Sham Sundar vs. Puran*, AIR 1991 SC 8; *Mangal Singh vs. State of UP*, AIR 1975 SC 76.

98   Adopted by the UN General Assembly in 1966.

99   The UN General Assembly adopted the Second Optional Protocol to the ICCPR. Its goal is the abolition of the death penalty, however, Bangladesh did not ratify the said Protocol yet.

crimes".'[100] Essentially, the *Committee* stated that "the expression the most serious crimes must be read restrictively to mean that the death penalty should be quite an exceptional measure.[101] Besides, the *UN Human Rights Committee* has interpreted "most serious crimes" not to include economic offences, embezzlement by official's robbery, abduction not resulting in death, apostasy and drug-related crimes.[102] Interestingly, expressing particular concern about very vague categories of offences relating to internal and external security, it has excluded political offences otherwise the imposition of the death penalty may be subject to essentially subjective criteria in practice.'[103]

Again, Article 1 of the '*Safeguards Guaranteeing Protection of the Rights of those Facing the Death Penalty, Approved by Economic and Social Council resolution 1984/50 of 25 May 1984*' very clearly stated that '[i]n countries which have not abolished the death penalty, capital punishment may be imposed only for the most serious crimes, it being understood that their scope should not go beyond intentional crimes with lethal or other extremely grave consequences.'[104] In this regard, the *United Nations Commission on Human Rights*, a subsidiary body of the *UN Economic and Social Council (ECOSOC)*, replaced by the Human Rights council in 2006,

---

[100] Human Rights Committee, General Comment 6, Article 6 (Sixteenth session, 1982), Compilation of General Comments and General Recommendations Adopted by Human Rights Treaty Bodies, U.N. Doc. HRI/GEN/1/Rev.1 at 6 (1994) <https://www1. umn.edu/humanrts/gencomm/hrcom6.htm>.

[101] *Id.*

[102] *Id.*

[103] *Ibid; Kamaruzzaman, op. cit. no. 79, at page 20.*

[104] 'Safeguards Guaranteeing Protection of the Rights of those Facing the Death Penalty, Approved by Economic and Social Council resolution 1984/50 of 25 May 1984'; <http://www.ohchr.org/EN/ ProfessionalInterest/Pages/DeathPenalty.aspx>.

interpreted "most serious crimes" as not including 'non-violent acts such as financial crimes, religious practice or expression of conscience and sexual relations between consenting adults.'[105]

In addition to that, in 2012 report to the UN General Assembly, the 'UN Special Rapporteur on Extrajudicial Killings' in the UN General Assembly of 2012 specified that 'the death penalty should only be applied for offenses of intentional killings, based on the practices of retentionist States and the jurisprudence of the UN and other bodies.'[106] Moreover, as per the report of 2014 by the Amnesty International, it has found that 'many of the countries that carry out executions justify their action as a response to threats – real or perceived – to state security and public safety posed by terrorism, crime or internal instability.'[107]Apart from all the above discussion, it must be mentioned here that albeit the International Criminal Tribunal for Rwanda (ICTR) statute excludes death sentence, in the Prosecutor vs. Semanza[108] its Tribunal very lucidly held that 'Rwanda Organic Law indicates that even for genocide and Crimes against Humanity, the ordinary Penal Code sentences shall apply with certain modifications, which include heightened penalties of death and life imprisonment, respectively, for categories 1 and 2 perpetrators.'[109]

Under the above circumstances, it can be said that there might be certain arguments in abolishing death penalty; however, it should not be abolished unquestionably rather in the rarest of

---

[105]   Kamaruzzaman, op. cit. no. 79, at page 20.

[106]   Ricky Gunawan, 'Death penalty does not deter drug traffickers,' Jakarta (Online), December 10, 2014 <http://www.thejakartapost. com/news/2014/12/10/death-penalty-does-not-deter-drug-traffickers.html>.

[107]   Kamaruzzaman, op. cit. no. 79, at pages 20-21.

[108]   The Prosecutor vs. Semanza, (ICTR Trial Chamber), May 15, 2003.

[109]   See also Kamaruzzaman, op. cit. no. 79, at page 19.

the rare cases it has to be ensured to the convicts. Otherwise, the doctrine of proportionality will be of no value and the general people might lose confidence upon the criminal justice system of Bangladesh.

As regards of giving other kind of punishments except death sentence, it is found in the case concerning *Ghulam Azam*[110] that the honourable Tribunal held that having considered the attending facts, legal position, and the gravity as well as magnitude of the offences committed by the accused, the accused certainly deserves the death sentence as provided under Section 20(2) of the *ICT Act* of 1973.[111] Nonetheless, since Ghulam Azam was 91 years old then, the Tribunal took this matter into its consideration as a mitigating factor of sentencing him with a view to meeting the ends of justice.[112] Therefore, the Tribunal sentenced him for 90 years of imprisonment instead of death sentence.[113]

Likewise, another accused, Md. Abdul Jabbar Engineer,[114] who was an old man of more than 82 years during his trial before the Tribunal. Corresponding to the mitigating factor considered in the *Ghulam Azam* case, the Tribunal sentenced Md. Abdul Jabbar Engineer life imprisonment till his natural death rather than death sentence.[115]

---

[110] *The Chief Prosecutor vs. Professor Ghulam Azam*, ICT-BD Case No. 06 of 2011 [ICT-BD 1].

[111] *Ibid*, at page 241 at para 392.

[112] *Ibid*, at page 241 at para 394.

[113] *Id.*

[114] *The Chief Prosecutor vs. Md. Abdul Jabbar Engineer*, ICT-BD Case No. 01 of 2014 [ICT-BD 1].

[115] *Ibid*, at pages 137-138 at para 310.

3.9 Right of Appeal

The right of appeal to a higher Court or Tribunal is recognised and protected in both continental and common law jurisdictions. This right is considered as a means of preventing miscarriages of justice and securing the legitimacy of the criminal justice process.[116] Generally, appeal processes are operated to achieve consistency in trial Courts; even though, this is, arguably, inapplicable in the context of "Ad-hoc International Military Courts" without a jury. In many jurisdictions, acquittals are considered final immediately and are not subjected to appeals. On appeal, the appeals chamber may affirm, revise, or reverse the appealed decision. Alternatively, it may set aside the judgment and order a new trial before a different chamber. Detailed procedures are set forth for each jurisdiction.

In the international arena, the Nuremberg and Tokyo Tribunal did not provide for appeals but today ICTY, ICTR, ICC all allow appeals.[117] In case of Nuremberg, Article 26 of the *Charter of the International Military Tribunal* provided that the judgment of the Tribunal as to guilt or innocence shall give reasons, and shall be final and not subject to appeal or review. Thereby, the right of appeal was altogether denied and so there was no appellate instance to neither affirm nor reject the judgments or sentences. In the interests of time and expense, the Allies desired a full and final judgment.[118] However, deprivation of this fundamental

---

[116] Peter D Marshall, "A Comparative Analysis of the Right to Appeal," (2011) *Duke Journal of Comparative and International Law* at page 11; Mirjan Damaska, "Structures of Authority and Comparative Criminal Procedure," (1975) 84 *Yale Law Journal* at page 489.

[117] The *ICTY Statute*, Article 25; The *ICTR Statute*, Article 24(2); The *ICC Statute*, Article 81.

[118] Andreas Krieg, "The Nuremberg Trials: An Attempt of Bringing War Criminals to Justice," (2009) *The Pica Project* <www.thepicaproject.

right to have the Nuremberg judgments evaluated at a higher appellate level was considered as one of the most "procedurally dubious" and controversial elements of the trial.[119] Later, the defendants, in general, of Nuremberg trials were permitted to appeal to the United States Military Governor.[120] They were given the right to seek clemency and pardons based on firstly, a review of the evidence against them, secondly, any legal issues, and thirdly, personal circumstances.[121] Besides, in *Eichmann's case*, hearings of appeal took place between 22 and 29 March, 1962 in the Israeli Supreme Court which rejected the appeal and upheld the District Court's judgement on all counts.[122]

In regards to ICTY and ICTR, the process of appeal was limited to correcting errors of law invalidating decision and errors of facts resulting "miscarriage of justice".[123] Thus, against this limited scope of appeal process, the ICTY and ICTR Appeals Chambers established an inherent power deriving from their judicial function.[124] As a result, the burden of proof on appeals

org> at page 7.

[119] Jonathan A Bush, "Lex Americana: Constitutional Due Process and the Nuremberg Defendants," (2001) 45 *Saint Louis University Law Journal* at page 530.

[120] Nuremberg Trial Proceedings (Volume 2), 23 November 1945, at page 214; Freda Utley, *The High Cost of Vengeance* (Chicago: Henry Regnery Company, 1949).

[121] Tessa Mckeown, "Nuremberg: Procedural Due Process at the International Military Tribunal," (2013) *Victoria University of Wellington*, at page 30.

[122] *Eichmann's Case*, Matěj Jungwirth, The Aspirations and Shortcomings of Nazi Trials: Cases of the Nuremberg and Eichmann <http://postnito.cz/the-aspirations-and-shortcomings-of-nazi-trials-cases-of-the-nuremberg-and-eichmann/>.

[123] The *ICTY Statute*, Article 25; The *ICTR Statute*, Article 24(2).

[124] The Prosecutor vs. *Delalic et.al.*, (ICTY Trial Chamber), 16

is not absolute regarding point of law, but the party must, at least, identify the alleged error, present arguments and explain how the errors invalidate the decision. The ICC statute lists the grounds of appeal as procedural error, error of facts, and error of law, and as an additional ground in case of conviction, 'any other ground that affects the fairness or reliability of the proceedings or decision.[125] Regarding sentences, the main ground of appeal is disproportion between the crime and the sentence.[126]

Concerning trials of the ICT-BD, the right to appeal has been recognized under Section 21 of the 1973 *Act*, which was amended by the *International Crimes (Tribunals) (Amendment) Act*, 2013.[127] Adding the possibility of appeal of an "order of sentence", this amendment has been given retrospective effect from 14 July, 2009, bringing the judgment and sentence in the *Quader Molla case* within the purview of the amended provisions. The amendment allows such an appeal to be filed by "the complainant or the informant," whereas previously only the Government was given that right.[128] Additionally, where under the original *Act* a period

---

November, 1998, at para 16; *The Prosecutor vs. Kambanda*, (ICTR Appeal Chamber), 19 October, 2000, at para 178.

[125] The *ICC Statute*, Article 83.

[126] *Ibid*, Article 83(2).

[127] Act No. III of 2013.

[128] The *International Crimes (Tribunals) Act*, 1973, Section 21 reads as follows:

'(1) A person convicted of any crime specified in section 3 and sentenced by a Tribunal shall have the right of appeal to the Appellate Division of the Supreme Court of Bangladesh against such conviction and sentence.

(2) The Government shall have the right of appeal to the Appellate Division of the Supreme Court of Bangladesh against an order of acquittal.

of 60 days was allowed for the filing of a case, the Amendment limits that period to 30 days after the date of conviction, sentence or acquittal.[129] The Amendment also imposes an entirely new duty on the Appellate Division, requiring them to dispose of any appeal within a maximum of 60 days from the date of its filing.[130] Essentially, the distinguishing feature of exercising the right to appeal under the 1973 *Act* is that the appeal shall lie in the Appellate Division (AD) of the Supreme Court of Bangladesh with a view to ensuring the due process of law.

3.10 The Right to Invoke Review Proceedings

From the international perspectives, the scope of invoking review proceedings is recognized, *inter alia*, under the ICTY, ICTR, SCSL statutes. These statutes analogously states, 'where a new fact has been discovered which was not known at the time of the proceedings before the Trial Chambers or the Appeals Chamber and which could have been a decisive factor in reaching the decision, the convicted person or the Prosecutor may submit to the International Tribunal an application for review of the judgment.'[131] It is seen from the concerned provisions of review proceedings under the said statutes that these statutes provide for the review of final judgments upon the discovery of a 'new fact' that could have affected the judgments. The term 'new fact' so far is interpreted to mean new information related to a

---

(3) An appeal under sub-section (1) or (2) shall be preferred within sixty days of the date of order of conviction and sentence or acquittal.'

[129] *Ibid*; Section 21(3).

[130] *Id.*

[131] The *ICTY Statute*, Article 26; The *ICTR Statute*, Article 25; The *SCSL Statute*, Article 21.

matter that was not at issue during the original trial, as opposed to simply meaning new information of a factual nature.[132]

In the question of invoking review proceedings of the cases, firstly decided by the ICT-BD, it was argued in view of Article 47A(2) of the *Constitution of Bangladesh* that review petitions are not maintainable from the judgment of this Division, in the absence of any provision for review in the 1973 *Act*.[133] It was contended that against a conviction or sentence or an order of acquittal or inadequacy of sentence, there is only one remedy of appeal available to a convicted person, and the Government and the informant and the complainant, as the case may be, can prefer an appeal under Section 21 of the *Act* of 1973 before the AD.[134] Further, after the disposal of the appeals, the judgment attains finality and it cannot be challenged by resorting to the constitutional provision, which has totally been ousted by the *Constitution (Fifteenth Amendment) Act*, 2011 and the *Constitution (First Amendment) Act*, 1973 respectively.[135] It is added that no person to whom the *Act* of 1973 applies shall have the right to move this Division for any of the remedies available under the Constitution other than the one provided in the *Act* of 1973.[136]

On the other hand, it is argued that the review petition is maintainable in view of Article 105 of the *Constitution of Bangladesh* read with Order XXVI of the *Supreme Court of Bangladesh (Appellate Division) Rules*, 1998.[137] Besides, it is

---

[132]   Jean Galbraith, "New Facts' in ICTY and ICTR Review Proceedings," (2008) 21(1) *Leiden Journal of International Law*, at page 131.

[133]   *Abdul Quader Mollah vs. The Chief Prosecutor*, Criminal Review Petition Nos.17-18 of 2013 at pages 5-6.

[134]   *Id.*

[135]   *Id.*

[136]   *Id.*

[137]   *Id.*

contended that there is, nevertheless, no prohibition, either expressly or by implication, to move a review petition from the judgment of this Division on appeal from the judgment of the Tribunal.[138] A plain reading of this non-obstante clause of the Constitution will manifest that a review petition from the judgment of this Division passed on appeal from the judgment of the Tribunal has not been ousted.[139] Alternatively, it may be said that the power of this Division as the appellate forum to review its judgment has not been ousted, either directly or indirectly, by Article 47A(2) of the constitution.[140]

In this regard, it is also claimed that if any law contains no specific provisions to meet the necessity of a particular case, the inherent power of a Court merely saves by expressly preserving to the Court which is both a Court of equity and law, to act according to *justice, equity and good conscience* and make such orders as may be necessary for the ends of justice or to prevent the abuse of the process of the Court.[141] It is an enabling provision by virtue of which inherent powers have been vested in a Court so that it does not find itself helpless for administering justice.[142] They are not intended to enable the Tribunal to create rights for the parties, but they are meant to enable the Tribunal to pass such orders for ends of justice as may be necessary.[143] For instance, it has been an established principle that generally in the rarest of the rare cases a mercy petition or a review petition is allowed.[144]

---

[138] *Ibid*, at pages 7-8.

[139] *Id.*

[140] *Id.*

[141] *Ibid*, at page 11.

[142] *Id.*

[143] *Ibid*, at page 12.

[144] *Ibid*, at page 48.

Moreover, it is an established jurisprudence that a review is by no means an appeal in disguise whereby an erroneous decision is reheard and corrected, but lies only against patent error of law.[145] Where without any elaborate argument one could point to the error and say that here is a substantial point of law which stares one in the face, and there could reasonably be no two opinions to be entertained about it, a clear case of error apparent on the face of the record would be made out.[146] It is only a clerical mistake or mistake apparent on the face of the record that can be corrected but does not include the correction of any erroneous view of law taken by the Court.[147] Further, it has now been settled that an error is necessary to be a ground for review but it must be one which is so obvious that keeping it on the record will be legally wrong.[148] The moot point is, a party to litigation is not entitled to seek a review of judgment merely for the purpose of rehearing or a fresh decision of the case.[149] The power can be extended in a case where something obvious has been overlooked-some important aspects of the matter has not been considered, the Court can reconsider the matter.[150]

Now the question is as to what would be period of limitation for filing a review petition from the judgment of AD passed against a judgment of the Tribunal set up under the *Act* of 1973. As per rules of this Division review petitions shall be filed within thirty days but this period of limitation is not only inconsistent with the provisions of the *Act* but also not applicable. Therefore, the Court provides reasonable time to file a review petition which

[145] *Ibid*, at page 45.

[146] *Id.*

[147] *Id.*

[148] *Ibid*, at pages 45-46.

[149] *Id.*

[150] *Id.*

is considered in the context of particular matter and there is no hard and fast rule in this regard.[151] Besides, an aggrieved party can file a review petition against any order of the Tribunal within seven days as per Rules framed by it. In the Courts of small causes, a period of fifteen days limitation is provided for filing review petition from its judgment.[152] In some cases, it has been observed that if this bar of time is not placed on the power of review it would mean that a judgment can never become final.[153]

Hence, from the above-mentioned discussion, it is clear that the review petitions are maintainable in the cases decided by the ICT-BD. However, a review petition should not be equated with an appeal. In criminal matters, the power of review must be limited to an error which has a material, real ground on the face of the case. The finality attached to a judgment at the apex level of the judicial hierarchy upon a full-fledged hearing of the parties should be re-examined in exceptional cases and a review is not permissible to embark upon a reiteration of the same points. The period of limitation provided in the AD Rules will not be applicable in respect of a review petition from a judgment on appeal under the *Act* of 1973. The period of limitation is fifteen days and the review petition should be disposed of on priority basis.

3.11 Right to Apply for Presidential Pardon

Both the ICTY and ICTR provide that if a convicted person becomes eligible for pardon or commutation of sentence under the law of the enforcing State, that State must notify the Court accordingly.[154] The President of the Court, in consultation with

---

[151]   *Ibid*, at pages 20-21.

[152]   *Id.*

[153]   *Id.*

[154]   The *ICTY Statute*, Article 28 reads as follows:

the members of the Bureau which comprises the President, Vice-President and the presiding judges of the trial chambers of the Court, and any permanent judges of the sentencing chamber who remain judges of the Court, must decide whether pardon or commutation is appropriate, on the basis of the interests of justice, and the general principles of law.[155] In ICTR, the President must notify the government of Rwanda before he or she, in consultation with the other judges, decides on the matter.[156] Factors to be considered by the judges include the gravity of the crime or crimes, the treatment of similarly-situated prisoners and any substantial cooperation of the prisoner with the prosecutor.[157] The governing instruments of the SCSL have largely similar provisions in relation to pardon and commutation of sentences.[158]

'If, pursuant to the applicable law of the State in which the convicted person is imprisoned, he or she is eligible for pardon or commutation of sentence, the State concerned shall notify the International Tribunal accordingly. The President..., in consultation with the judges, shall decide the matter on the basis of the interests of justice and the general principles of law.'

The *ICTR Statute*, Article 27 reads as follows:

'If, pursuant to the applicable law of the State in which the convicted person is imprisoned, he or she is eligible for pardon or commutation of sentence, the State concerned shall notify the International Tribunal for Rwanda accordingly. There shall only be pardon or commutation of sentence if the President of the International Tribunal for Rwanda, in consultation with the judges, so decides on the basis of the interests of justice and the general principles of law.'

[155] *Id.*

[156] *Id.*

[157] *Id.*

[158] The *SCSL Statute*, Article 23 reads as follows:

'If, pursuant to the applicable law of the State in which the convicted person is imprisoned, he or she is eligible for pardon

In case of trials under the 1973 *Act*, if a warrant of death for execution is communicated to the jail authority after it is confirmed or imposed by the AD of the Supreme Court, it is established that the condemned prisoner should be afforded an opportunity to file a mercy petition and he should also be afforded an opportunity to meet his near ones before the execution of the sentence.[159] In this regard, it must be mentioned that 'the President shall have power to grant pardons, reprieves and respites and to remit, suspend or commute any sentence passed by any court, tribunal or other authority.'[160] Thereby, if the jail authority fixes a date for execution of the sentence, the same cannot be taken as has been done hurriedly.[161] Moreover, if any mercy petition is filed or pending, the sentence cannot be executed unless the petitions are disposed of.[162]

3.12 Conclusion

To conclude, it can be said that the 1973 *Act* includes mainly the crimes of "genocide, crimes against humanity, and war crimes" to try the perpetrators responsible for committing the same during the Liberation War, 1971 in Bangladesh. Again, it recognized most of the required procedural mechanisms as well as rights for the parties to ensure justice and due process of law. Therefore, this chapter discusses the significant features of this particular

---

or commutation of sentence, the State concerned shall notify the Special Court accordingly. There shall only be pardon or commutation of sentence if the President of the Special Court, in consultation with the judges, so decides on the basis of the interests of justice and the general principles of law.'

[159] *Ibid*, at pages 64-65.

[160] The *Constitution of Bangladesh*, Article 49.

[161] *Id*.

[162] *Id;* This is also applicable where review petition is filed or pending.

law. Firstly, it confers the matter of including the international crimes in the ambits of the 1973 *Act* which is a domestic law, and establishes that under the constitutional safeguards internalization of international law is undoubtedly permitted in the jurisdiction of Bangladesh. Secondly, this chapter talks about the question of supremacy of the 1973 *Act* as recognized under the *Constitution of Bangladesh* that the constitution itself compromises its supremacy to the extent of dealing with the main crimes as entailed in the *Act*. Thirdly, the discussion draws the experiences of formation of domestic tribunals in many jurisdictions as well as in Bangladesh. Subsequently, the historical surroundings of defining genocide as a crime is placed in this chapter to address the realm of this definition in many laws and conventions, and the differences among the definitions such as the political group is not recognized as a protected group under the *Genocide Convention* while the 1973 *Act* recognizes this group as a protected group. Further, this chapter shows that the trial in *absentia* is found in many jurisdictions; for example, the IMT, STL, SCSL etc. conducted a significant number of trials in *absentia* under the respective provisions of concerned statutes. Next, this chapter focuses on the sentencing consideration including the issue of death sentence, and demonstrates that the death sentence should be awarded to the offenders of grave offences based on consideration of the circumstances of each case. Finally, the rights of accused under the 1973 *Act* has been elaborated in this chapter, including the right to bail, right to appeal, right to invoke review proceedings, and right of application for pardon to the President.

Chapter 4

Trials under the International Crimes (Tribunals) Act, 1973

4.1 Introduction

It has been stated in *Chapter 2* of this particular book that the ICT-1 has decided 19 cases and ICT-2 has decided 11 cases till now. However, in this Chapter, brief discussions have been made on the first 20 cases emphasizing on the charges brought against the convicts and the sentences awarded to them by the respective Tribunal.

4.2 *The Chief Prosecutor vs. Moulana Abdul Kalam Azad*[1]

On the basis of the report and documents submitted by the Investigation Agency, the Chief Prosecutor submitted the formal charge against the accused *Moulana Abdul Kalam Azad*

---

[1]   ICT-BD Case No. 05 of 2012 [ICT-BD 2].

@ *Bachchu*[2] on 2 September, 2012 before the concerned Tribunal.[3] There were 8 charges brought against the accused in relation to the offence of 'genocide' for 'killing the members of Hindu community'[4] (Charge No. 7); the offences of abduction, confinement and torture as 'crimes against humanity'[5] (Charge Nos. 1, 2 and 8); the offence of murder as 'crimes against humanity'[6] (Charge Nos. 3, 4 and 6); and the offence of rape as

---

[2] *Ibid*, at pages 5-6 at para 12: 'Moulana Abdul Kalam Azad @ Bachchu was born on 5th March, 1947 at village *'Barakhardia'*. He studied in Faridpur Rajendra College and was a close associate of Ali Ahsan Mohammad Mujahid, the then President of East Pakistan Islami Chatra Sangha (ICS). Till formal formation of Razakar force, Moulana Abdul Kalam Azad @ Bachchu actively aided the Pakistani army as an armed member of volunteer Razakar Force formed in Faridpur in committing criminal acts alleged. He, during the war of liberation in 1971, assisted the Pakistani occupation force initially in the capacity of 'Razakar' and subsequently as chief of Al-Badar *Bahini* of Faridpur. At one time, Moulana Abdul Kalam Azad @ Bachchu was *'rokan'* of Jamat-E-Islami and now he is not associated with any political party. He is the chairman of 'Masjid Council, a non-government organization [NGO]. On 21 April, 1971 he being united with the local anti-liberation circle welcomed the Pakistani army in Faridpur District. He was a close associate of Pakistani army, and actively and substantially assisted them as a potential member of Razakar (Volunteer) force in committing atrocities targeting the civilians and Hindu community and pro-liberation Bangalee people. In Faridpur, he was in charge of Razakar Bahini which was equipped with rifles.'

[3] *Ibid*, at page 2 at para 1: the charges have been submitted under Section 9(1) of the *ICTA*, 1973.

[4] The *ICTA* of 1973, Section 3(2)(c)(i).

[5] *Ibid*, Section 3(2)(a).

[6] *Id.*

'crimes against humanity'[7] (Charge No. 5).[8] The Tribunal took cognizance of the alleged offences accordingly.[9]

During trial of this particular case, the Prosecution adduced and examined 22 witnesses which took 13 working days to complete.[10] Within this said period, the learned State Defence Counsel cross-examined each witness.[11] However, after closing of the Prosecution witnesses, the learned State Defence Counsel informed the Tribunal that he would not adduce and examine any witness in support of defence as he could not have been able to submit the list of witnesses and required documents before the Tribunal in due time.[12] Finally, the judgment of the case was delivered by the Tribunal on 21 January, 2013.[13]

The Tribunal unanimously found the accused *Abdul Kalam Azad @ Bachchu* guilty of the offence of 'genocide' as listed in Charge No.7 and the offences of 'crimes against humanity' as listed in Charge Nos. 3, 4 and 6.[14] Hence, he was sentenced to death by hanging by the neck till he is dead under Section 20(2) of the *ICTA*, 1973.[15] Even though he had been found guilty of the offences of 'crimes against humanity' as listed in Charge Nos. 1, 5 and 8, no

---

[7]   *Id.*

[8]   ICT-BD Case No. 05 of 2012 [ICT-BD 2] at pages 109-110 at para 332.

[9]   *Ibid*, at page 2 at para 2: the Tribunal took cognizance under Rule 29(1) of the *Rules of Procedure* ['ROP'] of the alleged offences as mentioned in section 3(2) (a)(c)(g)(h) of the *ICTA*, 1973.

[10]   *Ibid*, at pages 11-12 at para 28.

[11]   *Id.*

[12]   *Id.*

[13]   *Ibid*, at page 1.

[14]   *Ibid*, at page 111.

[15]   *Ibid*, at pages110-111.

separate sentence of imprisonment was provided to him as the 'sentence of death' had already been awarded to him in respect of four other charges as noted above.[16]

Here, it can be mentioned that there was only one charge on genocide (Charge No. 7) in this case which had been successfully proved by the Prosecution and thereby, the accused was provided sentence in this particular charge.

4.3 *The Chief Prosecutor vs. Abdul Quader Molla*[17]

In this distinct case against the accused *Abdul Quader Molla*,[18] the Chief Prosecutor submitted the formal charge on 18 December, 2011 based on the investigation report of the Investigation Agency.[19] There were 6 charges brought against the accused in regards of the offence of 'complicity' to commit murder as

---

[16]   *Id.*

[17]   ICT-BD Case No. 02 of 2012 [ICT-BD 2].

[18]   *Ibid*, at page 8 at para 17: 'Abdul Quader Molla was born in 1948. While he was a student of BSC (Bachelor of Science) in Rajendra College, Faridpur in 1966, he joined the student wing of JEI known as 'Islami Chatra Sangha' (ICS) and he held the position of president of the organization. While he was student of the Dhaka University, he became the president of Islami Chatra Sangha of Shahidullah Hall unit. In 1971, he organized the formation of Al-Badar Bahini with the students belonging to Islami Chatra Sangha (ICS) which allegedly being in close alliance with the Pakistani occupation army and Jamat-E-Islami actively aided, abetted, facilitated and substantially assisted, contributed and provided moral support and encouragement in committing appalling atrocities in 1971 in the territory of Bangladesh.'

[19]   *Ibid*, at page 9 at para 20: the charges were submitted under Section 9(1) of *ICTA*, 1973.

'crimes against humanity'[20] (Charge Nos. 1, 2 and 3); the offence of 'abetting' or in the alternative 'complicity' to commit murders as 'crimes against humanity'[21] (Charge No. 4); the offence of murders as 'crimes against humanity'[22] (Charge No. 5); and the offences of murder and rape as 'crimes against humanity'[23] (Charge No. 6).[24] Later on, the Tribunal took cognizance of the offences as mentioned in the charges accordingly.[25]

The Prosecution adduced and examined 12 witnesses and a total 04 exhibits were admitted into evidence during the trial process.[26] On the other hand, the defence submitted a list of 965 witnesses together with the documents and materials upon which it proposed to rely.[27] However, after hearing both the sides on an application of the Prosecution pursuing for limiting the defence witnesses, the Tribunal limited the same to 06 witnesses, keeping the matter of 'defence case' and *plea of alibi*' into account.[28] Thereby, the defence called the 06 witnesses including the accused *Abdul Quader Molla*.[29] Following the entire trial process, the Tribunal delivered judgment of the case on 5 February, 2013.[30]

---

[20]   The *ICTA* of 1973, Section 3(2)(a)(h).

[21]   *Id.*

[22]   *Ibid*, Section 3(2)(a).

[23]   *Id.*

[24]   ICT-BD Case No. 02 of 2012 [ICT-BD 2], at page 130 at para 427.

[25]   *Ibid*, at page 3 at para 1.

[26]   *Ibid*, at page 25 at para 10.

[27]   *Id.*

[28]   *Ibid*, at page 11 at para 27.

[29]   *Id.*

[30]   *Ibid*, at page 1.

The Tribunal unanimously found the accused *Abdul Quader Molla* guilty of the offences of 'crimes against humanity' as listed in Charge Nos. 1, 2, 3, 5 and 6.[31] For Charge Nos. 5 and 6, he was convicted and condemned to a single sentence of 'imprisonment for life' and for Charge Nos. 1, 2 and 3, he was given a single sentence of 'imprisonment for fifteen (15) years' under Section 20(2) of the *ICTA*, 1973.[32] As the convict *Abdul Quader Molla* was sentenced to 'imprisonment for life', the sentence of 'imprisonment for (fifteen) 15 years' naturally got merged into the sentence of 'imprisonment for life'.[33]

It can be noted here that there was no charge on genocide in this specific case.

4.4 *The Chief Prosecutor vs. Delowar Hossain Sayeedi*[34]

The Chief Prosecutor submitted the formal charge against the accused *Delowar Hossain Sayeedi alias Delu*[35] on 11 July, 2011

---

[31]   *Ibid*, at page 141.

[32]   *Id.*

[33]   *Ibid*, at page 142; this sentence shall be carried out under Section 20(3) of the *Act* of 1973.

[34]   ICT-BD Case No. 01 of 2011 [ICT-BD 1].

[35]   *Ibid*, at pages 7-8 at para 15: Delowar Hossain Sayeedi alias Delu @ Abu Nayeem Mohammad Delowar Hossain@ Allama Delowar Hossain Sayeedi was born on 1 February, 1940. He passed Dakhil Examination from Darns Sunnat [Madrassa] Sarsina in 1957 and he also passed the Alim Examination in 1960 from Barroipara [Madrassa]. He was elected Member of the parliament in the election held in 1996 and 2001. He joined Jamaat-E-Islam and was the Nayb-e-Amir of Jamaat-E- Islami Central Committee. He is a writer by profession and known all over the Muslim world as a renowned Oazin and Orator. On perusal of the papers submitted by the accused with the form filled up in the 9th Parliament Election of

before the Tribunal.[36] There were 20 charges brought against the accused as regards the offences of murder, persecution, genocide, abduction and torture which fall within the purview of 'crimes against humanity' and 'genocide'[37] (Charge Nos. 1-4 and 13); the offences of murder, abduction and abetment which fall within the purview of 'crimes against humanity'[38] (Charge No. 5); the offence of persecution which falls within the purview of 'crimes against humanity'[39] (Charge Nos. 6 and 9); the offences of persecution and torture which fall within the purview of 'crimes against humanity'[40] (Charge Nos. 7 and 11); the offences of murder, abduction, torture and persecution which fall within

---

2008, it is found that a part of his name "Abu Nayeem Mohammad" is cut off from his name and new names such as 'Allamma' and 'Sayeedi' have been added with his name. In the same form he wrote his name "Allama Delowar Hossain Sayeedi" and signed it. It is alleged by the prosecution that after passing Alim Examination he did not receive any higher degree nor he obtained doctorate degree in any subject of Islamic religion and as such he is not legally entitled to use the title 'Allama' or 'Maulana' with his name. During the War of Liberation in 1971 the accused was a grocery shopkeeper, he used to sell oil, salt, onion and pepper at Parerhat Bazar and as such his economic condition was not good. He could speak Urdu well as he obtained 'Alim' degree from [Madrassa]. He welcomed the Pakistani Army at Parerhat Bazar and formed local peace committee and subsequently as a member of Rajakar Bahini actively participated in the atrocities committed by Pakistani Army and Rajakar Bahini targeting civilians, Hindu Community and pro-liberation people. By adopting illegal means became a rich man and now he is the owner of huge properties including multi-storied buildings in Dhaka and Khulna.

[36]   *Ibid*, at pages 21-22 at para 34.

[37]   The *ICTA* of 1973, Sections 3(2)(a) and 3(2)(c)(i).

[38]   *Ibid*, Section 3(2)(a).

[39]   *Id*.

[40]   *Ibid*, Section 3(2)(a) and (g).

the purview of 'crimes against humanity'[41] (Charge No. 8); the offences of murder and persecution which fall within the purview of the 'crimes against humanity'[42] (Charge No. 10); the offence of genocide which falls within the purview of 'genocide'[43] (Charge Nos. 12 and 15); the offences of persecution and rape which fall within the purview of 'crimes against humanity'[44] (Charge No. 14); the offences of abduction, confinement, rape and abetment which fall within the purview of 'crimes against humanity'[45] (Charge No. 16); the offence of rape which falls within the purview of 'crimes against humanity'[46] (Charge No. 17); the offences of torture and murder which fall within the purview of 'crimes against humanity'[47] (Charge No. 18); the offence of other inhumane act by forcing Hindus to convert into Muslims which falls within the purview of 'crimes against humanity'[48] (Charge No. 19); and the offences of abduction, torture and rape which fall within the purview of the 'crimes against humanity'[49] (Charge No. 20).[50] The Tribunal upon consideration of the submitted the formal charge and documents took cognizance of offence on 14 July, 2011.[51]

---

[41]   *Ibid*, Section 3(2)(a).

[42]   *Id.*

[43]   *Ibid*, Section 3(2)(c)(i).

[44]   *Ibid*, Section 3(2)(a).

[45]   *Ibid*, Section 3(2)(a) and (g).

[46]   *Ibid*, Section 3(2)(a).

[47]   *Ibid*, Section 3(2)(a)(g).

[48]   *Ibid*, Section 3(2)(a).

[49]   *Id.*

[50]   ICT-BD Case No. 01 of 2011 [ICT-BD 1] at pages 115-118 at para 249.

[51]   *Ibid*, at pages 21-22 at para 34.

In this case, the Prosecution submitted a list of 138 witnesses whereas the defence submitted a list of 48 witnesses to examine.[52] Nonetheless, at the time of trial, the Prosecution examined 28 witnesses of whom 20 were witnesses of occurrence, 07 were seizure list witnesses and 01 was the investigation officer.[53] On the other hand, the defence examined 17 witnesses of whom 14 were listed witnesses and the rest three unlisted witnesses were examined by the defence even though the Tribunal allowed the defence to examine maximum 20 witnesses.[54] Finally, the Tribunal delivered judgment in this case on 28 February, 2013.[55]

The Tribunal found the accused *Delowar Hossain Sayeedi alias Delu* guilty of the offences of crimes against humanity as listed in Charge Nos. 8 and 10, and thereby, he was convicted and sentenced to death and was punished to be hanged by the neck till he was dead under Section 20(2) of the *ICTA*, 1973.[56] In the Tribunal's due consideration, the gravity of the offences as listed in Charge Nos. 6, 7, 11, 14, 16 and 19 appear to be lesser than that of as listed in Charge Nos. 8 and 10.[57] As the Tribunal awarded death sentence to the accused for the offences as listed in Charge Nos. 8 and 10, it did not pass any separate sentence of imprisonment for the offences as listed in the rest Charge Nos. 6, 7, 11, 14, 16 and 19 *albeit* these noted charges had also been proved beyond reasonable doubt.[58]

---

[52] *Ibid*, at page 24 at para 36.

[53] *Id.*

[54] *Id.*

[55] *Ibid*, at page 1.

[56] *Ibid*, at page 119.

[57] *Id.*

[58] *Ibid*, at pages 119-120 at para 253.

It is mentionable here that in this case there were 7 charges on genocide (Charge Nos. 1-4, 12, 13 and 15) while no charge had been successfully proved by the Prosecution before the Tribunal.

4.5 *The Chief Prosecutor vs. Muhammad Kamaruzzaman*[59]

On 11 December, 2011 the Chief Prosecutor firstly submitted the formal charge before the Tribunal against the accused *Muhammad Kamaruzzaman*[60] on the basis of the investigation report.[61] Subsequently, the Prosecution re-submitted the formal

---

[59]   ICT-BD Case No. 03 of 2012 [ICT-BD 2].

[60]   *Ibid*, at page 8 at para 17: Muhammad Kamaruzzaman was born on 4 July. 1952. In 1967, while he was a student of class X of Sherpur GKM Institution he started student politics as a supporter of Islami Chatra Sangha [ICS]. He was the secretary of ICS, Jamalpur Ashek Mahmud Degree College hall unit, while he was student of degree class. He contested in college student sangsad against the post of Assistant Cultural Secretary but could not succeed. At the end of 1970, he was assigned with the charge of president, Islami Chatra Sangha [ICS] of greater Mymensingh. Kamaruzzaman was holding the post of office secretary, of Islami Chatra Sangha of the then East Pakistan. It is alleged that the accused Muhammad Kamaruzzaman, in 1971, as the president of Islami Chatra Sangha, greater Mymensingh played the role of a key organizer in formation of Al-Badar Bahini with the selected students of Ashek Mahmud College belonging to Islami Chatra Sangha. It is also alleged that within a month, under the leadership of Kamaruzzaman, all the students belonging to Islami Chatra Sangha of greater Mymensingh, were absorbed to Al-Badar Bahini and they received summary training. He allegedly being in close association with the Pakistani army, actively aided, abetted, facilitated and substantially contributed in committing dreadful atrocities during the War of Liberation in 1971 in the territory of greater Mymensingh.

[61]   *Ibid*, at page 9 at para 20.

charge on 15 January, 2012 as per the order of the Tribunal.[62] There were 7 charges brought against the accused in respect of the offence of 'complicity' to commit murder as 'crime against humanity'[63] (Charge Nos. 1, 3, 4 and 7); the offence of 'complicity' to commit 'other inhumane acts' as 'crime against humanity'[64] (Charge No. 2); and the offence of murders as 'crimes against humanity'[65] (Charge Nos. 5 and 6).[66] Having found the *prima facie* case, the Tribunal took cognizance of the offences against the accused *Muhammad Kamaruzzaman* on 31 January, 2012.[67]

In this case, the Prosecution adduced and examined 18 witnesses including 3 female witnesses who had been permitted to depose in camera under Section 10(4)[68] of the *ICTA*, 1973.[69] On the other hand, the Defence submitted a list consisting of 1354 witnesses together with documents and materials upon which it intended to rely upon.[70] Nonetheless, the Defence examined only 4 witnesses.[71] After concluding the trial process, the Tribunal delivered judgment of the case on 9 May, 2013.[72]

---

[62]   *Id.*

[63]   The *ICTA*, 1973, Section 3(2)(a)(h).

[64]   *Id.*

[65]   *Ibid*, Section 3(2)(a).

[66]   ICT-BD Case No. 03 of 2012 [ICT-BD 2] at pages 210-211 at para 641.

[67]   *Ibid*, at pages 9-10 at para 22.

[68]   Section 10(4) reads as follows:
The proceedings of the Tribunal shall be in public: Provided that the Tribunal may, if it thinks fit, take proceedings in camera.

[69]   *Ibid*, at page 11 at para 29.

[70]   *Ibid*, at page 11 at para 28.

[71]   *Ibid*, at page 13 at para 35.

[72]   *Ibid*, at page 1.

The Tribunal unanimously found the accused *Muhammad Kamaruzzaman* guilty of the offences of 'crimes against humanity' enumerated in Section 3(2) of the *ICTA*, 1973 as listed in Charge Nos. 1, 2, 3, 4 and 7.[73] Thereby, he was convicted and condemned to a 'single sentence of death' for the crimes as listed in Charge Nos. 3 and 4, and he was sentenced to be hanged by the neck till he was dead under Section 20(2) of the *ICTA*,1973.[74] Additionally, he was condemned to a single sentence of 'imprisonment for life' for the crimes as listed in Charge Nos. 1 and 7 and to the sentence of 'imprisonment for ten (10) years' for the crimes as listed in Charge No. 2 under Section 20(2) of the *ICTA*, 1973.[75] However, as the convict *Muhammad Kamaruzzaman* had been provided 'death sentence', the sentence of 'imprisonment for life' and the sentence of 'imprisonment for ten (10) years' naturally got merged into the 'sentence of death'.[76]

It may be mentioned here that there was no charge on genocide in this individual case.

4.6 *The Chief Prosecutor vs. Professor Ghulam Azam*[77]

On perusal of the investigation report, statement of witnesses and the documents collected during investigation, the Prosecutors prepared the formal charge against the accused *Professor Ghulam Azam*[78] and then the Chief Prosecutor submitted

---

[73]   *Ibid*, at page 214.

[74]   *Id*.

[75]   *Id*.

[76]   *Id*.

[77]   ICT-BD Case No. 06 of 2011 [ICT-BD 1].

[78]   *Ibid*, at pages 9-10 at para 15: 'Professor Ghulam Azam was born on 7 November, 1922. In his early days, he studied in Madrassa and later obtained Master's degree in Political Science from the

University of Dhaka in 1950. He served as a Professor in Rangpur Carmichael College from 1950 to 1955. He joined Jamaat-E-Islami in 1954 and was the Secretary of that party from 1957 to 1960 and held the post of 'Ameer' (Head) of the said party from 1969 to 1971. At the time of the War of Liberation in 1971, under the leadership of the accused, all the subordinate leaders and workers of Jammat-E-Islami and its student wing Islami Chhatra Sangha actively opposed the Liberation movement. He, as the 'Ameer' of East Pakistan Jamaat-E-Islami, not only controlled the organizational framework of Jamaat-E-Islami and Islami Chhatra Sangha but also played the pivotal role in forming Shanti Committee, Razakars, Al-Badr, Al-shams, etc., to collaborate Pakistani occupation forces. While Bangalee people were fighting for liberation, at that time the accused participated in an election and was elected uncontested as a Member of National Assembly from District Tangail in 1971. While he realized that Bangladesh was going to be liberated soon, then he left for Pakistan on 22nd November, 1971. After Liberation of Bangladesh on 16 December 1971, he formed a Committee named "Purbo Pakistan Punoruddhar Committee" (East Pakistan Restoration Committee) as a part of his campaign in the 1st part of 1972. As a leader of the committee upto March 1973, he tried to create public opinion against Bangladesh in the Islamic Countries of the Middle East and campaigned internationally against recognizing Bangladesh as an independent and Sovereign State. He left Pakistan for London in the middle of 1973 and set up the head office of the "Purbo Pakistan Punoruddhar Committee" there. He also published a weekly newspaper named "Sonar Bangla" in London which propagated against independent Bangladesh. His citizenship was cancelled by the Bangladesh Government on 18 April, 1973. He visited Saudi Arabia in March, 1975 and met King Foisal where he also canvassed against Bangladesh. He told the King that Hindus had captured East Pakistan, Holy Qurans had been burnt, mosques had been destroyed and converted into Mandirs (prayer place) and many Muslims had been killed. On the basis of such propaganda, he collected funds from Middle East in the name of re-establishing mosques and Madrassas. Following the assassination of the Father of the Nation Bangabandhu Sheikh

the same on 12 December, 2011 before the Tribunal.[79] There were 5 charges brought against the accused in relation to the offences of conspiracy (Charge No.1) and planning (Charge No. 2) in respect of 'crimes against humanity' and 'genocide'[80]; the offence of incitement for committing 'crimes against humanity' and 'genocide'[81] (Charge No. 3); the offence of complicity for involving himself in the commission of 'genocide', 'crimes against humanity', etc.[82] (Charge No. 4); and the offences of murder and torture which fall within the purview of 'crimes against humanity'[83] (Charge No. 5).[84] After receiving the formal charge, the Tribunal took cognizance of offence on 26 December, 2011 against the accused.[85]

The Prosecution submitted a list of 88 witnesses while the Defence submitted a huge list of 2939 witnesses.[86] During continuance of the trial, the Prosecution examined only 16 witnesses of whom 07 were seizure list witnesses, 08 were witnesses of occurrence and 01 was Investigation Officer.[87] On the other hand, this

---

Mujibur Rahman, he came back to Bangladesh on 11 August, 1978 with a Pakistani passport and since then he has been residing in this country. He got back his citizenship through Court and resumed the office of 'Ameer' of Jamaat-E-Islami and he continued till Motiur Rahman Nizami was elected Ameer of Jamaat-E-Islami.'

79   *Ibid*, at pages 23-24 at para 33.
80   The *ICTA*, 1973; Section 3(2) read with Section 4(2).
81   *Id.*
82   *Id.*
83   *Ibid*, Section 3(2)(a) read with Section 4(1).
84   ICT-BD Case No. 06 of 2011 [ICT-BD 1] at pages 238-239 at para 387.
85   *Ibid*, at pages 23-24 at para 33.
86   *Ibid*, at page 27 at para 35.
87   *Id.*

Tribunal allowed the Defence to examine maximum number of 12 witnesses out of listed 2939 proposed witnesses.[88] Nevertheless, the Defence examined only one witness who is one of the sons of the accused.[89]As a matter of fact, the Defence took 10 (ten) working days to complete the examination of the said witness while the Prosecution took 5 (five) working days to complete cross-examination of that witness.[90] At the end of the trial process, the Tribunal delivered the verdict of this case on 15 July, 2013.[91]

In this particular case, the Tribunal unanimously held that the accused *Professor Ghulam Azam*, being a *de facto* superior, is guilty of the offences mentioned in all 5 charges for the commission of crimes as specified in Section 3(2) read with Sections 4(1) and 4(2) of the *ICTA*, 1973.[92] He was convicted and sentenced to suffer imprisonment for ten years (10) for the offences mentioned in Charge Nos. 1 and 2 where each of the offences totaling 20 years under Section 20(2) of the said *Act*.[93] Moreover, the accused was held guilty of the offence of incitement in the commission of crimes as listed in Charge No. 3 and he was convicted and sentenced to suffer imprisonment for 20 years under Section 20(2) of the said *Act*.[94] Further, the accused was held guilty of the offence of complicity in the commission of 'genocide', 'crimes against humanity' etc. as listed in Charge No. 4 and he was convicted and sentenced to suffer imprisonment for

---

[88]   *Ibid*, at page 27 at para 35; the Tribunal exercised the power under Rule 51A(2) of the *Rules of Procedure*.

[89]   *Id*.

[90]   *Ibid*, at page 27 at para 36.

[91]   *Ibid*, at page 1.

[92]   *Ibid*, at page 241.

[93]   *Id*.

[94]   *Id*.

20 years under Section 20(2) of the said *Act*.[95] In addition to that, the accused was held guilty to the offence of torture and murder as listed in Charge No. 5 and he was convicted and sentenced to suffer imprisonment for 30 years under Section 20(2) of the said *Act*.[96] As a result, the total period of sentences provided to the accused was 90 years.[97]

It can be stated here that there was no distinct charge on directly committing genocide against the accused in this above mentioned case rather complicity in, and planning as well as incitement for commission of genocide are themselves separate crimes under the *ICTA*, 1973[98] for which he had been given punishment by the Tribunal.

4.7 *The Chief Prosecutor vs. Ali Ahsan Muhammad Mujahid*[99]

The Chief Prosecutor submitted the formal charge against the accused *Ali Ahsan Muhammad Mujahid*[100] on 11 December,

---

[95]   *Id.*

[96]   *Id.*

[97]   *Ibid*, at page 242.

[98]   Section 3(2)(g)(h) of the *ICTA*, 1973 read as follows:
      '(g) attempt, abetment or conspiracy to commit any such crimes;
      (h) complicity in or failure to prevent commission of any such crimes.'

[99]   ICT-BD Case No. 04 of 2012 [ICT-BD 2].

[100] *Ibid*, at page 7 at para16: 'Ali Ahsan Muhammad Mujahid was born on 2nd January, 1948. He obtained SSC in 1964 and thereafter, studied in Faridpur Rajendra College when he joined the Islami Chatra Sangha. During 1968-1970, he was the president of Faridpur District *Islami Chatra Sangha*. In 1970, he got himself admitted in the Department of Law, University of Dhaka. He was nominated

2011.[101] There were 7 charges presented against the accused as regards the offence of 'abetting' and facilitating the commission of the offence of 'murder' as 'crimes against humanity'[102] (Charge No. 1); the offence of 'abetting' to commit 'genocide'[103] (Charge No. 2); the offence of 'abetting' and facilitating the commission of offence of 'confinement' as 'crimes against humanity'[104] (Charge No. 3); the offence of 'abetting' and 'facilitating' the commission of offence of confinement and causing inhumane act as 'crimes against humanity'[105] (Charge No. 4); the offence of 'abetting' and facilitating the commission of offence of murders as 'crimes against humanity'[106] (Charge No. 5); the offence of 'abetting' and 'planning' and facilitating the commission of offence of 'extermination' and 'murder' as 'crimes against humanity'[107] (Charge No. 6); and the offence of 'participating' and 'facilitating' the commission of offence of 'murders' and

---

as the President of Dhaka District *Islami Chatra Sangha* and in the same year, in the month of August/September, he was assigned with the responsibility of Secretary, *East Pakistan Islami Chatra Sangha*. Thereafter, in the month of October, 1971 he was elected as Provincial President of the organization and also became the Chief of *Al-Badar Bahini*. Ali Ahsan Muhammad Mujahid belonged to a political family. His father late Moulana Abdul Ali was a member of 'Provincial Assembly' of the then East Pakistan since 1962-1964. Ali Ahsan Muhammad Mujahid contested the parliamentary election in 1986, 1991, 1996 and 2008 but could not succeed even for once. He was the social welfare Minister of the BNP-Jamat alliance government during 2001-2006.'

[101]   *Ibid*, at page 8 at para19.

[102]   The *ICTA*, 1973; Section 3(2)(a)(g).

[103]   *Id.*

[104]   *Id.*

[105]   *Id.*

[106]   *Id.*

[107]   *Id.*

'persecution' as 'crimes against humanity'[108] (Charge No. 7).[109] Considering the formal charge and the documents submitted by the Chief Prosecutor, the Tribunal took cognizance of the offences against the accused *Ali Ahsan Muhammad Mujahid* on 26 January, 2012.[110]

The Prosecution adduced and examined 17 witnesses including Investigating Officer and 02 seizure list witnesses who were also duly cross-examined by the Defence counsel.[111] The Defence submitted a list of 1315 witnesses while the Tribunal allowed the Defence to adduce and examine 3 witnesses preferably from the list submitted.[112] However, the Defence duly produced and examined 1 witness who mainly proved and exhibited some of the documents and books.[113] Finally, the Tribunal delivered judgment of this case on 17 July, 2013.[114]

The Tribunal found the accused *Ali Ahsan Muhammad Mujahid* as guilty of the offences of 'crimes against humanity' enumerated in Charge Nos. 1, 3, 5, 6 and 7.[115] Hence, the accused was condemned to the sentence of 'imprisonment for 05 (five) years' for the crimes as listed in Charge No. 3, and to the sentence of 'imprisonment for life' for the crimes as listed in Charge No. 5 under Section 20(2) of the *Act* of 1973.[116] Further, he was condemned to a 'single sentence of death' for the crimes as listed in Charge Nos.

---

108 *Id.*

109 ICT-BD Case No. 04 of 2012 [ICT-BD 2], at page 201 at para 633.

110 *Ibid,* at page 9 at para 22.

111 *Ibid,* at page 10 at para 28.

112 *Ibid,* at page 11 at para 29.

113 *Ibid,* at page 11 at para 30.

114 *Ibid,* at page 1.

115 *Ibid,* at pages 208-209.

116 *Id.*

6 and 7 and he was sentenced to be hanged by the neck till he was dead under Section 20(2) of the *ICTA*, 1973.[117] However, as the convict *Ali Ahsan Muhammad Mujahid* was 'sentenced to death', the sentence of 'imprisonment for life' and the sentence of 'imprisonment for five years' naturally got merged into the 'sentence of death'.[118]

In this particular case, there wasno separate charge brought on genocide.

4.8 The Chief Prosecutor vs. Salauddin Quader Chowdhury[119]

On perusal of the investigation report, statement of witnesses and the documents collected during investigation, the Prosecutors prepared the formal charge against the accused *Salauddin Quader Chowdhury*[120] and submitted the same on 14

---

[117]   *Id.*

[118]   *Ibid*, at page 209.

[119]   ICT-BD Case No. 02 of 2011 [ICT-BD 1].

[120]   *Ibid*, at pages 8-10 at para 15: '*Salauddin Quader Chowdhury* is the eldest son of late *Fazlul Quader Chowdhury* who was born on 13 March, 1949 at Chittagong. His father was the General Secretary of Muslim League of Chittagong since before partition of India in 1947. Late *Fazlul Quader Chowdhury* was one of the Ministers in the Cabinet of President *Ayub Khan* in 1962 and subsequently he became the Speaker of the National Assembly of Pakistan. In the General Election of 1970, late *Fazlul Quader Chowdhury* being the President of Convention Muslim League contested the said election but he was defeated. While Pakistan army launched "Operation Search Light" in Bangladesh in the night following 25 March 1971, the father of the accused formed para-Militia *Bahinies* in collaboration with Pakistan-army to resist the independence of Bangladesh. *Salauddin Quader Chowdhury* and his father joined

November, 2011 in the Tribunal.[121] There were 23 charges brought against the accused in respect of the offences of abduction, torture, confinement, murder and race-killing as 'crimes against humanity' and 'genocide'[122] (Charge Nos. 9, 13, 15, 16, 21 and 22); the offences of abduction, torture and race-killing as 'crimes against humanity' and 'genocide'[123] (Charge No. 1); the offences of killing of a religious group as 'genocide'[124] (Charge No. 2); the offence of murder as 'crimes against humanity'[125] (Charge No. 3); the offences of persecution on religious ground and deportation as 'crimes against humanity' and offence of 'genocide'[126] (Charge

---

their hands with Pakistan-army and auxiliary forces to commit crimes against humanity and genocide in Chittagong area during the War of Liberation in 1971. The accused actively participated in the killing of unarmed Hindu people of Chittagong in a large scale and also committed offences of abduction, torture, looting, deportation, genocide and all other atrocities during the War of Liberation of Bangladesh in collaboration with Pakistan army, *Razakars*, *Al-Badrs* and *Al-shams*. For anti-liberation role, accused *Salauddin Quader Chowdhury* was attacked by throwing grenade on 20 September, 1971 by the Freedom-Fighters causing injuries on his person. Thereafter, he left this Country for his misdeeds and he came back to Bangladesh in 1974. He joined the politics at Chittagong and he was elected Member of Parliament (M.P.) for five times being the candidate of different political parties, namely, Muslim League, *Jatio* Party, N.D.P. and BNP since 1979 to 2008. He and his father used their own residence named "Goods Hill" situated at Chittagong town as torture centre and he as self-declared Brigadier used to conduct operations under his leadership in different places of Chittagong.'

[121] *Ibid*, at page 3 at para 3.
[122] The *ICTA*, 1973, Section 3(2)(a) and 3(2)(c).
[123] *Ibid*, Section 3(2)(a)(h) and 3(2)(c).
[124] *Ibid*, Section 3(2)(c)(i) and (ii).
[125] *Ibid*, Section 3(2)(a).
[126] *Ibid*, Section 3(2)(a) and 3(2)(c)(i) and (ii) and 3(2)(g)(h).

No. 4); the offence of killing of a religious group as 'genocide' and persecution as 'crimes against humanity'[127] (Charge No. 5); the offences of killing people of a religious group as 'genocide' and deportation as 'crimes against humanity'[128] (Charge No. 6); the offence of murder as 'crimes against humanity'[129] (Charge No. 7); the offences of abduction and murder as 'crimes against humanity'[130] (Charge No. 8); the offences of looting and arson as 'crimes against humanity'[131] (Charge No. 10); the offences of killing of the members of a political and religious group as 'genocide' and deportation as 'crimes against humanity'[132] (Charge No. 11); the offence of killing of religious group as 'genocide'[133] (Charge No. 12); the offence of murder, abduction, torture and confinement as 'crimes against humanity'[134] (Charge Nos. 14 and 19); the offences of abduction, confinement and torture as 'crimes against humanity'[135] (Charge Nos. 17, 18 and 23); and the offences of murder, torture and confinement as 'crimes against humanity'[136] (Charge No. 20).[137] The Tribunal took cognizance of the offences mentioned in the formal charge on 17 November, 2011.[138]

---

[127] *Ibid*, Section 3(2)(c)(i).

[128] *Ibid*, Section 3(2)(c)(i) and (ii) and 3(2)(a).

[129] *Ibid*, Section 3(2)(a).

[130] *Ibid*, Section 3(2)(a)(h).

[131] *Ibid*, Section 3(2)(a).

[132] *Ibid*, Section 3(2)(c)(i) and 3(2)(a).

[133] *Ibid*, Section 3(2)(c)(i).

[134] *Ibid*, Section 3(2)(a).

[135] *Id*.

[136] *Id*.

[137] ICT-BD Case No. 02 of 2011 [ICT-BD 1], at pages 164-168 at para 288.

[138] *Ibid*, at pages 22-23 at para 39.

In this case, the Prosecution submitted a list of 133 witnesses whereas the Defence submitted a huge list of 1153 witnesses.[139] At the time of trial, the Prosecution examined total 41 witnesses including seizure list witnesses and the Investigation Officer.[140] On the other hand, the Tribunal allowed the Defence to examine maximum number of 5 witnesses out of listed 1153 witnesses.[141] In fact, the defence examined only 4 witnesses to prove the defence plea.[142] The accused *Salauddin Quader Chowdhury* deposed himself as one of the witnesses of the case for 9 working days while the learned prosecutor cross-examined him for only 2 working days.[143] The verdict of this case was delivered by the Tribunal on 01 October, 2013.[144]

The concerned Tribunal unanimously found the accused *Salauddin Quader Chowdhury* as guilty in the Charge Nos. 2, 3, 4, 5, 6, 7, 8, 17 and 18. The Tribunal held that under the purview of the Charge Nos. 3, 5, 6 and 8, the accused was held guilty of the offences of 'crimes against humanity' and 'genocide' for substantially contributing to the commission of crimes as brought in the said four charges.[145] The accused was convicted and sentenced to death for each charge mentioned above under Section 20(2) of the said *Act* for committing the gravest offences, and accordingly, he was sentenced to be hanged by the neck till he was dead.[146] Further, the Tribunal found the accused guilty of the offences of 'crimes against humanity' and 'genocide' for

---

[139]   *Ibid*, at page 25 at para 41.

[140]   *Id.*

[141]   *Id.*

[142]   *Id.*

[143]   *Id.*

[144]   *Ibid*, at page 1.

[145]   ICT-BD Case No. 02 of 2011 [ICT-BD 1], at page 171.

[146]   *Id.*

substantially contributing to the commission of offences as envisaged in Charge Nos. 2, 4 and 7.[147] Thus, the accused was convicted and sentenced to suffer imprisonment for twenty (20) years for each charge mentioned above under Section 20(2) of the said *Act*.[148] Finally, the accused was held guilty of the offences of 'crimes against humanity' as included in Charge Nos. 17 and 18.[149] Hence, the accused was convicted and sentenced to suffer imprisonment for five (5) years for each charge mentioned above under Section 20(2) of the said *Act*.[150]

It is mentionable here that there were 13 charges on genocide (Charge Nos. 1, 2, 4, 5, 6, 9, 11, 12, 13, 15, 16, 21, and 22) brought against the accused in this case while only 4 charges had been proved by the Prosecution before the Tribunal.

4.9 *The Chief Prosecutor vs. Md. Abdul Alim @ M. A. Alim*[151]

The Chief Prosecutor submitted the formal charge against the accused *Md. Abdul Alim*[152]on 15 March, 2012 relying on the

---

[147] *Id.*

[148] *Id.*

[149] *Id.*

[150] *Ibid*, at page 172.

[151] ICT-BD Case No. 01 of 2012 [ICT-BD 2].

[152] *Ibid*, at pages 6-7 at para 14: '*Md. Abdul Alim* was born on 1st November, 1930 in the village Pandua under police station *Hooghli*, West Bengal, India. He and his family migrated to the then East-Pakistan in the year of 1950-51 and settled at *Joypurhat*. After having M.A. and LL.B. degree he joined the legal profession. In 1958, he joined the Muslim League and got the responsibility of divisional organizing secretary of the party in 1962. In 1971, he was an influential leader of the Convention Muslim League

investigation report of the Investigating Agency.[153] There were 17 charges brought against the accused in relation to the offences of 'participating', 'abetting' and 'substantially contributing' to the commission of the offence of 'deportation' as 'crimes against humanity'[154] (Charge No. 1); the offence of 'abetting' and 'substantially contributing' to the commission of the offence of 'genocide'[155] (Charge No. 2); the offence of 'abetting' and substantially contributing to commit 'murder' as 'crime against humanity'[156] (Charge Nos. 3, 4, 5, 11, 13, 15 and 17); the offence of 'abetting' and facilitating the commission of offence of 'murder' as 'crime against humanity'[157] (Charge Nos. 6, 7, 9, 12 and 14); the offence of 'abetting' and facilitating the commission of offence of 'genocide'[158] (Charge No. 8); the offence of participating, substantially abetting and contributing to the actual commission of offence of 'killing a group' as 'genocide'[159] (Charge No. 10); the offence of 'abetting' and substantially contributing to commit

---

and Vice-chairman, *Bogra* District council. It is alleged by the prosecution that he established an army camp, peace committee office and training center for *Razakars* and lodging arrangement for one Pakistani Major *Afzal* by occupying the '*gadighar*' (trading office) and trading and homestead premises of one *Shaonlal Bajla*, a significant Marwari jute trader of *Joypurhat* when they became compelled to deport to India leaving all of their assets. Accused *Alim* was the chairman of *Joypurhat* Municipality for twice. In 1979, he joined the Bangladesh Nationalist Party (BNP) and was elected Member of Parliament and then a Cabinet Minister of *Ziaur Rahman's* government.'

[153] *Ibid*, at page 8 at para17.

[154] The *ICTA* of 1973, section 3(2)(a)(g).

[155] *Ibid*, Section 3(2)(c)(g).

[156] *Ibid*, Section 3(2)(a)(g).

[157] *Id*.

[158] *Ibid*, Section 3(2)(c)(g).

[159] *Ibid*, Section 3(2)(c)(i)(g).

'confinement' as 'crime against humanity'[160] (Charge No. 16).[161] Having found *prima facie* case in consideration of the documents together with the formal charge, statement of witnesses submitted by the Prosecution, the Tribunal took cognizance of offences against the accused on 27 March, 2012.[162]

The Prosecution adduced and examined 35 witnesses including Investigating Officer and two seizure list witnesses.[163] On the contrary, the Defence submitted a list of 3328 witnesses while the Tribunal permitted the Defence to examine 03 witnesses preferably from the list.[164] After the entire trial process, the Tribunal provided judgment of the case on 9 October, 2013.[165]

The Tribunal unanimously found that the accused *Md. Abdul Alim* is guilty of the offences of 'genocide' as listed in Charge Nos. 2 and 8; and 'crimes against humanity' as listed in Charge Nos. 1, 6, 7, 9, 10, 12 and 14 enumerated in Section 3(2) of the *ICTA*,1973.[166] Thereby, he was condemned to the sentence of imprisonment for ten years for the crimes as listed in Charge No. 1 under Section 20(2) of the *Act* of 1973.[167] He was also condemned to a single sentence of imprisonment for twenty years for the crimes as listed in Charge No. 6, 7, 9 and 12 under Section 20(2) of the *Act* of 1973.[168] Moreover, he was condemned to a single sentence

---

160   *Ibid*, Section 3(2)(a)(g).

161   ICT-BD Case No. 01 of 2012 [ICT-BD 2]; at pages 183-185 at para 667.

162   *Ibid*, at page 8 at para 18.

163   *Ibid*, at page 9 at para23.

164   *Ibid*, at page 9 at para 25.

165   *Ibid*, at page 1.

166   *Ibid*, at page 190.

167   *Id*.

168   *Id*.

of 'imprisonment for remaining part of his life' *i.e.* the sentence awarded shall be served in full, till his natural death for the crimes as listed in Charge Nos. 2, 8, 10 and 14 under Section 20(2) of the *Act* of 1973.[169] However, as the convict is condemned to a single sentence of 'imprisonment for remaining part of his life', the sentence of 'imprisonment for ten years' and the single sentence of 'imprisonment for twenty years' would naturally get merged into the sentence of 'imprisonment for remaining part of his life'.[170]

It can be noted here that there were 2 charges on genocide (Charge Nos. 2 and 10) brought against the accused where these 2 charges have been successfully proved by the Prosecution.

4.10 *The Chief Prosecutor vs. Ashrafuzzaman Khan @ Naeb Ali Khan & Chowdhury Mueen Uddin*[171]

On the basis of the report and documents submitted by the Investigation Agency, the Chief Prosecutor submitted the formal charge against both the accused *Chowdhury Mueen Uddin*[172] and

---

[169] *Ibid*, at page 191.

[170] *Id.*

[171] ICT-BD Case No. 01 of 2013 [ICT-BD 2].

[172] *Ibid*, at page 8 at para 15: 'Chowdhury Mueen Uddin was a student of Dhaka University till independence of Bangladesh. He had served as staff reporter of the *Daily Purbadesh*. He was allegedly a central leader *of Islami Chatra Sangha*. During the war of liberation in 1971, he was allegedly a significant leader of *Al-Badar* and had allegedly played active and key role to wipe out the intellectuals including the university teachers. He was a student of M.A. class in the department of Bengali, University of Dhaka [1969-70 session] and a non-resident student of *Haji Muhammad Mohsin* Hall, Dhaka University. After independence of Bangladesh *Chowdhury Mueen Uddin* went to Pakistan and then to London and since then he

Ashrafuzzaman Khan @ Naeb[173] on 28 April, 2013.[174] There were 11 charges brought against the accused where all the charges were related to the offences for participation by 'abetting' and for 'complicity' to the commission of the offence of abduction and killing as 'crimes against humanity'[175] (Charge Nos. 1-11).[176] The concerned Tribunal took cognizance of the offences as mentioned in the formal charge on 2 May, 2013.[177]

The Prosecution examined 25 witnesses including the Investigation Officer[178] where the Defence did not adduce and examine any witness.[179] They, however, submitted some

---

has been there at 1, Jonson Road, *Tottenham*, London NJ54JU, UK and there he has been the Chairman of *Tottenham* Mosque, Vice Chairman of National Health Service, Director, Muslim Spiritual Care Provision in the National Health Service, as alleged. The family members of *Chowdhury Mueen Uddin* were allegedly against the war of liberation in 1971.'

[173] *Ibid*, at pages 8-9 at para 16: '*Ashrafuzzaman Khan @ Naeb Ali Khan* was born on 28 February 1948. He passed HSC examination in 1967 from *Siddeswari* Degree College and got admitted in the University of Dhaka in Islamic Studies department [session 1967-68] and was a non-resident student of Haji Muhammad Mohsin Hall of Dhaka University. He obtained B.A. [Hons] in 1970. He was a central committee member of *Islami Chatra Sangha*. During the war of liberation in 1971, he was allegedly assigned with the responsibility of member of *Al-Badar* high command in Dhaka and had allegedly acted as the chief executor of intellectual killings. As a key member of *Al-Badar* he allegedly led the killings. He allegedly served as commander of *Gaji Salahuddin* Company of *Al-Badar*.'

[174] *Ibid*, at page 10 at para 19.

[175] The *ICTA* of 1973, Section 3(2)(a)(g)(h).

[176] ICT-BD Case No. 01 of 2013 [ICT-BD 2]; at pages 145-47 at para432.

[177] *Ibid*, at page 10 at para 20.

[178] *Ibid*, at page 11 at para26.

[179] *Id*.

documents, in course of trial, which have been kept with the record for consideration.[180] The judgment of the case was delivered on 3 November, 2013.[181]

Considering all the evidences and arguments presented by both the parties, the Tribunal unanimously found that the accused *Ashrafuzzaman Khan @ Naeb Ali Khan* and *Chowdhury Mueen Uddin* were guilty in the Charge Nos. 1, 2, 4, 5, 6, 7, 8, 9, 10 and 11.[182] The Tribunal held that the accused *Ashrafuzzaman Khan @ Naeb Ali Khan*and *Chowdhury Mueen Uddin* were guilty of the offences of 'extermination' as 'crimes against humanity' enumerated in Section 3(2) of the *ICTA*, 1973.[183] Accordingly, the accused *Ashrafuzzaman Khan @ Naeb* Ali Khan and *Chowdhury Mueen Uddin* hadbeen convicted and condemned to the 'single sentence of death' for the crimes listed in all the charges and they were sentenced to be hanged by the neck till they were dead under Section 20(2) of the *ICTA*, 1973.[184]

Since the convicted accused persons have been absconding, the 'sentence of death' as awarded above would be executed after causing their arrest or when they surrender before the Tribunal, whichever would be earlier.[185] The 'sentence of death'awarded as above under Section 20(2) of the *ICTA*, 1973 would be carried out and executed in accordance with the order of the government as required under Section 20(3) of the said *Act*.[186]

---

[180]   *Id.*

[181]   *Ibid*, at page 1.

[182]   *Ibid*, at page 145 at para 432.

[183]   *Ibid*, at page 153.

[184]   *Ibid*, at pages 153-154.

[185]   *Ibid*, at page 154.

[186]   *Id.*

It is mentionable here that there was no particular charge on genocide in this case.

4.11 *The Chief Prosecutor vs. Motiur Rahman Nizami*[187]

The Chief Prosecutor submitted the formal charge in this case against the accused *Motiur Rahman Nizami*[188] on 11 December,

---

[187] ICT-BD Case No. 03 of 2011 [ICT-BD 1].

[188] *Ibid*, at pages 9-10 at para 18: 'Motiur Rahman Nizami was born on 31st March, 1943. In his early life, he studied in Boalmari [Madrassa] at Sathia and passed his Dakhil examination in 1955, and then he passed Alim examination in 1959 and Fazil examination in 1961. He got his Kamil degree in Figh from [Madrassa]-e-Alim, Dhaka in 1963. He also obtained graduation degree in 1967 from the University of Dhaka, as a private student. During the War of Liberation in 1971, he was the President of Pakistan Islami Chhatra Sangha (ICS), the student wing of Jamaat-E-Islami (JEI) and also the Chief of Al-Badr Bahini. The Al-Badr Bahini was mainly formed by the members of Islami Chhatra Sangha under the leadership of the accused. Both Jamaat-E-Islami and Islami Chhatra Sangha actively opposed the Liberation War of Bangladesh and those organizations formed Razakar Bahini, Al-Badr Bahini and Al-Shams. After completion of student life he joined the Jamaat-E-Islami and became Ameer of Dhaka city Unit as well as member of central executive committee of Jamaat-E-Islami from 1978 to 1982. He held the post of Assistant Secretary General of Jamaat-E-Islami from 1983 to 1988. He became the Secretary General of the said party in December, 1988 and held the said post up to 2000. He became the 'Ameer' (Chief) of Jamaat-E-Islami in 2000 and since then he has been holding the post of 'Ameer' of the said party till now. During the War of Liberation, he assisted the then 'Ameer' of Jamaat-E-Islami Professor Ghulam Azam in forming Shanti Committees, Razakars, Al-Badr and Al-Shams to collaborate Pakistan occupation forces. He was elected as a Member of Parliament in 1991 and was the leader of Parliamentary

2011 in the Tribunal.[189] There were 16 charges brought against the accused in relation to the offences of abetting, contributing to and participating in the commission of the offences of arrest, detention, torture and murder as 'crimes against humanity'[190] (Charge No. 1); the offences for the commission of conspiracy, murder, rape and deportation as 'crime against humanity'[191] (Charge No. 2); the offences of committing different international crimes at physical training including conspiracy, complicity and contributing to the commission of the offences of torture and murder as 'crimes against humanity'[192] (Charge No. 3); the offences of 'conspiracy' and complicity and contributing to the commission of the offences of murder, rape and persecutions as 'crimes against humanity'[193] (Charge No. 4); the offences of mass killing as 'crimes against humanity'[194] (Charge No. 5); the offence of murder as 'crime against humanity'[195] (Charge No. 6); the offence of complicity and contributing to the commission of the offences of abduction, torture and murder as 'crimes against humanity'[196] (Charge No. 7); the offence of contributing to the commission of the offences of torture and murder as 'crimes against humanity'[197] (Charge No. 8); the offences of 'genocide'

---

party of Jamaat-E-Islami. He was also elected as a Member of Parliament in 2001 and he became the Minister for Agriculture from 2001-2003 and Minister for Industries from 2003-2006 under the Bangladesh Nationalist Party (BNP) led government.'

[189] *Ibid*, at page 3 at para 3.

[190] The *ICTA* of 1973, Section 3(2)(a)(g) read with Section 4(1).

[191] *Ibid*, Section 3(2)(a)(g) read with Section 4(1).

[192] *Ibid*, Section 3(2)(a)(g)(h) read with Sections 4(1) and 4(2).

[193] *Id.*

[194] *Ibid*, Section 3(2)(a).

[195] *Id.*

[196] *Ibid*, Section 3(2)(a)(h) read with Section 4(1).

[197] *Ibid*, Section 3(2)(a) read with Section 4(1).

and persecutions as 'crimes against humanity'[198] (Charge No. 9); the offence of persecutions as 'crime against humanity'[199] (Charge No. 10); the offence of incitement enumerated as 'any other crimes under international law'[200] (Charge Nos. 11, 12, 13 and 14); the offence of conspiracy and complicity visiting the Rajakaar's camp to commit crimes[201] (Charge No. 15); and the offence of committing 'genocide'[202] (Charge No. 16).[203] On perusal of the formal charge and documents, the Tribunal took cognizance of offences as noted above on 28 May, 2012.[204]

The Prosecution submitted a list of 67 witnesses while the Defence submitted a voluminous list of 10,111 witnesses.[205] During the trial process, the Prosecution examined total 26 witnesses including seizure list witnesses and the Investigation Officer.[206] On the other hand, the Tribunal allowed the Defence to examine maximum number of 04 witnesses out of listed defence witnesses and the Defence examined 04 witnesses to cast doubt upon the Prosecution case.[207]At the end, the judgment of the case was delivered by the Tribunal on 29 October, 2014.[208]

---

[198] *Ibid*, Section 3(2)(a)(c)(i).

[199] *Ibid*, Section 3(2)(a).

[200] *Ibid*, Section 3(2)(f).

[201] *Ibid*, Section 3(2)(g)(h).

[202] *Ibid*, Section 3(2)(a)(h) read with Section 4(2).

[203] ICT-BD Case No. 03 of 2011 [ICT-BD 1], at pages 194-196 at para 419.

[204] *Ibid*, at page 3 at para 4.

[205] *Ibid*, at page 25 at para 50.

[206] *Id*.

[207] *Id*.

[208] *Ibid*, at page 1.

This Tribunal unanimously found the accused *Motiur Rahman Nizami* as guilty in Charge Nos. 1, 2, 3, 4, 6, 7, 8 and 16. Since the accused was held guilty of the offences of 'crimes against humanity' as listed in Charge Nos. 2, 4, 6 and 16, he was convicted and 'sentenced to death' for each of the said four charges and he was sentenced to be hanged by the neck till he was dead under Section 20(2) of the *ICTA*, 1973.[209] Moreover, the accused was held guilty of the offences of 'crimes against humanity' as listed in Charge Nos. 1, 3, 7 and 8, and he was convicted and sentenced to 'imprisonment for life' for each of the said four charges under Section 20(2) of the *Act* of 1973.[210] However, as and when any one of the four 'sentences to death' would be executed the other three sentences of death and the sentences to 'imprisonment for life' would naturally get merged into the sentence to death first executed.[211]

In this case, 2 charges (Charge Nos. 9 and 16) had been brought on genocide against the accused but only one charge had been successfully proved by the Prosecution.

---

[209]   ICT-BD Case No. 03 of 2011 [ICT-BD 1], at page 203.

[210]   *Ibid*, at page 203.

[211]   *Id*.

4.12 *The Chief Prosecutor vs. Mir Quasem Ali*[212]

The Prosecution filed the formal charge on 26 May, 2013 against the accused *Mir Quasem Ali*[213] in the form of a petition.[214] There were 14 charges brought against the accused relating to the offence of 'abetting' and facilitating the commission of the offences of 'abduction' 'confinement' and 'torture' as 'crimes against humanity'[215] (Charge Nos. 1, 2, 3, 4, 5, 6, 7, 8, 9, 10, 13 and 14); and the offence of 'abetting' and facilitating the commission of the offences of 'murder' as 'crime against humanity'[216] (Charge Nos. 11 and 12).[217]

---

[212] ICT-BD Case No. 03 of 2013 [ICT-BD 2].

[213] *Ibid*, at page 8 at para 14: 'Mir Quasem Ali was born on 31 December in 1952. He was a student of Chittagong Government College and passed H.S.C in 1969 and got admitted in B.S.C (Hons) class in the same college and was elected President of Islami Chhatra Sangha [ICS], the student wing of Jamat-E-Islami [JEI] for the period of 1970 to 25 March 1971. He was the President of Islami Chhatra Sangha, Chittagong Town unit up to 6 November, 1971. He also held the post of General Secretary of East Pakistan Islami Chhatra Sangha [ICS] till the surrender of Pakistani occupation army to the joint command of Liberation War. During the War of Liberation, the accused was one of the central commanders of Razakars, Al-Badar and Al-Shams Bahini as alleged by the prosecution. He was allegedly involved in the commission of offences of crimes against humanity in Chittagong and subsequently discontinuing his education he went into hiding and passed B.A. from Ideal College, Dhaka in 1974. He joined the Jamaat-E-Islami in 1980 and has been performing as Sura Member of Jamaat-E-Islami [JEI] since 1985.'

[214] *Ibid*, at page 3 at para1.

[215] The *ICTA*, 1973, Section 3(2)(a)(g)(h).

[216] *Id.*

[217] ICT-BD Case No. 03 of 2013 [ICT-BD 2], at pages 226-28 at para725.

Having found *prima facie* case considering the formal charge and documents submitted by the Chief Prosecutor, the Tribunal took cognizance of the offences brought against the accused *Mir Quasem Ali* on 26 May, 2013.[218] During trial, the Prosecution adduced and examined 24 witnesses including the Investigating Officer and three seizure witnesses.[219] The Defence Counsel cross-examined the witnesses as well.[220] On the other hand, the Defence Counsel examined 03 witnesses.[221] Finally, the judgment of the case was delivered on 2 November, 2014.[222]

The concerned Tribunal unanimously found the accused *Mir Quasem Ali* guilty of the offences of abduction, confinement and torture as 'crimes against humanity' as listed in Charge Nos. 2, 3, 4, 6, 7, 9, 10 and 14.[223] Accordingly, he had been convicted and condemned to the sentence of imprisonment for 20 years for the crimes as listed in Charge No.2; imprisonment for 7 years for the crimes as listed in Charge Nos. 3, 4, 6, 7, 9 and 10 respectively; and imprisonment for 10 years for the crimes as listed in Charge No.14.[224] The sentence so awarded above in respect of Charge Nos. 2, 3, 4, 6, 7, 9, 10 and 14 would run concurrently.[225] Additionally, the accused was condemned unanimously to a 'sentence of death' for the crimes as listed in this Charge No. 11 and he was sentenced to be hanged by the neck till he was dead under Section 20(2) of the *ICTA*, 1973.[226]Also, the accused was

---

[218]   *Ibid*, at page 9 at para 17.

[219]   *Ibid*, at page 11 at para 30.

[220]   *Id*.

[221]   *Ibid*, at page 12 at para 32.

[222]   *Ibid*, at page 1.

[223]   *Ibid*, at pages 349-350.

[224]   *Id*.

[225]   *Id*.

[226]   *Ibid*, at page 350.

found guilty by majority of the offence of 'murder' as 'crimes against humanity' enumerated as listed in Charge No.12.[227] Thus, he was convicted and condemned by majority to a 'sentence to death' for the crimes as listed in this charge and he was sentenced to be hanged by the neck till he was dead, under Section 20(2) of the *ICTA, 1973*.[228] This sentence would get merged into the 'sentence of death' so awarded in respect of Charge No.11.[229] However, as the convict had been condemned to 'single sentence of death', as above, the 'sentences of imprisonment' awarded in respect of Charge Nos. 2, 3, 4, 6, 7, 9, 10 and 14 would get merged into the 'sentence of death '.[230]

Here, it is mentionable that there was no charge on genocide in this specific case.

4.13 *The Chief Prosecutor vs. Zahid Hossain Khokon @ M. A. Zahid @ Khokon Matubbar @ Khokon*[231]

The Chief Prosecutor submitted the formal charge against the accused *Zahid Hossain Khokon @ M.A. Zahid Khokon @ Khokon Matubbar @ Khokon*[232]in the Tribunal on 23 June, 2013 on the

---

[227] *Id.*

[228] *Id.*

[229] *Id.*

[230] *Id.*

[231] ICT-BD Case No. 04 of 2013 [ICT-BD 1].

[232] *Ibid*, at page 4 at para 7: 'Zahid Hossain Khokon @ M. A Zahid Khokon @ Khokon Matubbar @ Khokon was born on 11th January, 1942. He was the local leader of Jamaat-E-Islami. He took training of arms for becoming a Razakar in April, 1971. In the month of May, 1971 the accused along with his elder brother late Zafor formed a Razakar Bahini in their locality. After the death of his elder brother Razakar Zafor in a combat with freedom fighters, he took absolute

basis of investigation report of the Investigation Agency.[233] There were 11 charges brought against the accused given that the offences of abduction, confinement and torture as 'crimes against humanity'[234] (Charge No. 1); the offences of deportation and torture by way of forceful conversion as 'crimes against humanity' and 'genocide'[235] (Charge No. 2); the offences of forceful conversion into Muslim religion, deportation, persecution as 'crimes against humanity' and 'genocide'[236] (Charge No. 3); the offences of confinement, deportation and rape as 'crimes against humanity'[237] (Charge No. 4); the offences of genocide, abduction, confinement, torture, murder and other inhumane acts [plundering and arson] as 'crimes against humanity'[238] (Charge No. 5); the offences of murder and other inhumane acts [plundering and arson] as 'crimes against humanity'[239] (Charge Nos. 6, 7, 8 and 9); the offences of 'genocide', murder and other inhumane acts [plundering and arson] as 'crimes against humanity'[240] (Charge No. 10); and the offences of torture and other inhumane act as 'crimes against humanity'[241] (Charge No.

---

leadership of local Razakar Bahini as a commander. He was directly involved in the commission of 'crimes against humanity' and genocide as committed in different places of Nagarkanda, Faridpur. Subsequently, he joined Bangladesh Nationalist Party (BNP) giving up Jamaat-E-Islami politics.'

[233] *Ibid*, at page 4 at para 8.

[234] The *ICTA* of 1973, Section 3(2)(a)(g).

[235] *Ibid*, Section 3(2)(a)(g)(h) and Section 3(2)(c)(ii) read with Section 4(1).

[236] *Ibid*, Section 3(2)(a)(c)(g)(h) read with Section 4(1).

[237] *Ibid*, Section 3(2)(a)(g) and (h) read with Section 4(1).

[238] *Id*.

[239] *Id*.

[240] *Id*.

[241] *Id*.

11).[242] Observing the submitted the formal charge, statement of witnesses, and the documents, the Tribunal took cognizance of the offences mentioned above against the accused on 18 July, 2013.[243]

The Prosecution submitted a list of 50 witnesses, nevertheless, the Prosecution has examined 24 witnesses including the Investigation Officer.[244] Further, the Prosecution had adduced some documentary evidences.[245] On the other hand, the Defence filed a list of Defence witnesses, in total 30 in numbers; but, later on, the learned Defence Counsel filed an application for withdrawal of the said list and as per the approval of the Tribunal the Defence had denied adducing any evidence both oral and documentary.[246] At the end, the verdict of the case was delivered by the Tribunal on 13 November, 2014.[247]

The Tribunal found that the accused *Zahid Hossain Khokon alias M. A. Zahid Khokon alias Khokon Matubbar alias Khokon* was guilty of the offences of 'crimes against humanity' as listed in Charge Nos. 2, 3, 4, 5, 6, 7, 8, 9, 10 and 11, and so he was sentenced to death for each charge mentioned above and was sentenced to behanged by the neck till he was dead under Section 20(2) of the *ICTA*, 1973.[248] Further, he was convicted and sentenced to suffer rigorous imprisonment for 5 (five) years for committing the 'crimes against humanity' as listed in Charge No.2 under Section

---

[242] ICT-BD Case No. 04 of 2013 [ICT-BD 1], at pages 104-106.

[243] *Ibid*, at page 5 at para 8.

[244] *Ibid*, at page 23 at para 46.

[245] *Id*.

[246] *Ibid*, at page 23 at para 50.

[247] *Ibid*, at page 1.

[248] *Ibid*, at page 107.

20(2) of the *Act* of 1973.[249] Moreover, he had been convicted and sentenced to suffer rigorous imprisonment for 10 (ten) years for committing the 'crimes against humanity' as listed in Charge No.3 under Section 20(2) of the *Act* of 1973.[250] The accused *Zahid Hossain Khokon alias M. A. Zahid Khokon alias Khokon Matubbar alias Khokon* was convicted and sentenced to suffer rigorous imprisonment for 20 (twenty) years for the crimes as listed in Charge No.4 under Section 20(2) of the *Act* of 1973.[251] Finally, he was convicted and sentenced to suffer rigorous imprisonment for 5 (five) years for the crimes as listed in Charge No. 11 under Section 20(2) of the *Act* of 1973.[252] However, all the aforesaid sentences awarded to the accused would naturally get merged into a single sentence of death.[253]

It can be noted here that there were 4 charges brought in relation to genocide in this case, nonetheless, the particular matter of genocide concerning the charges could not be successfully proved before the Tribunal by the Prosecution.

4.14 *The Chief Prosecutor vs. Md. Mobarak Hossain @ Mobarak Ali*[254]

The Chief Prosecutor submitted the formal charge against the accused *Md. Mobarak Hossain*[255] on 25 February, 2013 on the basis

---

[249] *Id.*

[250] *Id.*

[251] *Id.*

[252] *Ibid*, at page 108.

[253] *Id.*

[254] ICT-BD Case No. 01 of 2013 [ICT-BD 1].

[255] *Ibid*, at page 4 at para 7: 'Md. Mobarak Hossain alias Mobarak Ali was born on 10th January, 1950. He studied upto class-VIII. His profession is business but he is known as a collaborator in

of investigation report of the Investigation Agency.[256] There were 5 charges brought against the accused concerning the offences of murder, torture and abduction as 'crimes against humanity' and also for conspiracy to commit such offences[257] (Charge No. 1); the offences of murder, abduction, confinement, torture and other inhumane acts as 'crimes against humanity'[258] (Charge No. 2); the offences of murder, abduction, confinement, torture and other inhumane acts as 'crimes against humanity'[259] (Charge No. 3); the offences of abduction, confinement and torture as 'crimes against humanity'[260] (Charge No. 4); and the offences of murder, abduction, confinement, torture and other inhumane acts as 'crimes against humanity'[261] (Charge No. 5).[262] On perusal of the formal charge and the documents submitted, the Tribunal found *prima-facie* case and took cognizance of offences on 12 March, 2013.[263]

The Prosecution submitted a list of 22 witnesses along with the formal charge and documents.[264] Nonetheless, at the time of the trial, the Prosecution had examined 12 witnesses including

---

his locality. During the War of Liberation he was a member of Razakar Bahini and associated with the politics of Jamaat-e-Islami and after Liberation he became a Rokon of Jamaat-e-Islami at union parishad level and eventually, he has joined the politics of Bangladesh Awami League.'

[256] *Ibid*, at page 4 at para 9.

[257] The *ICTA* of 1973, Section 3(2)(a)(g)(h) read with Section 4(1).

[258] *Ibid*, Section 3(2)(a).

[259] *Ibid*, Section 3(2)(a)(g)(h) read with Section 4(1).

[260] *Ibid*, Section 3(2)(a).

[261] *Id*.

[262] ICT-BD Case No. 01 of 2013 [ICT-BD 1], at page 88-89 at para 167.

[263] *Ibid*, at page 5 at para 10.

[264] *Ibid*, at page 22 at para 47.

the investigation officer and adduced certain documentary evidences.[265] On the contrary, the Defence Counsel had examined 2 witnesses including the accused himself and the son of the accused.[266] Moreover, the Defence Counsel had produced some documentary evidences.[267] The decision of this case was provided by the Tribunal on 24 November, 2014.[268]

On the basis of the evidences produced and arguments made by both the parties, the Tribunal found the accused guilty in the Charge Nos. 1 and 3. The Tribunal held the accused guilty of the offences of 'crimes against humanity', 'conspiracy' and 'complicity' as listed in Charge No.1 and thereby, he was sentenced to death for the said charge and was sentenced to be hanged by the neck till he was dead under Section 20(2) of the said *Act*, 1973.[269] The accused was also held guilty of the offences of 'crimes against humanity', 'conspiracy' and 'complicity' enumerated in Section 3(2)(a)(g)(h) of the *ICTA*, 1973 as listed in Charge No. 3 and so he was sentenced to 'imprisonment for life' for the said charge under Section 20(2) of the said *Act* of 1973.[270] However, as and when the 'sentence of death' would be executed, the other sentence of 'imprisonment for life' would naturally get merged into the sentence of death executed.[271]

It can be mentioned here that there was no charge on genocide in this case.

---

[265] *Id.*

[266] *Ibid*, at page 23 at para 48.

[267] *Id.*

[268] *Ibid*, at page 1.

[269] ICT-BD Case No. 01 of 2013 [ICT-BD 1], at page 91.

[270] *Id.*

[271] *Id.*

4.15 *The Chief Prosecutor vs. Syed Md. Qaiser*[272]

The Chief Prosecutor submitted the formal charge against the accused *Syed Md. Qaiser @ Md. Qaiser @ Syed Qaiser @ SM Qaiser @ Qaiser*[273]on 10 November, 2013 based on the investigation

---

[272] ICT-BD Case No. 04 of 2013 [ICT-BD 2].

[273] *Ibid*, at page 9 at para 24: 'Syed Md. Qaiser @ Md. Qaiser @ Syed Qaiser @ SM Qaiser @ Qaiser was born on 19 June 1940. He obtained matriculation from Armanitola New Government High School, Dhaka and studied in Jagannath College Dhaka. He, however, studied up to B. A. class as found from the registration form filled up and submitted to the Habiganj Election Office. Accused Qaiser is an industrialist and owns a number of industrial concerns. It is alleged that Syed Md. Qaiser became associated with the politics of Convention Muslim League in 1962 and was elected Member of Sylhet District Board in 1966 and occupied the chair till 1971. Qaiser contested Provincial Assembly Election in 1970 as an independent contestant and was defeated. During the war of liberation in 1971 he was allegedly associated with the local occupation army and carried out atrocious criminal activities throughout the period of war in the localities of Habiganj and Brahamanbaria sub-division [now district], as alleged by the prosecution. Instantly either before or after the victory achieved on 16 December 1971, accused Qaiser allegedly went into hiding and fled to London, UK, quitting Bangladesh. The prosecution also alleges that the accused Syed Md. Qaiser returned back home in 1978. In 1979 he contested second parliamentary election as an independent candidate and was elected in Sylhet-17 constituency and afterwards joined the Bangladesh Nationalist Party [BNP] and became the President of Habiganj District BNP. In 1982 he became the Joint Secretary General of BNP [Shah Azizur Rahman group]. Afterwards, he joined the Jatio Party of General Ershad and was elected as President of Habiganj Jatio Party. In 1986, and 1988 he was elected Member of Parliament contesting the Jatio Parishad election as a candidate of Jatio Party, in Habiganj-4 constituency [Madhabpur-Chunarughat]. Later on, he became the State Minister for the Agricultural Ministry. In 1991, 1996 and

report.[274] There were 16 charges brought against the accused as to the offences of abetting, facilitating and contributing to the actual commission of the offences of murder and other inhumane acts as 'crime against humanity'[275] (Charge No. 1); the offence of encouraging and substantially facilitating the commission of other inhumane act as 'crime against humanity'[276] (Charge No. 2); the offence of substantially inducing and facilitating the commission of murder as 'crimes against humanity'[277] (Charge No. 3); the offence of abetting, facilitating and contributing to the actual commission of murder as 'crimes against humanity'[278] (Charge No. 4); the offence of substantially aiding, abetting, facilitating and contributing to the actual commission of killing constituting the offence of murder as 'crime against humanity'[279] (Charge No. 5); the offence of substantially abetting, facilitating and contributing to the actual commission of killing constituting the offence of murder as 'crime against humanity'[280] (Charge No. 6); the offence of abetting, facilitating and contributing to the actual commission of the offence of other inhumane acts as 'crime against humanity'[281] (Charge No. 7); the offence of abetting the act of rape as 'crime against humanity'[282] (Charge No. 8); the offence

---

2001 he contested the parliamentary elections as a candidate of Jatio Party, but was defeated. At a stage, he, quitting Jatio Party, joined PDP.'

[274] Ibid, at page 10 at para 27.

[275] The ICTA of 1973, Section 3(2)(a)(g)(h).

[276] Ibid, Section 3(2).

[277] Ibid, Section 3(2)(a)(g)(h).

[278] Id.

[279] Id.

[280] Id.

[281] Id.

[282] Id.

of abetting, murder as 'crimes against humanity'[283] (Charge No. 9); the offence of abetting, facilitating and contributing to the actual commission of the offence of murder as 'crime against humanity' and also the commission of abduction, confinement, and torture as 'crimes against humanity'[284] (Charge No. 10); the offence of abetting, and facilitating the commission of the offences of abduction, confinement and other inhumane act as 'crimes against humanity'[285] (Charge No. 11); the offence of significantly aiding, abetting and contributing to the commission of rape as 'crime against humanity'[286] (Charge No. 12); the offence of participating, abetting, facilitating and contributing to the actual commission of the offence of murder as 'crimes against humanity'[287] (Charge No. 13); the offence of participating, abetting and substantially contributing to the commission of the murder as 'crimes against humanity'[288] (Charge No. 14); the offence of participating, abetting, facilitating and substantially contributing to the commission of murder as 'crimes against humanity'[289] (Charge No. 15); and the offence of 'genocide' or in the alternative the offence of abetting, facilitating and participating in the commission of the offence of extermination as 'crimes against humanity'[290] (Charge No. 16).[291] Subsequently, having found *prima facie* case, the Tribunal took cognizance of

---

[283] *Id.*

[284] *Id.*

[285] *Id.*

[286] *Id.*

[287] *Id.*

[288] *Id.*

[289] *Id.*

[290] *Id.*

[291] ICT-BD Case No. 04 of 2013 [ICT-BD 2], at pages 287-289 at para 965.

offences against the accused on the basis of the investigation report.[292]

In this particular case, the Prosecution examined 3 witnesses in support of the charges submitted.[293] On the other hand, the Defence Counsel did not submit any list of witness and hence, the learned Defence Counsel explicitly refrained from adducing and examining any witness in support of the Defence case.[294] The Tribunal delivered verdict of this case on 23 December, 2014.[295]

The Tribunal found the accused as guilty on Charge Nos. 1, 2, 3, 5, 6, 7, 8, 9, 10, 12, 13, 14 and 16.[296] Therefore, he was sentenced to imprisonment for life in respect of Charge Nos. 1, 9, 13 and 14 which would construe to be served till the natural death of the convict.[297] The convict was sentenced to death in Charge Nos. 3, 5, 6, 8, 10, 12 and 16 and he was sentenced to be hanged by the neck till he was dead.[298] Since he was sentenced to death in respect of Charge Nos. 3, 5, 6, 8, 10, 12 and 16, the sentence of imprisonment for life for Charge No. 1, 10 (ten) years of imprisonment for Charge No. 2, 07 (seven) years of imprisonment for Charge No. 7, imprisonment for life for charge No. 9, imprisonment for life for Charge No. 13, and imprisonment for life for Charge No. 14 would obviously get merged into the sentence of death.[299]

---

[292]   *Ibid*, at page 10 at para 28.

[293]   *Ibid*, at page 215 at para 724.

[294]   *Ibid*, at page 12 at para 34.

[295]   *Ibid*, at page 1.

[296]   *Ibid*, at page 287 at para 965.

[297]   *Ibid*, at page 481.

[298]   *Id.*

[299]   *Id.*

It can be mentioned here that there was only one charge on genocide (Charge No. 16) in this case, however, the Prosecution could not prove the charge indicating genocide before the Tribunal.

4.16 *The Chief Prosecutor vs. A. T. M. Azharul Islam*[300]

On the basis of the investigation report of the Investigation Agency, the Chief Prosecutor submitted the formal charge against the accused *A. T. M. Azharul Islam*[301] on 18 July, 2013.[302] There were 6 charges brought against the accused with regard to the offences of abduction, confinement, torture and murder as 'crimes against humanity'[303] (Charge No. 1); the offences of murder and plundering, arson [other inhumane act] as 'crimes against humanity'[304] (Charge No. 2); the offences of murder, genocide and other inhumane act[plundering and arson] as 'crimes against

---

[300]   ICT-BD Case No. 05 of 2013 [ICT-BD 1].

[301]   *Ibid*, at page 16 at para 27: 'A. T. M. Azharul Islam was born on 28th February, 1952. He was a student of H.S.C in Rangpur Carmichael College during 1969 to 1971. At that time, he was the President of Islami Chhatra Sangha (ICS), the student wing of Jamaat-E-Islami (JEI) Rangpur unit and also Commander of Al-Badr Bahini of Rangpur District. In 1971, during the War of Liberation of Bangladesh, the accused collaborated Pakistani army to execute their plan and design in committing crimes against humanity and genocide all over Rangpur District. He, being the commander of Al-Badr Bahini, resisted the War of Liberation and committed atrocities in all over the district through his members of *Al- Badr Bahini*.'

[302]   *Ibid*, at page 17 at para 30.

[303]   The *ICTA* of 1973, Section 3(2)(a).

[304]   *Ibid*, Section 3(2)(a)(g) and (h) read with Section 4(1).

humanity'[305] (Charge No. 3); the offence of 'genocide', and abduction and murder as 'crimes against humanity'[306] (Charge No. 4); the offences of abduction, confinement, torture, rape and other inhumane acts as 'crimes against humanity'[307] (Charge No. 5); and the offences, in part, of abduction, confinement and torture as 'crimes against humanity'[308] (Charge No. 6).[309] The Tribunal took cognizance of offences as mentioned above on 25 July, 2013 against the accused.[310]

The Prosecution submitted a list of 22 witnesses along with the formal charge and documents.[311] However, at the time of the trial, the Prosecution had examined19 witnesses including the Investigation Officer.[312] The Prosecution has also adduced some documentary and material evidences.[313] On the contrary, the Defence had examined only 01 witness and exhibited certain documents.[314] The judgment of the case was delivered by the Tribunal on 30 December, 2014.[315]

The Tribunal found the accused as guilty in the Charge Nos. 2, 3, 4, 5 and 6. Thus, the Tribunal held that the accused was guilty of the offences of 'genocide' and 'crimes against humanity' as listed in Charge Nos. 2, 3 and 4 and thereby, he was sentenced

---

[305] *Id.*

[306] *Ibid,* Section 3(2)(c)(i)(g) and (h) read with Section 4(1).

[307] *Ibid,* Section 3(2)(a)(g) and (h) read with Section 4(1).

[308] *Id.*

[309] ICT-BD Case No. 05 of 2013 [ICT-BD 1], at page 145 at para 307.

[310] *Ibid,* at page 17 at para 30.

[311] *Ibid,* at page 18 at para 34.

[312] *Id.*

[313] *Id.*

[314] *Id.*

[315] *Ibid,* at page 1.

to death for each of the said three charges mentioned above and was sentenced to be hanged by the neck till he was dead under Section 20(2) of the said *Act* of 1973.[316] Moreover, he is held guilty of the offences of 'crimes against humanity' as listed in Charge No. 6 and he was sentenced to suffer rigorous imprisonment for 5 years for the said charge under Section 20(2) of the said *Act* of 1973.[317] Here, as and when any one of the three 'sentences to death' would be executed, the other two 'sentences to death' and the sentences to 'rigorous imprisonments' would naturally get merged into the sentence to death first executed.[318]

Here, it can be noted that there were 2 charges on genocide brought against the accused in this particular case where only one charge (Charge No. 4) had been proved successfully by the Prosecution.

4.17 *The Chief Prosecutor vs. Moulana Abdus Sobhan*[319]

The Chief Prosecutor submitted the formal charge against the accused *Abdus Sobhan @ Abul Basar Mohammad Abdus Sobhan*

---

[316] ICT-BD Case No. 05 of 2013 [ICT-BD 1], at page 155.

[317] *Id.*

[318] *Id.*

[319] ICT-BD Case No. 01 of 2014 [ICT-BD 2].

Mia @ Moulana Sobhan[320] on 15 September, 2013.[321] There were 9 charges brought against the accused namely the offences of participating the commission of murder as 'crimes against humanity'[322] (Charge No. 1); the offence of substantially facilitating and contributing to the commission of murder as 'crimes against humanity'[323] (Charge No. 2); the offence of substantially facilitating and contributing to the commission of abduction, confinement and torture as 'crimes against humanity'[324] (Charge

---

[320] *Ibid*, at page 7 at para 22: 'Abdus Sobhan @ Abul Basar Mohammad Abdus Sobhan Mia @ Moulana Sobhan was born on 19 February, 1936. He obtained 'Aleem' degree from Serajganj Alia Madrasa in 1950, 'Fazil' degree in 1952 and 'Kamil' degree in 1954. He joined Pabna Alia Madrasa as its 'Head Moulana' in 1952. Later, he served as the Superintendent of Gopal Chandra Institute and Arifpur Ulot Madrasa. Moulana Sobhan was actively associated with student politics. He had acted as the secretary of Pabna District 'East Pakistan Jamiat-E-Talebae Arabia'. He served as the 'Ameer' of Pabna district JEI and later on, he was elected a member of central Majlish e Sura of JEI. In 1962 and 1965 he was elected member of East Pakistan Provincial Assembly. He contested the election held in 1970 for MNA from Pabna-6 constituency but was defeated. In 1971, the accused Moulana Sobhan was an active collaborator of the Pakistani occupation armed force and was the Secretary of Pabna peace committee first and then its Vice-President, prosecution alleges. The accused was a potential organizer of local Razakar force too, prosecution avers. Accused Moulana Sobhan was elected MNA uncontested against the vacant seat in a by election in 1971, prosecution contends. In 1991 accused Moulana Sobhan was elected as an MP and served as the deputy leader of JEI in the Parliament. In 2001 he was elected MP as a candidate of four parties' alliance from Pabna Sadar constituency and currently he is the Naeb e Ameer of central executive council of JEI.'

[321] *Ibid*, at page 8 at para 24.

[322] The *ICTA* of 1973, Section 3(2)(a)(h).

[323] *Ibid*, Section 3(2)(a)(g).

[324] *Ibid*, Section 3(2)(a)(g)(h).

No. 3); the offence of substantially facilitating, contributing to and participating in the commission of murder as 'crimes against humanity'[325] (Charge No. 4); the offence of murder as 'crimes against humanity'[326] (Charge No. 5); the offence of abetting, facilitating and participating in the commission of extermination as 'crimes against humanity'[327] (Charge No. 6); the offence of abetting, facilitating the commission of abduction and murder as 'crimes against humanity'[328] (Charge No. 7); the offence of abduction, torture and murder as 'crimes against humanity'[329] (Charge No. 8); and the offence of abduction and murder as 'crimes against humanity'[330] (Charge No. 9).[331] Considering the formal charge, documents, and statement of witnesses submitted by the Prosecution, the Tribunal took cognizance of offences against the accused on 19 September, 2013.[332]

The Prosecution examined 31 witnesses including the Investigation Officer and seizure witnesses who were duly cross-examined by the Defence Counsel.[333] However, the learned Defence Counsel did not adduce any witness on its behalf.[334] Finally, the judgment of this case was delivered on 18 February, 2015.[335]

---

[325] *Id.*

[326] *Id.*

[327] *Id.*

[328] *Id.*

[329] *Id.*

[330] *Id.*

[331] ICT-BD Case No. 01 of 2014 [ICT-BD 2], at pages 157-158 at para 570.

[332] *Ibid*, at page 8 at para 25.

[333] *Ibid*, at page 8-9 at para 28.

[334] *Id.*

[335] *Ibid*, at page 1.

The Tribunal found the accused *Moulana Abdus Sobhan* as guilty of the offences of 'murder', 'abduction', 'confinement', 'torture' and 'extermination' as 'crimes against humanity' in respect of Charge Nos. 1, 2, 3, 4, 6 and 7.[336] Accordingly, he was condemned to the sentence of imprisonment for life till death for the crimes as listed in Charge No. 2; sentence of imprisonment for 5 years for the crimes as listed in Charge No. 3; and sentence of imprisonment for life till death for the crimes as listed in Charge No. 7.[337] Therefore, the sentence of imprisonment as awarded above in respect of Charge Nos. 2, 3 and 7 would run concurrently.[338] In addition to that, he was found guilty of the offence of 'murder' and 'extermination' as 'crimes against humanity' concerning Charge Nos. 1, 4 and 6.[339] Hence, he was condemned to 'sentence to death' for the crimes as listed in Charge No. 1 and he was sentenced to be hanged by the neck till he was dead; 'sentence of death' for the crimes as listed in Charge No.4 and he was sentenced to be hanged by the neck till he was dead; and 'sentence to death' for the crimes as listed in Charge No.6 and he was sentenced to be hanged by the neck till he was dead under Section 20(2) of *ICTA*, 1973 in all the three said charges. Thereby, the 'sentences to death' as awarded above, in respect of Charge Nos. 1, 4 and 6 would get merged.[340] Here, as the convict had been condemned to 'sentences to death', as above, the 'sentences of imprisonment' awarded in respect of Charge Nos. 2, 3 and 7 would get merged into the 'sentences of death'.[341]

---

[336] *Ibid*, at pages 163-164.

[337] *Id.*

[338] *Id.*

[339] *Id.*

[340] *Id.*

[341] *Id.*

It can be mentioned here that there was no charge on genocide brought against the accused in this case.

4.18 *The Chief Prosecutor vs. Md. Abdul Jabbar Engineer*[342]

The Chief Prosecutor submitted the formal charge against *Md. Abdul Jabbar alias Md. Abdul Jabbar Engineer*[343] in the Tribunal on 11 May, 2014 based on the investigation report of the Investigation Agency.[344] There were 5 charges presented against the accused concerning the offences of murder, plundering and arson as 'crimes against humanity'[345] (Charge Nos. 1 and 2); the offences of 'genocide', murder and other inhumane acts [plundering and arson] as 'crimes against humanity'[346] (Charge No. 3); the offence of persecution (conversion) as 'crimes against

---

[342] ICT-BD Case No. 01 of 2014 [ICT-BD 1].

[343] *Ibid*, at page 14 at para 27: 'Md. Abdul Jabbar alias Md. Abdul Jabbar Engineer was born on 30th November, 1932. After obtaining BSC Engineering degree from Dhaka, he joined the politics of Muslim League and became an influential leader of that political party as well as elected as an MPA (Member of Provincial Assembly) in 1964. He was also elected as a Member of Parliament (MP) in 1986 and 1988 respectively as a nominee of the Jatio Party (JP). Later on, he became Vice-Chairman of the central committee of JP. Afterwards, he joined the Bangladesh Nationalist Party (BNP). During the Liberation War of Bangladesh, being an influential leader of Muslim League, he formed *Shanti Committee* in Mothbaria area under presently Pirojpur District. He then became its Chairman to collaborate the Pakistani occupation Army and its auxiliary forces *e.g.* Razakar, Al-Badr, Al-Shams etc.'

[344] *Ibid*, at page 14 at para 28.

[345] The *ICTA* of 1973, Section 3(2)(a)(g) and(h) read with Section 4(1).

[346] *Id.*

humanity'[347] (Charge No. 4); and the offences of abduction, murder, persecutions and other inhumane act [plundering] as 'crimes against humanity'[348] (Charge No. 5).[349] The tribunal took cognizance of the offences as stated in the charges on 12 May, 2014 on perusal of the formal charge, the statement of witnesses and the documents submitted by the Prosecution.[350]

The Prosecution submitted a list of 40 witnesses, although the Prosecution had examined 24 witnesses including the Investigation Officer at the time of the trial.[351] The Prosecution had also presented particular documentary and material evidences.[352] On the other hand, the learned State Defence Counsel had cross-examined all the Prosecution witnesses while he did not adduce any Defence witness.[353] Finally, the Tribunal delivered the judgment of this case on 24 February, 2015.[354]

The Tribunal found the accused as guilty in all the charges.[355] He was firstly found guilty of the offences of 'crimes against humanity' as listed in Charge Nos. 1, 2 and 5.[356] Secondly, hewas held guilty of the offences of 'genocide' and 'crimes against humanity' as listed in Charge No. 3.[357] Therefore, he was sentenced to suffer imprisonment for life till his natural death, for

---

[347]   *Id.*

[348]   *Id.*

[349]   ICT-BD Case No. 01 of 2014 [ICT-BD 1], at pages 132-133 at para 291.

[350]   *Ibid*, at page 15 at para 28.

[351]   *Ibid*, at pages 15-16 at para 31.

[352]   *Id.*

[353]   *Ibid*, at page 16 at para 32.

[354]   *Ibid*, at page 1.

[355]   *Ibid*, at page 140 at para 317.

[356]   *Id.*

[357]   *Id.*

each of the said four charges mentioned above.[358] Furthermore, he was held guilty of the offence of 'crimes against humanity' as listed in Charge No. 4 and thereby, he was sentenced to suffer rigorous imprisonment for 20 years and to pay a fine of Tk. 10, 00,000/- (ten lakh) in default to suffer further simple imprisonment for 2 (two) years for the Charge no. 4.[359] However, the above mentioned five sentences would run concurrently.[360]

Here, it is important to mention that there was only 1 charge on genocide in this case which was proved successfully by the Prosecution before the Tribunal.

4.19 *The Chief Prosecutor vs. Md. Mahidur Rahman & Md. Afsar Hossain @ Chutu*[361]

The Chief Prosecutor submitted the formal charge before the Tribunal against *Md. Mahidur Rahman*[362] and *Md. Afsar Hossain @ Chutu*[363] on the basis of the report of the Investigation

---

[358] *Id.*

[359] *Ibid*, at pages 140-141 at para 318.

[360] *Ibid*, at page 141 at para 319.

[361] ICT-BD Case No. 02 of 2014 [ICT-BD 2].

[362] *Ibid*, at page 2 at para 5: 'Md. Mahidur Rahman studied up to class IX. In 1971, he used to maintain his livelihood by agricultural activities. Since prior to 1971, he was involved with politics of Muslim League. He joined the peace committee and Razakar force in 1971 intending to collaborate with the Pakistani occupation army. During the war of liberation in 1971, he used to stay at the local Razakar camp and commit atrocities around the localities jointly with other members of Razakars.'

[363] *Ibid*, at page 2 at para 5: 'Md. Afsar Hossain @ Chutu studied up to class V. He maintains his livelihood by agriculture activities. Since prior to 1971, he had been an active worker of Muslim League.

Agency.[364] There were 3 charges brought against both the accused in relation to the offences of abduction, confinement, and torture as 'crimes against humanity'[365] (Charge No. 1); the offence of wanton destructive activities constituting the offence of 'other inhumane acts'[366] (Charge No. 2); and the offences of abduction, confinement, torture, murder, and the offence of 'other inhumane acts' as 'crimes against humanity'[367] (Charge No. 3).[368] The Tribunal took cognizance of the offences as mentioned in charges on 24 November, 2014.[369]

In course of trial, the Prosecution adduced and examined 10 witnesses including the Investigating Officer.[370] The Defence duly cross-examined the witnesses.[371] On the contrary, the Defence submitted a list of 10 witnesses along with some documents.[372] However, the Defence examined only 1 witness but eventually the Defence refrained from adducing and examining any witness.[373]

During the war of liberation in 1971, he joined the peace committee and Razakar force. Being associated with the Razakar members of the local Razakar camp, he used to participate in carrying out criminal acts constituting the offence of crimes against humanity and genocide, around the locality.'

[364] *Ibid*, at page 3 at para 9.
[365] The *ICTA* of 1973, Section 3(2)(a)(g)(h).
[366] *Ibid*, Section 3(2)(a)(g)(h) read with Section 4(1).
[367] *Ibid*, Section 3(2)(a)(g)(h) read with Section 3(1) and Section 4(1).
[368] ICT-BD Case No. 02 of 2014 [ICT-BD 2], at pages 6-8.
[369] *Ibid*, at page 3 at para 10.
[370] *Ibid*, at page 6 at para 16.
[371] *Id.*
[372] *Ibid*, at page 6 at para 18.
[373] *Id.*

At the end, the judgment of the case was delivered on 20 May, 2015.[374]

The Tribunal unanimously found the accused *Md. Mahidur Rahman* and *Md. Afsar Hossain alias Chutu* as guilty of the offences of 'murder' as 'crimes against humanity' (Charge No. 1).[375] As a result, they were convicted and condemned to the 'sentences of imprisonment for life till death'.[376] Further, the accused *Md. Mahidur Rahman* and *Afsar Hossain Chutu* were found guilty of majority of the offences of 'other inhumane act' as 'crimes against humanity' (Charge No. 2).[377] Accordingly, they were convicted and condemned to the 'sentence of imprisonment for 5 years'.[378] The sentence of imprisonment as awarded above in respect of Charge Nos. 1 and 2 would run concurrently.[379] However, Charge No. 3 was dropped being barred by the doctrine of double jeopardy.[380]

It can be mentioned here that there was no charge on genocide in this case.

---

[374] *Ibid*, at page 1.

[375] *Ibid*, at page 132.

[376] *Id.*

[377] *Id.*

[378] *Id.*

[379] *Id.*

[380] *Ibid*, at page 133.

4.20 *The Chief Prosecutor vs. Syed Md. Hachhan alias Syed Md. Hasan alias Hachhen Ali*[381]

On the basis of investigation report of the Investigation Agency, the Chief Prosecutor submitted the formal charge against *Syed Md. Hachhan alias Syed Md. Hasan alias Hachhen Ali*[382] in the Tribunal on 24 August, 2014.[383] In this case, there were 6 charges brought against the accused as regards the offences of other inhumane acts [plundering and arson] as 'crimes against humanity'[384] (Charge No. 1); the offences of murder, abduction, confinement, torture and other inhumane [plundering] act as 'crimes against humanity'[385] (Charge No. 2); the offences of 'genocide', and murder, deportation and other inhumane acts [plundering and arson] as 'crimes against humanity'[386] (Charge No. 3); the offences of 'genocide', and murder, abduction, confinement and other inhumane acts as 'crimes against humanity'[387] (Charge No. 4); the offences of murder, abduction, torture and other inhumane acts [looting and mental harm] as 'crimes against humanity'[388] (Charge No. 5); and the offences of murder and other inhumane act [arson] as 'crimes against

---

[381] ICT-BD Case No. 02 of 2014 [ICT-BD 1].

[382] *Ibid*, at page 14 at para 17: 'Syed Md. Hachhan alias Syed Md. Hasan alias Hachhen Ali was born on 18th August, 1947. His father late Syed Muslehuddin was the Vice-President of *Pakistan Democratic Party (PDP)* and the Chairman of *Peace Committee* of Kishoreganj Sub-Division in 1971. During the Liberation War of Bangladesh, he joined the *Razakar Force*. At that time, he introduced himself as the Tarail Thana 'Commander' of *Razakar Force* and 'Daroga'.'

[383] *Ibid*, at page 14 at para 28.

[384] The *ICTA* of 1973, Section 3(2)(a)(g) and (h).

[385] *Ibid*, Section 3(2)(a)(g) and (h) read with Section 4(1).

[386] *Id.*

[387] *Id.*

[388] *Id.*

humanity'[389] (Charge No. 6).[390] On perusal of the formal charge, the statement of witnesses and the documents submitted by the Prosecution, the Tribunal took cognizance of the offences as mentioned in the charges on the same day of submitting the formal charge.[391]

In this case, the Prosecution submitted a list of 40 witnesses while the Prosecution examined 26 witnesses including the Investigation Officer.[392] Again, the Prosecution adduced certain documentary evidences.[393] On the other hand, the learned State Defence Counsel did not adduce any Defence witness but he had cross-examined all the Prosecution witnesses.[394] The judgment of this particular case was delivered on 9 June, 2015.[395]

The Tribunal found the accused *Syed Md. Hachhan alias Syed Md. Hasan alias Hachhen Ali* as guilty in the Charge Nos. 2, 3, 4, 5 and 6. As a result, he was sentenced to death for being guilty of the offences of 'genocide' and 'crimes against humanity' as enlisted in Charge Nos. 3 and 4.[396] In addition to that, he was sentenced to suffer from 'imprisonment for life till his natural death' as he was found guilty of the offences of 'crimes against humanity' as listed in Charge Nos. 2, 5 and 6.[397] Essentially, at the time of executing any one of the two 'sentences to death', the other 'sentence to death' and the sentences to suffer imprisonment

---

[389] *Id.*

[390] ICT-BD Case No. 02 of 2014 [ICT-BD 1], at pages 118-119 at para 246.

[391] *Ibid*, at page 15 at para 28.

[392] *Ibid*, at page 16 at para 32.

[393] *Id.*

[394] *Ibid*, at page 16 at para 33.

[395] *Ibid*, at page 1.

[396] ICT-BD Case No. 02 of 2014 [ICT-BD 1], at page 123.

[397] *Id.*

for life till natural death would be merged into the sentence to death first executed.[398]

In this case, there were 2 charges on genocide which had been proved by the Prosecution successfully.

4.21 *The Chief Prosecutor vs. Md. Forkan Mallik @ Forkan*[399]

The Chief Prosecutor submitted the formal charge against the accused *Md. Forkan Mollik @ Forkan*[400] on the basis of the report and documents submitted by the Investigation Agency.[401] There were 5 charges brought against the accused in relation to the offence of abetting, facilitating and contributing to the actual commission of murder as 'crimes against humanity'[402] (Charge No. 1); the offence of substantially abetting, facilitating and contributing to the actual commission of the act of forcible religious conversion to Islam constituting the offence of other inhumane act and deportation as 'crimes against humanity'[403] (Charge No. 2); the offence of participating, abetting, facilitating and contributing to the actual commission of the act of mass

---

[398] *Id.*

[399] ICT-BD Case No. 03 of 2014 [ICT-BD 2].

[400] *Ibid*, at pages 2-3 at para 5: 'Md. Forkan Mollik @ Forkan studied up to class IV. As per prosecution, the accused is an employee in a Non-Government Organization (NGO) in Dhaka and also a farmer, by profession. In 1971, he joined the local Razakar force and used to carry out criminal acts under the local Razakar commanders. He was an active supporter of Muslim League and subsequently since 1977 he has been with the political party BNP.'

[401] *Ibid*, at page 4 at para 9.

[402] The *ICTA* of 1973, section 3(2)(a)(g)(h).

[403] *Id.*

rape that resulted in death constituting the offence of rape and murder as 'crimes against humanity'[404] (Charge No. 3); the offence of participating, abetting and substantially contributing to the actual commission of the act of rape and deportation as 'crimes against humanity'[405] (Charge No. 4); and the offence of participating, abetting, facilitating and contributing to the actual commission of the act of murder and mass rape as 'crimes against humanity'[406] (Charge No. 5).[407] After that, the Tribunal took cognizance of offences as mentioned in the charges and fixed a date for hearing on charge framing matter accordingly.[408]

In order to prove the said charges, the Prosecution examined 5 witnesses including a rape survivor.[409] On the contrary, the Defence examined 04 witnesses.[410] The judgment of the case was delivered on 16 July, 2015.[411]

The Tribunal found the accused *Md. Forkan Mollik @ Forkan* as guilty of the offences of rape, murder and deportation as 'crimes against humanity' in respect of Charge Nos. 3, 4 and 5.[412] Accordingly, he was convicted and condemned to the sentence as below for three charges, under Section 20(2) of the *Act* of 1973.[413] Sentence of 'imprisonment for life till death' for

---

[404] *Id.*

[405] *Id.*

[406] *Id.*

[407] ICT-BD Case No. 03 of 2014 [ICT-BD 2], at pages 89-90 at para 277.

[408] *Ibid*, at page 4 at para 10.

[409] *Ibid*, at page 67 at para 204; The rape survivor PW 4 named Aleya Begum.

[410] *Ibid*, at pages 83-86 at paras 259-269.

[411] *Ibid*, at page 1.

[412] *Ibid*, at pages 97-98.

[413] *Id.*

the crimes as listed in Charge No.4[414]; 'sentence of death' for the crimes as listed in Charge No. 3 and he was sentenced to be hanged by the neck till he was dead, under Section 20(2) of the *ICTA, 1973*[415]; and 'sentence of death' for the crimes as listed in Charge No. 5 and he was sentenced to be hanged by the neck till he was dead, under Section 20 (2) of the *ICTA, 1973.*[416] However, as the convict has been condemned to 'sentences of death', as above, the 'sentences of imprisonment for life till death' awarded in respect of Charge No. 4 would get merged into the 'sentences of death '.

It can be noted here that there was no charge on genocide in this particular case.

4.22 Conclusion

From the above discussion, it has become certain that the Prosecution brought specific and direct genocide charges in 10 cases out of 20 cases of the ICT-BD and succeeded in proving its charge only in 7 cases. Here, there were 200 charges in total brought in these concerned 20 cases in which conviction took place in 130 charges. Among all, there were 35 charges brought in relation to genocide while the Prosecution could prove 12 charges as the crime of genocide in the Tribunal.

---

[414]   *Ibid*, at page 98.

[415]   *Id.*

[416]   *Id.*

Chapter 5

Notable Trends in the Genocide Counts

5.1 Introduction

This chapter endeavours to find the "trends" of the trials of the ICT-BD focusing on the charges in relation to genocide. Generally, trend analysis involves the practice of gathering information with a view to attempting to spot a pattern or trend based on the same. For this purpose, this chapter focuses on the first 20 cases of the ICT-BD, briefly discussed in the chapter 4.

This chapter mainly shows 6 separate trends including *i.e.* "Lesser Number of Genocide Charges", "Less Number of Genocide Charges Compared to Incidents of Mass Killing", "Categories of Genocide Charged", "Group Identification", "Conviction Rate of Genocide Charges", and "Punishment for Genocide Charges". The first trend demonstrates that in all the concerned cases, a few charges have been brought in relation to genocide in comparison with the charges concerning crimes against humanity. The second trend shows that even though many charges drew the incident of mass killing which took place during the 1971 Liberation War in Bangladesh, committed by the Pakistani Army and their local collaborators, the number of genocide charges brought by the prosecution is comparatively very less. The third trend is regarding the method of committing genocide which attracts that the groups of people of Bangladesh were targeted by the perpetrators, and they were killed. Thus, it is certain that the method of killing only was invoked by the perpetrators to commit genocide in 1971 Liberation War in Bangladesh. The fourth trend portrays that, most of the time, the religious groups *e.g.* Hindu religious groups were targeted, and killed with the intention of destroying such groups. Besides, it is found that in a very few cases, the other groups namely national, ethnic, racial, and political group(s) were targeted to commit genocide. Referring to the next trend, it can be noted that the first trend makes it evident that the number of genocide charges were very less; however, the fifth trend precisely demonstrates that the conviction rate of genocide charges was also not as much of the other charges. As a final point, the sixth trend lists the punishments given to the convicts for the commission of genocide making it evident that most of the perpetrators were sentenced to death while some of the convicts were awarded life imprisonment considering, *inter alia*, their age and physical conditions as the mitigating factors.

5.2 Trend 1: Lesser Number of Genocide Charges

The following *Table-1* shows that the prosecution brought 8 charges against *Abdul Kalam Azad*,[1] 6 charges against *Abdul Quader Molla*,[2] 20 charges against *Delowar Hossain Sayeedi*,[3] 7

---

[1]   *The Chief Prosecutor vs. Moulana Abdul Kalam Azad*, ICT-BD Case No. 05 of 2012 [ICT-BD 2].

[2]   *The Chief Prosecutor vs. Abdul Quader Molla*, ICT-BD Case No. 02 of 2012 [ICT-BD 2].

[3]   *The Chief Prosecutor vs. Delowar Hossain Sayeedi*, ICT-BD Case No. 01 of 2011 [ICT-BD 1].

charges against *Muhammad Kamaruzzaman*,[4] 5 charges against *Ghulam Azam*,[5] 7 charges against *Muhammad Mujahid*,[6] 23 charges against *Salauddin Quader Chowdhury*,[7] 17 charges against *Abdul Alim*,[8] 11 charges against both *Ashrafuzzaman Khan and Chowdhury Mueen Uddin*,[9] 16 charges against *Motiur Rahman Nizami*,[10] 14 charges against *Mir Quasem Ali*,[11] 11 charges against *Zahid Hossain Khokon*,[12] 5 charges against *Mobarak Hossain*,[13] 16 charges against *Md. Qaiser*,[14] 6 charges against *Azharul Islam*,[15] 9

---

[4] *The Chief Prosecutor vs. Muhammad Kamaruzzaman*, ICT-BD Case No. 03 of 2012 [ICT-BD 2].

[5] *The Chief Prosecutor vs. Professor Ghulam Azam*, ICT-BD Case No. 06 of 2011 [ICT-BD 1].

[6] *The Chief Prosecutor vs. Ali Ahsan Muhammad Mujahid*, ICT-BD Case No. 04 of 2012 [ICT-BD 2].

[7] *The Chief Prosecutor vs. Salauddin Quader Chowdhury*, ICT-BD Case No. 02 of 2011 [ICT-BD 1].

[8] *The Chief Prosecutor vs. Md. Abdul Alim @ M. A. Alim*, ICT-BD Case No. 01 of 2012 [ICT-BD 2].

[9] *The Chief Prosecutor vs. Ashrafuzzaman Khan @ Naeb Ali Khan & Chowdhury Mueen Uddin*, ICT-BD Case No. 01 of 2013 [ICT-BD 2].

[10] *The Chief Prosecutor vs. Motiur Rahman Nizami*, ICT-BD Case No. 03 of 2011 [ICT-BD 1].

[11] *The Chief Prosecutor vs. Mir Quasem Ali*, ICT-BD Case No. 03 of 2013 [ICT-BD 2].

[12] *The Chief Prosecutor vs. Zahid Hossain Khokon*, ICT-BD Case No. 04 of 2013 [ICT-BD 1].

[13] *The Chief Prosecutor vs. Md. Mobarak Hossain @ Mobarak Ali*, ICT-BD Case No. 01 of 2013 [ICT-BD 1].

[14] *The Chief Prosecutor vs. Syed Md. Qaiser*, ICT-BD Case No. 04 of 2013 [ICT-BD 2].

[15] *The Chief Prosecutor vs. A. T. M. Azharul Islam*, ICT-BD Case No. 05 of 2013 [ICT-BD 1].

charges against *Abdus Sobhan*,[16] 5 charges against *Abdul Jabbar*,[17] 3 charges against both *Mahidur and Afsar Hossain*,[18] 6 charges against *Md. Hachhan*,[19] and 5 charges against *Md. Forkan Mallik*.[20]

Thus, the total number of charges in all these 20 cases was 200.

Table-1 also demonstrates that the prosecution brought genocide charges in 12 cases out of total 20 cases. It means only 60% cases of total 20 cases had charges on genocide.

Table-1 further shows that the prosecution brought only 1 genocide charge against *Abdul Kalam Azad*,[21] 4 genocide charges against *Delowar Hossain Sayeedi*,[22] 2 genocide charges against *Muhammad Mujahid*,[23] 9 genocide charges against *Salauddin Quader Chowdhury*,[24] 3 genocide charges against *Abdul Alim*,[25] 2 genocide charges against *Motiur Rahman Nizami*,[26] 4 genocide

---

[16]   *The Chief Prosecutor vs. Moulana Abdus Sobhan*, ICT-BD Case No. 01 of 2014 [ICT-BD 2].

[17]   *The Chief Prosecutor vs. Md. Abdul Jabbar Engineer*, ICT-BD Case No. 01 of 2014 [ICT-BD 1].

[18]   *The Chief Prosecutor vs. Md. Mahidur Rahman & Md. Afsar Hossain @ Chutu*, ICT-BD Case No. 02 of 2014 [ICT-BD 2].

[19]   *The Chief Prosecutor vs. Syed Md. Hachhan alias Syed Md. Hasan alias Hachhen Ali*, ICT-BD Case No. 02 of 2014 [ICT-BD 1].

[20]   *The Chief Prosecutor vs. Md. Forkan Mallik @ Forkan*, ICT-BD Case No. 03 of 2014 [ICT-BD 2].

[21]   *Abdul Kalam Azad, op. cit. no. 1.*

[22]   *Delowar Hossain Sayeedi, op. cit. no. 3.*

[23]   *Ali Ahsan Muhammad Mujahid, op. cit. no. 6.*

[24]   *Salauddin Quader Chowdhury, op. cit. no. 7.*

[25]   *Md. Abdul Alim, op. cit. no. 8.*

[26]   *Motiur Rahman Nizami, op. cit. no. 10.*

charges against *Zahid Hossain Khokon*,[27] 1 genocide charge against *Md. Qaiser*,[28] 2 genocide charges against *Azharul Islam*,[29] 1 genocide charge against *Abdus Sobhan*,[30] 1 genocide charge against *Md. Abdul Jabbar*,[31] and 2 genocide charges against *Md. Hachhan*[32].

Therefore, the prosecution brought 32 genocide charges in total in the concerned cases. Consequently, the rate of genocide charges brought against the said convicts stands as 16% only. Thus, it is apparent that the Prosecutors are prone to bring lesser number of genocide charges.

According to Prosecutor Zead-al-Malum,[33] when the ICT-BD started its journey in 2010 the Office of the Chief Prosecutor had to face a lot of challenges. The most challenging part was to gather appropriate evidences to prove the charges. It was undoubtedly a difficult task, more so for the reason that the trial was to take place after a long 40 years of commission of the offence. The social and political atmosphere in the country during the initial years of the constitution of the ICT-BD was also a barrier for the prosecution team to produce relevant witnesses to prove the charges. Since the proof of genocide charges require to satisfy higher threshold of evidential burden (for example, proof of genocidal intent), the prosecution on strategic purposes opted more for Crimes Against Humanity charges than genocide

---

[27]   *Zahid Hossain Khokon, op. cit. no. 12.*
[28]   *Syed Md. Qaiser, op. cit. no. 14.*
[29]   *A. T. M. Azharul Islam, op. cit. no. 15.*
[30]   *Moulana Abdus Sobhan, op. cit. no. 16.*
[31]   *Md. Abdul Jabbar Engineer, op. cit. no. 17.*
[32]   *Hachhen Ali, op. cit. no. 19.*
[33]   Views expressed in an interview with the author.

charges. That explains why there have been less charges of genocide at the ICT-BD.

Similar explanations have been forwarded by the other prosecutors too. Prosecutor Sultan Mahmud[34] further stated that proving 'genocidal intent' in genocide charges is a must. However, to prove 'genocidal intent' in cases after 40 years puts an extra burden on the prosecution. Therefore, the prosecution thought that it would be better to frame charges under the Crimes Against Humanity category and could still ensure the highest punishment if the prosecution had been able to prove the relevant charge. As a result, the ICT-BD charges reflected comparatively less genocide charges.

However, according to Prosecutor Tapas Kanti Baul,[35] when the ICT-BD started its journey, both the Investigation Agency and the Office of the Chief Prosecutor had huge knowledge gap. Genocide was not a Penal Code offence; hence the investigators and the prosecutors did not have sufficient knowledge and efficiency as to how to investigate or to conduct a genocide charge. They were not fully aware of the evidential burden to prove the elements of genocide charges. Moreover, many of the events investigated even though could fall within the parameters of genocide charges, the investigation and the prosecutors could not appreciate the same. For example, the investigation and the prosecution members could not appreciate that the issue of religious conversion or rape could amount to genocide if other elements of genocide were present. The prosecution simply did not explore various methods of committing genocide except for genocide by killing. In turn, this resulted in lesser number of genocide charges at the ICT-BD.

---

[34]   *Id.*

[35]   *Id.*

Table 1

SL No.	Cases	Total Number of Charges	Total Number of Genocide Charges
1	*Chief Prosecutor v. Abdul Kalam Azad*	8	1
2	*Chief Prosecutor v. Abdul Quader Molla*	6	0
3	*Chief Prosecutor v. Delowar Hossain Sayeedi*	20	4
4	*Chief Prosecutor v. Muhammad Kamaruzzaman*	7	0
5	*Chief Prosecutor v. Ghulam Azam*	5	0
6	*Chief Prosecutor v. A. A. Muhammad Mujahid*	7	2
7	*Chief Prosecutor v. Salauddin Quader Chowdhury*	23	9
8	*Chief Prosecutor v. M. A. Alim*	17	3
9	*Chief Prosecutor v. Ashrafuzzaman & Mueenuddin*	11	0
10	*Chief Prosecutor v. Motiur Rahman Nizami*	16	2
11	*Chief Prosecutor v. Mir Quasem Ali*	14	0
12	*Chief Prosecutor v. Zahid Hossain Khokon*	11	4
13	*Chief Prosecutor v. Mobarak Hossain*	5	0
14	*Chief Prosecutor v. Syed Md. Qaiser*	16	1
15	*Chief Prosecutor v. A. T. M. Azharul Islam*	6	2
16	*Chief Prosecutor v. Abdus Sobhan*	9	1
17	*Chief Prosecutor v. Md. Abdul Jabbar*	5	1

18	*Chief Prosecutor v. Mahidur & Afsar Hossain*	3	0
19	*Chief Prosecutor v. Syed Md. Hachhan*	6	2
20	*Chief Prosecutor v. Md. Forkan Mallik*	5	0
Total		**200**	**32**

5.3 Trend 2: Less Number of Genocide Charges Compared to Incidents of Mass Killing

This trend explores that even though the charges brought by the ICT-BD prosecution had incidents of mass killing, not all mass killing were framed as genocide charges. There, however, remains a question as to what one should consider as mass killing.

As regards numerical threshold to determine 'mass killing', it has been well established in the cases of the 'International Criminal Tribunal for Rwanda (ICTR)' that 'large scale does not suggest a numerical minimum, it must be determined on case-by-case basis using a common-sense approach.'[36]

Likewise, in the cases of the 'International Criminal Tribunal for former Yugoslavia (ICTY)', it has also been settled that in respect

---

[36] *The Prosecutor vs. Gacumbitsi*, (ICTR Trial Chamber), June 17, 2004, at para 309; *The Prosecutor vs. Ntakirutimana*, (ICTR Appeals Chamber), December 13, 2004, at para 516; *The Prosecutor vs. Bagosora, Kabiligi, Ntabakuze* and *Nsengiyumva*, (ICTR Trial Chamber), December 18, 2008, at para 2191; *The Prosecutor vs. Karera*, (ICTR Trial Chamber), December 7, 2007, at para 552; *The Prosecutor vs. Rugambarara*, (ICTR Trial Chamber), November 16, 2007, at para 23; *The Prosecutor vs. Simba*, (ICTR Trial Chamber), December 13, 2005, at para 422; *The Prosecutor vs. Bagilishema*, (ICTR Trial Chamber), June 7, 2001, at para 87; *The Prosecutor vs. Kamuhanda*, (ICTR Trial Chamber), January 22, 2004, at para 692.

of the question as to whether the element of killings on a massive scale implies a numerical requirement, the Trial Chamber finds that there is no such requirement and the element of massive scale must be assessed on a case-by-case basis in light of the proven criminal conduct and all relevant factors.[37]

Henceforth, for the purpose of this research on the incidents of mass killing on the basis of the charges brought in the said 20 cases of the ICT-BD, killing of at least 10 people in a distinct attack has been considered as the minimum number to determine mass killing.

Now, the *Table-2* shows that total 1 charge was brought related to mass killing against *Abdul Kalam Azad*[38] and the same had been alleged as genocide; 1 charge was brought against *Abdul Quader Molla*[39] regarding mass killing but the same had been alleged as 'crimes against humanity'[40] instead of genocide; 4 charges were brought against *Delowar Hossain Sayeedi*[41] where all these

---

[37] *The Prosecutor vs. Blagojevic and Jokic*, (ICTY Trial Chamber), January 17, 2005, at para 573; *The Prosecutor vs. Brdjanin*, (ICTY Trial Chamber), September 1, 2004, at para 391; *The Prosecutor vs. Stakic*, (ICTY Trial Chamber), July 31, 2003, at para 640; *The Prosecutor vs. Vasiljevic*, (ICTY Trial Chamber), November 29, 2002, at para 227; *The Prosecutor vs. Krstic*, (ICTY Trial Chamber), August 2, 2001, at para 503.

[38] *Abdul Kalam Azad, op. cit. no. 1.*

[39] *Abdul Quader Molla, op. cit. no. 2.*

[40] In accordance with Section 3(2)(a) of the *ICTA* of 1973, committing murder, extermination, enslavement, deportation, imprisonment, abduction, confinement, torture, rape or other inhumane acts against any civilian population or persecutions based on political, racial, ethnic or religious grounds, whether or not in violation of the domestic law of the country where perpetrated, is called as 'Crime against Humanity (CAH)'.

[41] *Delowar Hossain Sayeedi, op. cit. no. 3.*

charges had been alleged as genocides; 1 charge was brought against *Muhammad Kamaruzzaman*[42] as regards mass killing but it had been alleged as 'crimes against humanity' instead of genocide; 3 charges were brought against *Muhammad Mujahid*[43] related to mass killing in which 2 charges had been considered as genocides while the other 1 was considered as 'crimes against humanity'; 9 charges were brought against *Salauddin Quader Chowdhury*[44] related to mass killing where all these 9 charges had been alleged as genocides; 10 charges were brought against *Abdul Alim*[45] regarding mass killing in which 3 charges had been alleged as genocides while the other 7 charges had been alleged as 'crimes against humanity'; 5 charges were brought against *Motiur Rahman Nizami*[46] related to mass killing in which 2 charges had been alleged as genocides and the other 1 charge had been alleged as 'crimes against humanity'; 4 charges were brought against *Zahid Hossain Khokon*[47] in relation to mass killing and the same had been alleged as genocide.

Table-2 further shows that only 1 charge was brought against *Mobarak Hossain*[48] as regards mass killing but the same had been alleged as 'crimes against humanity' instead of genocide; 2 charges were brought against *Md. Qaiser*[49] related to mass killing in which 1 charge had been alleged as genocide and the other 1 had been alleged as 'crimes against humanity'; 4charges were

---

[42]   *Muhammad Kamaruzzaman, op. cit. no. 4.*

[43]   *Ali Ahsan Muhammad Mujahid, op. cit. no. 6.*

[44]   *Salauddin Quader Chowdhury, op. cit. no. 7.*

[45]   *Md. Abdul Alim, op. cit. no. 8.*

[46]   *Motiur Rahman Nizami, op. cit. no. 10.*

[47]   *Zahid Hossain Khokon, op. cit. no. 12.*

[48]   *Md. Mobarak Hossain, op. cit. no. 13.*

[49]   *Syed Md. Qaiser, op. cit. no. 14.*

brought against *Azharul Islam*[50] in relation to mass killing in which 2 charges had been alleged as genocides and the other 2 charges had been alleged as 'crimes against humanity'; 3 charges were brought against *Abdus Sobhan*[51] related to mass killing in which 1 had been alleged as genocide and the other 2 had been alleged as 'crimes against humanity'; 2 charges were brought against *Abdul Jabbar*[52] as regards mass killing in which 1 charge had been alleged as genocide and the other 1 had been alleged as 'crimes against humanity'; 1 charge was brought against both *Mahidur and Afsar Hossain*[53] related to mass killing but the same had been alleged as 'crimes against humanity' instead of genocide; and 2 charges were brought against *Md. Hachhan*[54] in relation to mass killing where both of these 2 charges had been alleged as genocides.

Thus, the total number of charges related to mass killing in the said 20 cases was 53. However, the total number of genocide charges was 32 only *i.e.* only 60.3% charges of mass killing incidents was alleged as genocides.

From the above discussion and data, it is evident that even though there were more incidents of mass killing, genocide charges brought by the prosecution were less in number. Thus, it seems that the prosecution brought less number of genocide charges compared to the incidents of mass killings as stipulated in the said 20 cases.

---

[50]   *A. T. M. Azharul Islam, op. cit. no.* 15.

[51]   *Moulana Abdus Sobhan, op. cit. no.* 16.

[52]   *Md. Abdul Jabbar Engineer, op. cit. no.* 17.

[53]   *Md. Mahidur Rahman & Md. Afsar Hossain, op. cit. no.* 18.

[54]   *Hachhen Ali, op.cit. no.* 19.

Table 2

SL No	Cases	Total Charges Related to Mass Atrocities	Total Number of Genocide Charges
1	*Chief Prosecutor v. Abdul Kalam Azad*	1	1
2	*Chief Prosecutor v. Abdul Quader Molla*	1	0
3	*Chief Prosecutor v. Delowar Hossain Sayeedi*	4	4
4	*Chief Prosecutor v. Muhammad Kamaruzzaman*	1	0
5	*Chief Prosecutor v. A. A. Muhammad Mujahid*	3	2
6	*Chief Prosecutor v. Salauddin Quader Chowdhury*	9	9
7	*Chief Prosecutor v. M. A. Alim*	10	3
8	*Chief Prosecutor v. Motiur Rahman Nizami*	5	2
9	*Chief Prosecutor v. Zahid Hossain Khokon*	4	4
10	*Chief Prosecutor v. Mobarak Hossain*	1	0
11	*Chief Prosecutor v. Syed Md. Qaiser*	2	1
12	*Chief Prosecutor v. A. T. M. Azharul Islam*	4	2
13	*Chief Prosecutor v. Abdus Sobhan*	3	1
14	*Chief Prosecutor v. Md. Abdul Jabbar*	2	1
15	*Chief Prosecutor v. Mahidur & Afsar Hossain*	1	0

16	Chief Prosecutor v. Syed Md. Hachhan	2	2
Total		53	32

5.4 Trend 3: Categories of Genocide Charged

Genocide has been defined in Section 3(2)(c) of the *International Crimes (Tribunals) Act* of 1973 which entails five methods of committing genocide such as:

    (a) 'killing members of the group;
    (b) causing serious bodily or mental harm to members of the group;
    (c) deliberately inflicting on the group conditions of life calculated to bring about its physical destruction in whole or in part;
    (d) imposing measures intended to prevent births within the group; and
    (e) forcibly transferring children of the group to another group.'[55]

Therefore, it is clear that genocide as per the 1973 *Act* can be committed by 5 different methods. These are: (a) killing; (b) causing serious bodily or mental harm; (c) deliberately inflicting conditions of life calculated to bring about physical destruction; (d) imposing measures intended to prevent births; and (e) forcibly transferring children. It is to be stated that the above-mentioned five methods of committing genocide do basically form the *actus reus* of genocide.[56]

---

[55] Section 3(2)(c) of the *ICTA*, 1973.

[56] *Gacumbitsi, op. cit. no. 36*, at para 251; *Kamuhanda, op. cit. no. 36*, at para 631.

The *first* method *i.e.* genocide by killing would mean committing 'murder'.[57] It may also mean 'homicide committed with intent to cause death'.[58]

The *second* method of committing genocide includes causing serious bodily or mental harm.[59] In general terms, serious bodily or mental harm would mean 'an intentional act or omission causing serious bodily or mental suffering'.[60]

Serious harm needs not be *permanent* or *irremediable*,[61] but 'it must involve harm that goes beyond temporary unhappiness, embarrassment or humiliation'[62] or '[i]t must be harm that results in a grave and long-term disadvantage to a person's ability to

---

[57] *Blagojevic and Jokic, op. cit. no.* 37, at para 642.

[58] *The Prosecutor vs. Seromba,* (ICTR Trial Chamber), December 13, 2006, at para 317.

[59] *Kamuhanda, op. cit. no.* 36, at para 633; *The Prosecutor vs. Kajelijeli,* (ICTR Trial Chamber), December 1, 2003, at para 814.

[60] *Krstic, op. cit. no.* 37, at para 513.

[61] *Bagosora, op. cit. no.* 36, at para 2117; *The Prosecutor vs. Ntagerura, Bagambiki, and Imanishimwe,* (ICTR Trial Chamber), February 25, 2004, at para 664; *The Prosecutor vs. Semanza,* (ICTR Trial Chamber), May 15, 2003, at paras 320-322; *Bagilishema, op. cit. no.* 36, at para 59; *The Prosecutor vs. Musema,* (ICTR Trial Chamber), January 27, 2000, at para 156; *The Prosecutor vs. Rutaganda,* (ICTR Trial Chamber), December 6, 1999, at para 51; *The Prosecutor vs. Kayishema and Ruzindana,* (ICTR Trial Chamber), May 21, 1999, at para 108; *The Prosecutor vs. Akayesu,* (ICTR Trial Chamber), September 2, 1998, at para 502; *The Prosecutor vs. Muhimana,* (ICTR Trial Chamber), April 28, 2005, at para 502; *Gacumbitsi, op. cit. no.* 36, at para 291; *Seromba, op. cit. no.* 58, at para 317; *The Prosecutor vs. Muvunyi,* (ICTR Trial Chamber), September 12, 2006, at para 487; *Kamuhanda, op. cit. no.* 36, at para 634; *Kajelijeli, op. cit. no.* 59, at para 815.

[62] *Krstic, op. cit. no.* 37, at para 513.

lead a normal and constructive life'.[63] In other words, the harm inflicted needs not be permanent and irremediable, but needs to be serious.[64] It may also be mentioned that the harm does not require that its necessary result would be death of the victim.[65]

Sometimes, a list is suggested to include matters of serious bodily or mental harm. For example, serious bodily or mental harm may include acts of torture, inhuman or degrading treatment, sexual violence including rape,[66] interrogations combined with beatings, threats of death,[67] forcible transfer[68] and deportation.[69]

Bodily harm refers to harm that seriously injures the health, causes disfigurement or any serious injury to the external, internal organs or senses.[70] On the other hand, mental harm

---

[63] *Blagojevic and Jokic, op. cit. no. 37,* at para 645.

[64] *Brdjanin, op. cit. no. 37,* at para 690; *Stakic, op. cit. no. 37,* at para 516.

[65] *Muvunyi, op. cit. no. 61,* at para 487.

[66] *Seromba, op. cit. no. 58,* at para 46; *Akayesu, op. cit. no. 61,* at para 688.

[67] *Akayesu, op. cit. no. 61,* at paras 711-712.

[68] *Krstic, op. cit. no. 37,* at para 31; *Blagojevic and Jokic, op. cit. no. 37,* at paras 663, 665-666.

[69] *Blagojevic and Jokic, op. cit. no. 37,* at para 646; *Brdjanin, op. cit. no. 37,* at para 690; *Stakic, op. cit. no. 37,* at para 516; *Krstic, op. cit. no. 37,* at para 513; *Kamuhanda, op. cit. no. 36,* at para 634; *Kajelijeli, op. cit. no. 59,* at para 815; *Kayishema and Ruzindana, op. cit. no. 61,* at para 108; *Rutaganda, op. cit. no. 61,* at para 51; *Seromba, op. cit. no. 58,* at para 317; *Bagilishema, op. cit. no. 36,* at para 59; *Musema, op. cit. no. 61,* at para 156; *Akayesu, op. cit. no. 61,* at para 504.

[70] *Blagojevic and Jokic, op. cit. no. 37,* at para 645; *Muvunyi, op. cit. no. 61,* at para 487; *Gacumbitsi, op. cit. no. 36,* at para 291; *Muhimana, op. cit. no. 61,* at para 502; *Ntagerura, Bagambiki and Imanishimwe, op. cit. no. 61,* at para 664; *Seromba, op. cit. no. 58,* at para 317; *Kayishema and Ruzindana, op. cit. no. 61,* at para 109.

refers to 'more than minor or temporary impairment of mental faculties such as the infliction of strong fear or terror, intimidation or threat'.[71]

However, it is suggested in a number of cases that whether a particular act constitutes 'serious bodily or mental harm' or not, it must be assessed on a case-by-case basis, with due regard to the particular circumstances of the case.[72]

The *third* method of committing genocide includes deliberately inflicting on the group conditions of life calculated to bring about its physical destruction. This category of committing genocide covers methods of destruction by which the perpetrator does not immediately kill group members, but which, ultimately, seek their physical destruction.[73]

This method of committing genocide may include subjecting the group to a subsistence diet, systematic expulsion from homes and denial of the right to medical services, creation of circumstances that would lead to a slow death, such as lack of proper housing, clothing and hygiene or excessive work or physical exertion etc.[74]

---

71   *Seromba, op. cit. no.* 58, at para 46; *Ntagerura, Bagambiki and Imanishimwe, op. cit. no.* 61, at para 664; *Kamuhanda, op. cit. no.* 36, at para 634; *Kajelijeli, op. cit. no.* 59, at para 815; *Semanza, op. cit. no.* 61, at para 321; *Muvunyi, op. cit. no.* 61, at para 487; *Muhimana, op. cit. no.* 61, at para 502; *Gacumbitsi, op. cit. no.* 36, at para 291.

72   *Blagojevic and Jokic, op. cit. no.* 37, at para 646; *Kamuhanda, op. cit. no.* 36, at para 634; *Kajelijeli, op. cit. no.* 59, at para 815; *Kayishema and Ruzindana, op. cit. no.* 61, at paras 108, 113.

73   *Stakic, op. cit. no.* 37, at para 518; *Akayesu, op. cit. no.* 61, at paras 505-506; *Musema, op. cit. no.* 61, at para 157; *Rutaganda, op. cit. no.* 61, at para 52.

74   *Brdjanin, op. cit. no.* 37, at para 691; *Stakic, op. cit. no.* 37, at para 517; *Kayishema and Ruzindana, op. cit. no.* 61, at paras 115-116; *Akayesu, op. cit. no.* 61, at paras 505-506; *Musema, op. cit. no.* 61,

The *fourth* method of committing genocide involves imposing measures intended to prevent births within the target group. This may include sexual mutilation, the practice of sterilization, forced birth control, separation of the sexes and prohibition of marriages.[75] It may also be mentioned that rape can be a measure intended to prevent births when the person raped refuses subsequently to procreate, in the same way that members of a group can be led, through threats or trauma, not to procreate.[76]

The *fifth* method of committing genocide can be done by forcibly transferring children of the target group to another group. It is stated that the objective of this method of committing genocide is not only to sanction a direct act of forcible physical transfer, but also to sanction acts of threats or trauma which would lead to the forcible transfer of children from one group to another.[77]

Now, in the cases of the ICT-BD, the following *Table-3* shows that in all 12 cases in which the genocide charges were brought against the accused, the alleged common method of committing genocide was only 'killing members of the group(s)' *i.e.* 100% genocide charges were about genocide by killing. Charges alleging other methods of committing genocide had not been explored in the first 20 cases of the ICT-BD.

---

at para 157; *Rutaganda, op. cit. no.* 61, at para 52.

[75] *Akayesu, op. cit. no.* 61, at paras 507-508; *Musema, op. cit. no.* 61, at para 158; *Rutaganda, op. cit. no.* 61, at para 53; *Kayishema and Ruzindana, op. cit. no.* 61, at para 117.

[76] *Id.*

[77] *Id.*

Table 3

SL No.	Cases	Total Number of Genocide Charges	Method of Committing Genocide
1	*Chief Prosecutor v. Abdul Kalam Azad*	1	Killing
2	*Chief Prosecutor v. Delowar Hossain Sayeedi*	4	Killing
3	*Chief Prosecutor v. A. A. Muhammad Mujahid*	2	Killing
4	*Chief Prosecutor v. Salauddin Quader Chowdhury*	9	Killing
5	*Chief Prosecutor v. M. A. Alim*	3	Killing
6	*Chief Prosecutor v. Motiur Rahman Nizami*	2	Killing
7	*Chief Prosecutor v. Zahid Hossain Khokon*	4	Killing
8	*Chief Prosecutor v. Syed Md. Qaiser*	1	Killing
9	*Chief Prosecutor v. A. T. M. Azharul Islam*	2	Killing
10	*Chief Prosecutor v. Abdus Sobhan*	1	Killing
11	*Chief Prosecutor v. Md. Abdul Jabbar*	1	Killing
12	*Chief Prosecutor v. Syed Md. Hachhan*	2	Killing

5.5 Trend 4: Group Identification

According to Section 3(2)(c) of the *ICTA*, there are five protected groups, *i.e.* national, ethnic, racial, religious or political group who may be targeted by the perpetrators with the intent to destroy, in whole or in part.

Here, the following *Table-4* shows that in all the 12 cases where the genocide charges were brought, it has been mentioned that the perpetrators targeted the 'religious group' with the intent to destroy the same in whole or in part.

However, along with the religious group, in *Salauddin Quader Chowdhury*[78] and *Zahid Hossain Khokon*[79] cases 'political group'; in *Abdul Alim*[80] case 'freedom-fighters group'; in *Motiur Rahman Nizami*[81] case 'national, ethnic, and racial group'; and in *Abdus Sobhan*[82] case 'national group' have been mentioned as target groups by the perpetrators with the intent to destroy the same in whole or in part.

Table 4

SL No.	Cases	Total Number of Genocide Charges	Alleged Target Group
1	*Chief Prosecutor v. Abdul Kalam Azad*	1	Religious
2	*Chief Prosecutor v. Delowar Hossain Sayeedi*	4	Religious

---

[78]   *Salauddin Quader Chowdhury, op. cit. no. 7.*

[79]   *Zahid Hossain Khokon, op. cit. no. 12.*

[80]   *Md. Abdul Alim, op. cit. no. 8*

[81]   *Motiur Rahman Nizami, op. cit. no. 10.*

[82]   *Moulana Abdus Sobhan, op. cit. no. 16.*

3	*Chief Prosecutor v. A. A. Muhammad Mujahid*	2	Religious
4	*Chief Prosecutor v. Salauddin Quader Chowdhury*	9	Religious and Political
5	*Chief Prosecutor v. M. A. Alim*	3	Religious and Freedom-Fighters
6	*Chief Prosecutor v. Motiur Rahman Nizami*	2	Religious, National, Ethnic, and Racial
7	*Chief Prosecutor v. Zahid Hossain Khokon*	4	Religious and Political
8	*Chief Prosecutor v. Syed Md. Qaiser*	1	Religious
9	*Chief Prosecutor v. A. T. M. Azharul Islam*	2	Religious
10	*Chief Prosecutor v. Abdus Sobhan*	1	National, and Religious
11	*Chief Prosecutor v. Md. Abdul Jabbar*	1	Religious
12	*Chief Prosecutor v. Syed Md. Hachhan*	2	Religious

5.6 Trend 5: Conviction Rate of Genocide Charges

Table-5 displays that in *Abdul Kalam Azad*[83] case, 1 genocide charge was brought and the prosecution could prove the same; in

---

[83] *Abdul Kalam Azad, op. cit. no. 1.*

Delowar Hossain Sayeedi[84] case, 4 genocide charges were brought and the prosecution could prove none; in *Muhammad Mujahid*[85] case, 2 genocide charges were brought and the prosecution could prove none; in *Salauddin Quader Chowdhury*[86] case, 9 genocide charges were brought and the prosecution could prove only 4 charges; in *Abdul Alim*[87] case, 3 genocide charges were brought and the prosecution could prove only 2 charges; in *Motiur Rahman Nizami*[88] case, 2 genocide charges were brought and the prosecution could prove none.

Table-5 further shows that in *Zahid Hossain Khokon*[89] case, 4 genocide charges were brought and the prosecution could prove none; in *Md. Qaiser*[90] case, only 1 genocide charge was brought and the prosecution could not prove that; in *Azharul Islam*[91] case, 2 genocide charges were brought and the prosecution could prove only 1 charge; in *Abdus Sobhan*[92] case, only 1 genocide charge was brought and the prosecution could not prove that; in *Abdul Jabbar*[93] case, only 1genocide charge was brought and the prosecution could prove the same; and in *Md. Hachhan*[94] case, 2 genocide charges were brought and the prosecution could prove both the charges.

---

84   *Delowar Hossain Sayeedi, op. cit. no. 3.*

85   *Ali Ahsan Muhammad Mujahid, op. cit. no. 6.*

86   *Salauddin Quader Chowdhury, op. cit. no. 7.*

87   *Md. Abdul Alim, op. cit. no. 8.*

88   *Motiur Rahman Nizami, op. cit. no. 10.*

89   *Zahid Hossain Khokon, op. cit. no. 12.*

90   *Syed Md. Qaiser, op. cit. no. 14.*

91   *A. T. M. Azharul Islam, op. cit. no. 15.*

92   *Moulana Abdus Sobhan, op. cit. no. 16.*

93   *Md. Abdul Jabbar Engineer, op. cit. no. 17.*

94   *Hachhen Ali, op. cit. no. 19.*

Therefore, the total number of genocide conviction was 11 out of 32 alleged genocide charges. Consequently, the genocide conviction rate is 34.37% which is less than one third.

Table 5

SL No.	Cases	Total Number of Genocide Charges	Total Number of Genocide Conviction
1	Chief Prosecutor v. Abdul Kalam Azad	1	1
2	Chief Prosecutor v. Delowar Hossain Sayeedi	4	0
3	Chief Prosecutor v. A. A. Muhammad Mujahid	2	0
4	Chief Prosecutor v. Salauddin Quader Chowdhury	9	4
5	Chief Prosecutor v. M. A. Alim	2	2
6	Chief Prosecutor v. Motiur Rahman Nizami	2	0
7	Chief Prosecutor v. Zahid Hossain Khokon	4	0
8	Chief Prosecutor v. Syed Md. Qaiser	1	0
9	Chief Prosecutor v. A. T. M. Azharul Islam	2	1
10	Chief Prosecutor v. Abdus Sobhan	1	0
11	Chief Prosecutor v. Md. Abdul Jabbar	1	1
12	Chief Prosecutor v. Syed Md. Hachhan	2	2
Total		32	11

It may be mentioned that at the ICT-BD, the genocide conviction rate is much less than the overall conviction rate. As per the following *Table-6*, the overall conviction rate is 67% *i.e.* 134 out of 200 at the ICT-BD.

Table -6 demonstrates that in *Abdul Kalam Azad* case[95] 8 charges were brought and the prosecution could prove 7 charges, in the case against *Abdul Quader Molla*[96] 6 charges were brought but the prosecution could prove only 5 charges, in the case against *Delowar Hossain Sayeedi*[97] 20 charges were brought but the prosecution could prove only 8 charges, in the case against *Muhammad Kamaruzzaman*[98] 7 charges were brought but the prosecution could prove only 5 charges, in the *Ghulam Azam* case[99] 5 charges were brought and the prosecution could prove all the 5 charges, in the *Muhammad Mujahid* case[100] 7 charges were brought but the prosecution could prove only 5 charges, in the *Salauddin Quader Chowdhury* case[101] 23 charges were brought however the prosecution could only prove 9 charges, in the *Abdul Alim* case[102] 17 charges were brought but the prosecution could prove only 9 charges, in the case against *Ashrafuzzaman Khan and Chowdhury Mueen Uddin*[103] 11 charges were brought and the prosecution could prove all the 11 charges and in the

---

[95] *Abdul Kalam Azad, op. cit. no. 1.*

[96] *Abdul Quader Molla, op. cit. no. 2.*

[97] *Delowar Hossain Sayeedi, op. cit. no. 3.*

[98] *Muhammad Kamaruzzaman, op. cit. no. 4.*

[99] *Ghulam Azam, op. cit. no. 5.*

[100] *Ali Ahsan Muhammad Mujahid, op. cit. no. 6.*

[101] *Salauddin Quader Chowdhury, op. cit. no. 7.*

[102] *Md. Abdul Alim, op. cit. no. 8.*

[103] *Ashrafuzzaman Khan & Chowdhury Mueen Uddin, op. cit. no. 9.*

Motiur Rahman Nizami case[104] 16 charges were brought but the prosecution could prove only 8 charges.

Table-6 further shows that in the *Mir Quasem Ali* case[105] 14 charges were brought and the prosecution could prove only 10 charges, in the *Zahid Hossain Khokon* case[106] 11 charges were brought but the prosecution could prove 10 charges, in the *Mobarak Hossain* case[107] 5 charges were brought but the prosecution could prove only 2 charges, in the *Md. Qaiser* case,[108] 16 charges were brought but the prosecution could prove only 14 charges, in the *Azharul Islam* case[109] 6 charges were brought but the prosecution could prove only 5 charges, in the *Abdus Sobhan* case[110] 9 charges were brought but the prosecution could prove only 6 charges, in the *Abdul Jabbar* case[111] 5 charges were brought and the prosecution could prove all the 5 charges, in the *Mahidur and Afsar Hossain* case[112] 3 charges were brought but the prosecution could prove only 2 charges, in the *Md. Hachhan* case[113] 6 charges were brought but the prosecution could prove only 5 charges and in the *Md. Forkan Mallik* case[114] 5 charges were brought but the prosecution could prove only 3 charges.

---

[104]   *Motiur Rahman Nizami, op. cit. no.* 10.

[105]   *Mir Quasem Ali, op. cit. no.* 11.

[106]   *Zahid Hossain Khokon, op. cit. no.* 12.

[107]   *Md. Mobarak Hossain, op. cit. no.* 13.

[108]   *Syed Md. Qaiser, op. cit. no.* 14.

[109]   *A. T. M. Azharul Islam, op. cit. no.* 15.

[110]   *Moulana Abdus Sobhan, op. cit. no.* 16.

[111]   *Md. Abdul Jabbar Engineer, op. cit. no.* 17.

[112]   *Md. Mahidur Rahman & Md. Afsar Hossain, op. cit. no.* 18.

[113]   *Hachhen Ali, op. cit. no.* 19.

[114]   *Md. Forkan Mallik, op. cit. no.* 20.

Thus, the total number of charges in all these 20 cases was 200 while the prosecution could prove only 134 charges. Therefore, the overall conviction rate is only 67%. This average conviction rate is undoubtedly higher than the conviction rate in genocide charges *i.e.* 34.37%.

Table 6

SL No.	Cases	Number of Charges	Number of Conviction
1	*Chief Prosecutor v. Abdul Kalam Azad*	08	07
2	*Chief Prosecutor v. Abdul Quader Molla*	06	05
3	*Chief Prosecutor v. Delowar Hossain Sayeedi*	20	08
4	*Chief Prosecutor v. Muhammad Kamaruzzaman*	07	05
5	*Chief Prosecutor v. Ghulam Azam*	05	05
6	*Chief Prosecutor v. A. A. Muhammad Mujahid*	07	05
7	*Chief Prosecutor v. Salauddin Quader Chowdhury*	23	09
8	*Chief Prosecutor v. M. A. Alim*	17	09
9	*Chief Prosecutor v. Ashrafuzzaman & Mueenuddin*	11	11
10	*Chief Prosecutor v. Motiur Rahman Nizami*	16	08
11	*Chief Prosecutor v. Mir Quasem Ali*	14	10
12	*Chief Prosecutor v. Zahid Hossain Khokon*	11	10

13	*Chief Prosecutor v. Mobarak Hossain*	05	02
14	*Chief Prosecutor v. Syed Md. Qaiser*	16	14
15	*Chief Prosecutor v. A. T. M. Azharul Islam*	06	05
16	*Chief Prosecutor v. Abdus Sobhan*	09	06
17	*Chief Prosecutor v. Md. Abdul Jabbar*	05	05
18	*Chief Prosecutor v. Mahidur & Afsar Hossain*	03	02
19	*Chief Prosecutor v. Syed Md. Hachhan*	06	05
20	*Chief Prosecutor v. Md. Forkan Mallik*	05	03
Total		**200**	**134**

5.7 Trend 6: Punishment for Genocide Charges

Under the purview of Section 20(2) of the *ICTA*, the Tribunal can award 'sentence of death or such other punishment proportionate to the gravity of the crime as appears to the Tribunal to be just and proper'[115] to the convicts.

Table-7 portrays that in all the cases concerning *Abdul Kalam Azad*;[116] *Azharul Islam*;[117] and *Md. Hachhan*,[118] the Tribunal awarded 'sentence of death' to the genocide charges. However, the Tribunal awarded 'sentence of death' in two genocide charges and 'imprisonment for life' in other two charges to *Salauddin*

---

[115]   Section 20(2) of the *ICTA* of 1973.

[116]   *Abdul Kalam Azad, op. cit. no. 1.*

[117]   *A. T. M. Azharul Islam, op. cit. no. 15.*

[118]   *Hachhen Ali, op. cit. no. 19.*

Quader Chowdhury.[119] On the other hand, in both the *Abdul Alim*[120] and *Abdul Jabbar*[121] cases, the Tribunal awarded 'imprisonment for life' to the genocide charges.

Table 7

SL No.	Cases	Total Number of Genocide Conviction	Punishment
1	*Chief Prosecutor v. Abdul Kalam Azad*	01	Sentence of Death
2	*Chief Prosecutor v. Salauddin Quader Chowdhury*	04	Sentence of Death (Charges 5 & 6) Imprisonment for 20 Years (Charges 2 & 4)
3	*Chief Prosecutor v. M. A. Alim*	02	Imprisonment for Life
4	*Chief Prosecutor v. A. T. M. Azharul Islam*	01	Sentence of Death
5	*Chief Prosecutor v. Md. Abdul Jabbar*	01	Imprisonment for Life
6	*Chief Prosecutor v. Syed Md. Hachhan*	02	Sentence of Death

---

[119] *Salauddin Quader Chowdhury, op. cit. no. 7.*

[120] *Md. Abdul Alim, op. cit. no. 8.*

[121] *Md. Abdul Jabbar Engineer, op. cit. no. 17.*

5.8 Conclusion

Trend 1 portrays that out of the concerned 20 cases, genocide charges were brought in only 12 cases *i.e.* 60% cases. Besides, this trend also shows that out of 20 charges total 32 charges were brought in relation to genocide *i.e.* 16% charges. *Trend 2* represents that the total number of charges related to mass atrocities was 53 while the total number of genocide charges was only 32 *i.e.* 60.3% genocide charges. *Trend 3* explores that in all the 12 cases in which the genocide charges were brought against the accused, the common method of committing genocide was 'killing members of the group/s' *i.e.* 100% charges were genocide by killing. *Trend 4* puts on view that in all the 12 cases the perpetrators mostly targeted the 'religious group' with the intention to destroy such group while in a very few cases, it has been found that other groups such as political, racial, ethnic, and national were targeted by the perpetrators. *Trend 5* portrays that the total number of genocide convictions were 11 out of 32 *i.e.* genocide conviction rate is 34.37%, whereas overall conviction rate is 67%. Finally, *Trend 6* shows that the highest punishment awarded to the convicts under the genocide charges was death sentence while the lowest punishment is 20 years of imprisonment.

Chapter 6

Rationales behind the Trends in Genocide Charges

6.1 Introduction

The trends discussed in the previous chapter have been found from the thorough study of the genocide charges of the first 20 cases decided by the ICT-BD. The trends explored that the Prosecution brought lesser number of genocide charges; and less number of genocide charges compared to the "mass killing" incidents. Again, the Prosecution considered only "killing" as the method of committing the crime of genocide while in certain charges the Prosecution faced legal challenges to establish group identification requirement. Moreover, the overall conviction rate of the genocide charges and the punishments awarded for the same have been explored. After identifying such trends of the genocide charges of such cases, five rationales behind such trends have been explored with some critical appraisals.

For this purpose, this chapter focuses on the rationales that, the Prosecution faced legal challenges to prove in a number of cases, beyond reasonable doubt, both the target group as well as genocidal intent requirements which are essential to constitute genocide. Further, the Prosecution in a number of cases faced legal challenges to produce witnesses and adduce adequate evidences to prove the genocide charges. Finally, the ICT-BD changed the characterization of some of the genocide charges into the 'crimes against humanity' charges and simultaneously, the ICT-BD was reluctant in a number of cases to take into account the genocide charges.

6.2 The Prosecution Faced Legal Challenges to Prove the Group Requirement

In a number of genocide charges, the Prosecution faced legal challenges to prove, beyond reasonable doubt, the target group requirement of genocide. For illustrations, the subsequent discussion addresses the observations of the ICT-BD in the following cases:

In the *Zahid Hossain Khokon* case, the Charge No. 5 was on "genocide, murder, abduction, confinement, torture and other inhumane acts" in which the Prosecution alleged that the perpetrators targeted to destroy a "political group" *i.e.* the *Awami League* (AL) since the killed persons were the supporters of AL.[1] Nevertheless, the ICT-BD held that it does not appear from the evidence on record that the killed persons were the supporters of the AL. In its place, the Tribunal observed that the targeted people were unarmed innocent civilians including females and babies and thus, such killing constituted the offence of "murder" as crimes against humanity instead of the offence of "genocide".[2] The observation of the Tribunal reads as follows:

---

[1]   *The Chief Prosecutor vs. Zahid Hossain Khokon @ M. A. Zahid @ Khokon Matubbar @ Khokon*, ICT-BD Case No. 04 of 2013 [ICT-BD 1], at para 115 at pages 60-61.

[2]   *Id.*

'The Prosecution has argued that since the killed persons were the 'supporters of Awami League', they deserve to be considered to belong to a 'group' for the purpose of constituting the offence of 'genocide'. Conversely, the defence has contended that the 'supporters of Awami League' did not belong to any 'stable' group. The Genocide Convention does not protect all types of 'human groups'. Its application is confined to national, ethnical, racial or religious group. In addition to these four groups, the *Act* of 1973 protects the 'political group' as well. It does not appear from the evidence on record that the killed persons were the supporters of Awami League. Rather we have already found the accused responsible for the killing of eighteen unarmed innocent civilians including females and babies and for other crimes against humanity. We are persuaded to conclude that the killing of eighteen unarmed civilians constituted the offence of 'murder' as crimes against humanity, instead of the offence of 'genocide'.'[3]

Likewise, in the Charge No. 10 of this case which was also on "genocide, killing and other inhumane acts", as regards the killing of the family members of Mini Begum, a supporter of AL, the ICT-BD found that the perpetrators killed the unarmed civilian people as a part of "systematic attack". The findings of the Tribunal have been quoted below:

'[O]n examination of evidence we do not find satisfactory elements of genocide. The basic principle of the concept of 'genocide' is

---

[3]   *Id.*

indiscriminate and systematic destruction of members of a group because they belong to that particular group. Merely the killing of a number of individuals in a particular village in a 'systematic' manner cannot be the only object for an inference as to constitution of genocide. It is the Prosecution case that Mini Begum being a supporter of Awami League, ... was targeted by accused Zahid Hossain Khokon and the Rajakars and as such her family members were brutally killed by the accused and the Pakistani occupation army. But, from the evidence of PW-20 it reveals that she was a student of class IV in 1971 and thus it is not acceptable to us that the said witness belonged to the political party Awami-League in 1971 and as such her inmates were killed as targeted by the Rajakars and Pakistani army. But it has been well proved that the inmates of PW-20, the civilian unarmed people, were killed by accused Zahid Hossain Khokon and Pakistani army as a part of 'systematic' attack."[4]

Considering these findings, the Tribunal finally concluded that the charge of genocide on the ground of destructing "political group" has not been successfully proved by the Prosecution and so the offences of murder and other inhumane acts constitute as the "crimes against humanity".[5] The final observation of the ICT-BD reads as follows:

'[W]e are of the view that the charge of genocide has not been proved but accused Zahid Hossain Khokon has substantially contributed and

---

[4]   *Ibid,* at pages 96-97 at para 184.

[5]   *Id.*

participated in committing the offences of murder and other inhumane acts [plundering and arson] as crimes against humanity ...'[6]

In the *Syed Md. Qaiser case*, in the Charge No.16 of "genocide or in the alternative extermination", the Prosecution argued that the "Kaiser Bahini" targeted the civilians of Hindu "religious group" and killed them as well as fired their houses with the intent to vanish this particular group.[7] However, based on the statements of the witnesses, the Tribunal deliberated that the victims who were killed in such attack included both the Muslim and Hindu religious people.[8] In this regard, the Tribunal noted that:

> '... [t]hough Prosecution intents to argue that with the attack, the civilians mostly belonged to Hindu religion have been killed and their houses have been set ablaze. But from the testimony of PW -3 who proved ... to have accompanied Kaiser as the accomplices of 'Kaiser Bahini' and participated in the carnage has categorically admitted that both Muslim and Hindu lived in the villages where the crackdown had been perpetrated.'[9]

To be more specific, the Tribunal referred to the testimony of the Prosecution Witness (PW) no. 16 stating that:

> 'PW-16 did not state in his testimony the dead body 31 in number, he found after the carnage,

---

6   *Id.*

7   *The Chief Prosecutor vs. Syed Md. Qaiser,* ICT-BD Case No. 04 of 2013 [ICT-BD 2], at page 471 at para 1635.

8   *Id.*

9   *Id.*

belonged to Hindu community rather from the testimony of PW-31, we find that all the deceased he named in his chief belonged to Muslim community. So, in view of the above testimony of those sighted witnesses it can be concluded that, no crime of 'Genocide' has been perpetrated with the [k]illing and monstrous act perpetrated on the date of event.'[10]

Based on the above-mentioned findings and reasoning, the Tribunal concluded that instead of 'genocide', the perpetrator is responsible for committing the 'crimes against humanity' of 'extermination'. Concerning this observation, one of the Judges of the ICT-BD very lucidly mentioned that:

'I am of the view that, even a single killing would qualify the crime of 'extermination' if it is proved from the evidences and attending circumstances the attack had been designed to commit widespread killing on a large section of unarmed civilians where numerical accuracy, location and number of dead bodies killed and exact number of crime zone will in no way shake the charge like extermination, one of the component of 'Crimes against Humanity'.'[11]

In the Charge No. 3 of the *A.T.M. Azharul Islam case*, the Tribunal asserted similar deliberations that since the killed persons of the concerned event were not only Hindus but also Muslims, it could not be concluded that the alleged killing was committed with intent to destroy, in whole or in part, the Bangalee national

---

[10] *Ibid*, at page 472 at para 1636.

[11] *Ibid*, at page 472 at para 1638.

group or Hindu religious group.[12] Hence, the Tribunal concluded that, the crimes committed in such events did not constitute the crime of "genocide" for the above mentioned reason.[13] As regards the submission of the Prosecution and the defence, the Tribunal pointed out that:

> '... [t]he Prosecution has argued that since the [killed] persons were the Bangalees and Hindus they deserve to be considered to belong to 'Bangalee national group' and a 'Hindu religious group' respectively for the purpose of constituting the offence of 'genocide'. Conversely, the defence has contended that the [killed] persons were not only Hindus and they were not killed targeting them as a Bangalee national group.'[14]

Referring to the aforesaid arguments, the Tribunal concluded that'[i]t does not appear from the evidence on record that the [killed] persons were all Hindus. Rather we have already found that many Muslims were also killed.'[15]

The Charge No. 6 of the *Abdus Sobhan* case was about targeting both the "national and religious groups". As per the observation of the ICT-BD, it is apparent that the Prosecution faced legal challenges to produce adequate evidence before the Tribunal to establish "group requirement" of proving the crime of genocide.[16]

---

[12]   *The Chief Prosecutor vs. A. T. M. Azharul Islam*, ICT-BD Case No. 05 of 2013 [ICT-BD 1], at pages 72-73 at para 123.

[13]   *Id.*

[14]   *Ibid*, at pages 72-73 at para 129.

[15]   *Id.*

[16]   *The Chief Prosecutor vs. Moulana Abdus Sobhan*, ICT-BD Case No. 01 of 2014 [ICT-BD 2], at page 118 at para 420.

The Tribunal observed that '... [t]he evidence presented before us does not show the 'group requirement' and the 'intent requirement' the necessary elements to characterize the killing of civilians as the offence of 'genocide'.'[17]

Similarly, the Prosecution alleged in the Charge No. 10 of the *Abdul Alim* case that the perpetrators targeted the "freedom fighters group (!)" but the ICT-BD rightly stated that the "freedom fighters group" does not belong to the indelible groups.[18] To be more precise, the Tribunal's deliberations can be mentioned in the following:

> 'The accused has been indicted for abetting and contribution to the commission of the offence of 'genocide' by killing 26 'freedom fighters'. Prosecution argued that since the detained persons were 'freedom fighters' they deserve to be considered to belong to a 'group', for the purpose of constituting the offence of 'genocide'. We disagree. They did not belong to any 'stable' group.'[19]

On the basis of the above-mentioned reasoning, in respect of the event of killing of 26 civilians who were essentially "freedom fighters", the Tribunal took decision as regards Charge No. 10 that the killing constituted the offence of 'murder' as crimes against humanity instead of the offence of 'genocide'.[20]

---

[17] *Id.*

[18] *The Chief Prosecutor vs. Md. Abdul Alim @ M. A. Alim*, ICT-BD Case No. 01 of 2012 [ICT-BD 2], at page 127 at para 469.

[19] *Id.*

[20] *Id.*

6.3 The Prosecution Faced Legal Challenges to Prove the Genocidal Intent Requirement

In some of the cases of the ICT-BD, the Tribunal explicitly deliberated that the Prosecution faced legal challenges to prove, beyond reasonable doubt, the genocidal intent requirement of the perpetrators. However, it must be stated that proving the element of genocidal intent in a charge of genocide is always the most difficult task for the Prosecution. For instances, the observation of the two prominent cases have been discussed in the following:

In the *A.T.M. Azharul Islam* case, as regards Charge No. 3 on "murder, genocide, plundering and arson" the Tribunal noted that the persons who were killed belong to not only the Hindu religious group but also to the Muslim religious group.[21] Considering this fact, the ICT-BD concluded that it is not proved, beyond reasonable doubt, that the perpetrators killed the victims with the intent to destroy, in whole or in part, the Hindu religious group.[22] For this reason, the Tribunal held that the killing of the unarmed civilians amounted to the offence of "murder" as crimes against humanity in the place of the offence of "genocide".[23] Specifically, as regards the reason(s) as to why the Tribunal was not satisfied that the genocidal intent of the perpetrators was present in such incident of killing the civilians, the Tribunal stated that:

> '[w]e do not ... find any evidence on record that the alleged killing was committed with intent to destroy, in whole or in part, Bangalee national group or Hindu religious group. We are, therefore, persuaded to conclude that the killing

---

[21]   *A. T. M. Azharul Islam, op. cit. no.* 12, at pages 72-73 at para 129.

[22]   *Id.*

[23]   *Id.*

of unarmed civilians constituted the offence of 'murder' as crimes against humanity, instead of the offence of 'genocide'.'[24]

Hence, it is clear that along with the previous reason, another vital reason behind the fall of this charge was the challenges to prove the 'genocidal intent' requirement of the perpetrator.

Correspondingly, in the Charge No. 6 of the *Abdus Sobhan* case in which the Prosecution brought an allegation against the accused for committing the offence of "murder" as crimes against humanity and also for committing the offence of "genocide". Regarding this charge, the Tribunal focused on the factual circumstances mentioned in the charge as provided below:

> 'Accused Moulana Abdus Sobhan the acting Ameer of Pabna district JEI and vice-president of Pabna district peace committee by launching attack, with intent to destroy the Bangalee national group and Hindu religious group either whole or in part ... abducted 400 leaders and workers of Awami League, supporters of the war of liberation and people belonging to Hindu community and killed them... Therefore, the accused has been charged for abetting and facilitating commission of the offences of 'murder' as crimes against humanity and also for the offence of 'genocide'.'[25]

In this particular charge, the ICT-BD pointed out that the Prosecution has faced legal challenges to establish the constituent elements of the offence of 'genocide' on the ground

---

[24] *Id.*

[25] *Moulana Abdus Sobhan, op. cit. no.* 16, at page 90 at para 320.

that the evidences presented before the Tribunal were not sufficient enough to show the "genocidal intent requirement".[26] The Tribunal emphasized on the fact that it is a must to establish specific genocidal intent to prove the crime of genocide against the accused person.[27] For this purpose, the ICT-BD concluded that the attack for which the accused has been charged resulted in large scale killing to be characterized as the offence of 'extermination' instead of genocide.[28] The observation of the Tribunal has been quoted in the following:

> '... the Prosecution has failed to establish the constituent elements of the offence of 'genocide' ... However, it has been proved beyond reasonable doubt that the attack resulted in 'large scale killing' which may lawfully be characterized as the offence of 'extermination'.'[29]

6.4 The Prosecution Faced Challenges to Produce Witnesses and Adduce Adequate Evidences

The ICT-BD observed in many cases that either the Prosecution could not produce witnesses and/or adduce adequate evidences to establish the crime of genocide. For examples, to prove the genocide charges such as the Charge Nos. 2 and 4 of the *Delowar Hossain Sayeedi* case, and the Charge Nos. 9 and 13 of the *Salauddin Quader Chowdhury* case, the Prosecution could not produce a single witness before the Tribunal due to their non-availability.[30]

---

[26] *Ibid*, at page 118 at para 420.

[27] *Id.*

[28] *Id.*

[29] *Id.*

[30] *The Chief Prosecutor vs. Delowar Hossain Sayeedi*, ICT-BD Case No.

Concerning both Charge Nos. 2 and 4 of the *Delowar Hossain Sayeedi* case, the Tribunal noted the following observation:

> 'Facts remain that the Prosecution could not produce any oral or documentary evidence to prove the occurrences mentioned in Charge Nos. 2 and 4 except statement of seven witnesses recorded by the investigation officer ... It is undisputed that not a single maker of those statements has been examined to prove the occurrances [*sic*] and as such it is undeniable that the defence did not get an opportunity to cross-examine those makers of statements to find out the truth. The statements of witnesses recorded by the investigation officer are always considered as unsafe documents and if the maker of such statement is not confronted during trial, such unsafe statement loses its credibility.'[31]

Thus, it has been clear-cut that in the Charge Nos. 2 and 4 of the *Delowar Hossain Sayeedi* case, the Prosecution established such charges referring to the statements of the witnesses as recorded by the investigation officer; however, it has been conceded by the Prosecution that the relevant witnesses could not be presented before the Tribunal during the trial process.[32] Therefore, in relation to the responsibility of the accused, the Tribunal reflected the following opinion:

---

01 of 2011 [ICT-BD 1], at page 47 at para 86; *The Chief Prosecutor vs. Salauddin Quader Chowdhury*, ICT-BD Case No. 02 of 2011 [ICT-BD 1], at page 42 at para 73.

[31] *Ibid, Sayeedi,* at pages 49-50 at para 95.

[32] *Ibid,* at pages 47-48 at para 86.

'... we are of the opinion that the statements of witnesses recorded ... alone do not form the basis of conviction and such statement of witnesses may be used as corroborative evidence to prove a particular occurrence. It is further observed that the Tribunal may gather information about the conduct of the accused by using statement of witnesses but no one can be held criminally responsible solely on the basis of such statement of witnesses ...'[33]

In this same case, the Prosecution also faced legal challenges to produce documentary evidence to prove the said charges of genocide.[34] Therefore, the ICT-BD held that depending on the witnesses' statements simply the information can be gathered about the conduct of the accused person but he could not be held criminally responsible merely based on the same.[35]

Likewise, to establish the Charge No. 12 of the *Delowar Hossain Sayeedi* case, Charge No. 9 of the *Motiur Rahman Nizami* case, Charge No. 2 of the *Mohammad Mujahid* case, Charge Nos. 1, 11, and 12 of the *Salauddin Quader Chowdhury* case, Charge Nos. 2 and 3 of the *Zahid Hossain Khokon* case, the Prosecution could not produce any evidence before the ICT-BD to connect the accused with the commission of the crime of genocide.

Beginning with the Charge No. 12 of the *Delowar Hossain Sayeedi* case, the ICT-BD stipulated that even though the Prosecution produced witnesses during the trial process, they could not

---

[33]   *Ibid*, at page 50 at para 96.

[34]   *Ibid*, at pages 49-50 at para 95.

[35]   *Ibid*, at page 50 at para 96.

connect the witnesses' statements with the commission of the accused.[36] To quote:

> 'The Prosecution has examined as many as 28 witnesses to prove 20 charges as framed against the accused ... It is evident that Prosecution witnesses have narrated different incidents involving the accused but none has entengled [sic] him with the commission of genocide in question.'[37]

In the Charge No. 15 of this case, corresponding to the previous reasoning the Tribunal stated that '... [t]wo statements of witnesses recorded by the investigation officer ... have been perused but those statements could not connect the accused with the commission of genocide alleged committed.'[38] Upon scrutiny of the evidence on record it transpires that Prosecution could not produce any evidence before this Tribunal to connect the accused with the commission of crime of genocide as stated in Charge No. 15.[39]

In the *Motiur Rahman Nizami* case, the Tribunal pointed out that there was no eye witness presented during the trial process.[40] The Tribunal also noted that even though all the witnesses were hearsay witnesses, 'none of the victim families has been examined by the Prosecution to prove the charge against the accused, nor it has been explained by the Prosecution for non-examination of

---

[36]   *Ibid*, at pages 85-86 at paras 182-183.

[37]   *Id*.

[38]   *Ibid*, at page 93 at para 197.

[39]   *Id*.

[40]   *The Chief Prosecutor vs. Motiur Rahman Nizami*, ICT-BD Case No.03 of 2011 [ICT-BD 1], at pages 121-122 at para 246.

such person[s]'.[41] Moreover, concerning the liability of the accused in relation to this particular charge the Tribunal observed that:

> '... it appears to us that only the four witnesses adduced hearsay evidence having no probative value to rely upon. The involvement of the accused with the commission of those offences appears to be doubtful, and as such the benefit of doubt must be given to the accused. Consequently, we are inclined to hold that the Prosecution has failed to prove the instant charge beyond reasonable doubt ...'[42]

In the *Muhammad Mujahid* case, the Tribunal found that the Prosecution could not establish the involvement of the accused with the alleged crime.[43] The ICT-BD, therefore, decided that the accused was not liable for the specific offence for which he has been charged.[44] To be more precise, the deliberation of the Tribunal is given in the following:

> '...itappearsthattheeventofmasskillingdirecting the Hindu unarmed civilians constituting the offence alleged has been proved. From evidence it stands proved too that a group of Razakars, peace committee members, Pakistani army committed the crimes alleged. But Prosecution has failed to prove that the accused Ali Ahsan Muhammad Mujahid accompanied the group towards the crime sites. Reasonable doubt has

---

41   *Id.*

42   *Ibid*, at page 123 at para 248.

43   *The Chief Prosecutor vs. Ali Ahsan Muhammad Mujahid*, ICT-BD Case No. 04 of 2012 [ICT-BD 2], at page 92 at para 294.

44   *Id.*

been created as to the fact of accompanying the group of perpetrators by the accused the benefit of which goes in favour of him.'[45]

In the *Salauddin Quader Chowdhury* case, on the charge of genocide (Charge No. 1), the Tribunal negated to hold the accused responsible solely depending on uncorroborated single hearsay evidence.[46] The findings of the ICT-BD have been mentioned below:

> 'In order to prove this charge Prosecution has examined only one witness ... it is evident that Prosecution has failed to produce any reliable evidence to connect the accused with the commission of offences of crimes against humanity and genocide as specified in the above charge. ... In the above context it is our considered opinion that it is very much unsafe to convict a person on the basis of uncorroborated single hearsay evidence. Thus, we hold that the Prosecution has failed to prove Charge No. 1 beyond reasonable doubt.'[47]

Likewise, in two other charges (Charge Nos. 11 and 12) of this case, the Tribunal provided the reasoning that since the Prosecution could not adduce adequate evidence connecting the accused with the alleged crimes, he could not be held liable for the same based on such weak evidences. Interestingly, as regards charge 11, the Tribunal stipulated that:

---

[45]   *Id.*

[46]   *Salauddin Quader Chowdhury, op. cit. no.* 30, at pages 42-43 at para 78.

[47]   *Id.*

'PW 24 in cross-examination has stated that he does not know whether he told the name of accused *Salauddin Quader Chowdhury* to the investigation officer. He cannot remember whether he as the informant lodged the Boalkhali P.S. Case No. 49 dated 28-02-1972 regarding the killing of his father. He cannot remember whether he stated the date of his father's death as 16-05-1971 in that case. He has also stated in cross-examination that he cannot remember whether he inserted the name of accused *Salauddin Quader Chowdhury* in the first information report of that case. The evidence of PW 24 is considered a weak type of evidence as well as uncorroborated one and as such we are of the opinion that the Prosecution has failed to prove the Charge No.11 beyond reasonable doubt.'[48]

Finally, in the *Zahid Hossain Khokon* case, both the Charge Nos. 2 and 3 were related to "forceful conversion of the Hindus into Muslim religious group" which the Prosecution could not successfully prove before the Tribunal.[49] In detail, the observation of the Tribunal is being quoted below:

'... Considering the contention of the Prosecution it can be said that there is no necessity to prove the physical torture directly with the victim by adducing evidence. Torture may happen in different ways, like mental pressure, forceful conversion, intimidation for deportation, even

---

[48] *Ibid*, at pages 114-115 at para 182.

[49] *Zahid Hossain Khokon, op. cit. no. 1*, at pages 36-37 at paras 77 and 78 and at pages 42-43 at paras 90-91.

by way of making loudly sound of horn to the victims etc.'[50]

Based on the stated arguments of the Prosecution, the Tribunal depicted that:

'In the light of discussion as narrated above by a careful scrutiny of the evidence, it is crystal clear that offences of arson [inhumane act], torture by way of conversion from Hindus to Muslims and deportation committed by the accused during the Liberation War of 1971 as a Razakar as well as commander of Razakar Bahini of Nagarkanda Thana unit. The offence of genocide indicted in the charge against the accused has not been established as it lacks evidence.'[51]

6.5 The Tribunal Changed the Legal Characterization of Genocide Charges into CAH by Murder or Extermination (Non-Genocide Convictions)

In many of the ICT-BD cases, the Tribunal itself used to change the legal characterization of the genocide charges into mostly the crimes against humanity by murder or extermination. To begin with, the *A.T.M. Azharul Islam* case can be referred in which the ICT-BD changed the legal characterization of the genocide charge into the crimes against humanity of murder on the ground that the Prosecution could not adduce relevant evidence to prove the crime of genocide.[52] The findings of the Tribunal read as follows:

---

[50]   *Ibid*, at pages 42-43 at para 90.

[51]   *Ibid*, at page 43 at para 91.

[52]   *A. T. M. Azharul Islam, op. cit. no. 12*, at pages 72-73 at para 129.

'... it does not appear from the evidence on record that the [killed] persons were all Hindus. Rather we have already found that many Muslims were also killed ... We are, therefore, persuaded to conclude that the killing of unarmed civilians constituted the offence of 'murder' as crimes against humanity, instead of the offence of 'genocide'.'[53]

For this same reason, on the charge of genocide or alternatively 'extermination' in the case of *Syed Md. Qaiser*, the Tribunal made the accused liable for committing the crimes against humanity of extermination.[54] The Tribunal very specifically mentioned that the Prosecution tried to argue that with the attack, the civilians mostly belonged to Hindu religion have been killed and their houses have been set ablaze but from the evidences it has become clear that both the Muslim and Hindu lived in the villages where the crackdown had been perpetrated by the "*Kaiser Bahini*".[55] The findings of the Tribunal are quoted below:

'PW -16 did not state in his testimony the dead body 31 in number, he found after the carnage, belonged to Hindu community rather from the testimony of PW -31 we find that, all the deceased he named in his chief belonged to Muslim community. So, in view of the above testimony of those sighted witnesses it can be concluded that, no crime of 'Genocide' has been perpetrated with the [k]illing and monstrous act perpetrated on the date of event.'[56]

---

[53]   *Id.*

[54]   *Syed Md. Qaiser, op. cit. no. 7*, at page 471 at para 1635.

[55]   *Id.*

[56]   *Ibid*, at pages 472 at para 1636.

In the case of *Motiur Rahman Nizami*, the ICT-BD observed that 'the pattern and feature of the persecution lead us to conclude that it was a "large scale killing" having all the required elements to constitute the offence of extermination as crimes against humanity, although the accused has been charged for [committing genocide by killing professionals and intellectuals].'[57] Pointing out the requirements of proving genocide, the ICT-BD also pondered in the *Abdus Sobhan* case that the Prosecution could establish neither the group requirement nor the genocidal intent requirement but it has been established that the perpetrators launched an attack which caused "large scale killing".[58] Hence, the Tribunal considerably characterized such offence as the crimes against humanity of "extermination".[59] In detail, in the *Abdus Sobhan* case the Tribunal stated that:

> '... the evidence presented before us does not show the 'group requirement' and the 'intent requirement' the necessary elements to characterize the killing of civilians as the offence of 'genocide'. However, it has been proved beyond reasonable doubt that the attack resulted in 'large scale killing' which may lawfully be characterized as the offence of 'extermination'.'[60]

In the case of *Zahid Hossain Khokon*, in order to prove the charge on "destruction of houses and intimidations to the Hindus for conversion, and deportation and genocide", considering the evidences produced by the Prosecution, the ICT-BD stipulated that it is not essential to directly prove the physical torture against

---

[57]   *Motiur Rahman Nizami, op. cit. no. 40,* at pages 159-160 at para 327.

[58]   *Moulana Abdus Sobhan, op. cit. no. 16,* at page 118 at para 420.

[59]   *Id.*

[60]   *Id.*

the victim by adducing evidence because the same may happen in different ways.[61] The Tribunal specially referred to the ways by which torture can be committed *i.e.* by causing mental pressure, forceful conversion, intimidation for deportation, even by way of making loudly sound of horn to the victims *etc.*[62] Finally, the Tribunal depicted that as there are lack of evidences to establish the crime of genocide, the offences of deportation and torture by way of forceful conversion lawfully constitute the crimes against humanity.[63] In this case, the ICT-BD characterized another two charges of genocide as the crimes against humanity of "murder" and "other inhumane acts" (plundering and arson). Both the charges were allegedly related to the perpetrator's intent to destroy the "political group", wholly or partly.[64] The ICT-BD very rightly focused on the stand-point that merely the killing of the members of a definite locality in a "systematic" manner cannot be the only object for an inference as to constitution of genocide.[65] The Tribunal required to produce adequate evidences and to connect the same with the act of the accused but the Prosecution could not do so.

Surprisingly, in the *Mohammed Mujahid* case the ICT-BD changed the legal characterization of the charge of genocide into the crimes against humanity of "extermination".[66] The accused mainly charged for abetting and facilitating the commission of offence of 'murder as crime against humanity'.[67] Alternatively, he was charged for abetting as well as facilitating to commit the

---

[61]   *Zahid Hossain Khokon, op. cit. no. 1*, at pages 42-43 at para 90.

[62]   *Id.*

[63]   *Id.*

[64]   *Ibid*, at pages 60-61 at para 115 and at pages 96-97 at para 184.

[65]   *Id.*

[66]   *Ali Ahsan Muhammad Mujahid, op. cit. no. 43*, at pages 160 at para 499.

[67]   *Ibid*, at page 120 at para 386.

crime of 'genocide' with the target of destroying the 'intellectual group' either wholly or partly.[68] In the discussion of the criminal liability of accused focusing on this charge, the Tribunal noted that:'... the accused *Ali Ahsan Muhammad Mujahid*, for his acts, conduct, inciting statement, speech and culpable association with Al-Badar is criminally responsible for all the criminal acts resulting from the criminal design of this Al-Badar force and shall be punished as if he himself committed them, irrespective of whether and in what manner he himself directly participated in the commission of any of these acts ...'[69]

From the reasoning of the Tribunal on this charge, it is clear that the Tribunal did not provide any particular reason as to why it has changed the legal characterization of the crime of genocide into the crimes against humanity.[70]

6.6 ICT-BD Considered Lesser Number of Genocide Charges Compared to CAH Charges

Throughout the trial processes, the ICT-BD used to change the characterization of genocide charges into CAH. In *Motiur Rahman Nizami* case, the Tribunal viewed regarding genocide by killing professionals and intellectuals in Charge No. 16 that the accused substantially contributed to the commission of the crime 'exterminations' as crimes against humanity.[71] Stating so, the ICT-BD converted the genocide charge into the charge of the crimes against humanity. The findings of the ICT-BD as regards the scenario of this particular charge are mentioned in the following: '... it is proved beyond reasonable doubt that accused Motiur

---

[68]   *Id.*

[69]   *Ibid*, at pages 160 at para 499.

[70]   *Id.*

[71]   *Motiur Rahman Nizami, op. cit. no.* 40, at pages 159-160 at para 327.

Rahman Nizami was the president of Islami Chhatra Sangha since 1966 upto at least 30ᵗʰ September, 1971, and he was then ex-officio commander of Al- Badr Bahini and, as such, he was aware of consequence of his act and conduct that substantially encouraged, endorsed, approved, provided moral support to the Al-Badr men in committing the killing of intellectuals. The accused's authoritative position on Al-Badr, both as *de jure* and *de facto*, is a fair indication that he had 'effective control' and ability over the members of Al-Badr ... and thus he cannot be relieved from responsibility of planned crimes committed by Al-Badr men with whom he had a 'relationship'...'[72]

Now, the deliberation of the Tribunal concerning responsibility of the accused is given in the following:

> '... the accused as chief of Al-Badr Bahini exercised his superior status but he never tried to prevent his subordinates from committing atrocities ... He is thus found guilty for substantially contributing to the commission of the offence 'exterminations' as crimes against humanity.'[73]

Similarly, in the genocide Charge Nos. 2 and 3 of the *Zahid Hossain Khokon* case, it is very surprising that the argument of causing mental harm to members of Hindu religious group by forcing them to convert their religion into Muslim religion was not considered as a method of committing genocide.[74] The Tribunal observed that: '... it is found that the accused rendered mental pressure on the victims including PW 23 to be converted as Muslims against their will and the accused also forced them

---

[72]   *Id.*

[73]   *Id.*

[74]   *Zahid Hossain Khokon, op. cit. no. 1,* at pages 42-43 at para 90.

[victims] to follow Islamic rituals. Prosecution has argued that mental pressure to the victims by way of conversion against their will is also fallen in the form of torture as specified in the *Act*. Considering the contention of the Prosecution it can be said that there is no necessity to prove the physical torture directly with the victim by adducing evidence. Torture may happen in different ways, like mental pressure, forceful conversion, intimidation for deportation, even by way of making loudly sound of horn to the victims etc.'[75]

From the above views, the ICT-BD held that the accused is guilty of committing the offences of deportation and torture by way of forceful conversion as crimes against humanity under Section 3(2) (a)(g) and (h) of the *ICTA*.[76] The final observation of the Tribunal is given in the following: '... it is crystal clear that offences of arson [inhumane act], torture by way of conversion from Hindus to Muslims and deportation committed by the accused during the Liberation War of 1971 as a Razakar as well as commander of Razakar Bahini of Nagarkanda Thana unit. The offence of genocide indicted in the charge against the accused has not been established as its lack of evidence. Therefore, we are led to hold that the Prosecution has been able to prove the aforesaid offences in both the Charge Nos. 02 and 03 beyond all reasonable doubt against the accused that had direct participation in the commission of those atrocities. As such, accused Zahid Hossain Khokon is criminally liable and held him guilty for his substantial contributions to the actual commission of the offences of deportation and torture by way of forceful conversion as crimes against humanity.'[77]

---

[75] *Id.*

[76] *Ibid,* at page 43 at para. 91.

[77] *Id.*

Hence, it can be concluded that the ICT-BD was certainly unwilling to consider the genocide charges in some cases.

6.7 Conclusion

The conclusion of this chapter can be drawn by stipulating that the challenges that the Prosecution faced to prove the genocide charges is found as the major reason behind the trends explored in the chapter 5. However, in respect of the discussed rationales behind such trends, it must be mentioned that proving "genocidal intent and group requirements" demands a higher threshold of producing witnesses and adducing adequate evidences. Thus, to prove "genocidal intent" in the cases of the ICT-BD after 40 years of happening of the concerned incidents puts an extra burden on the Prosecution. Hence, the Prosecution, on strategic purposes, mostly preferred to frame and to prove the charges of the ICT-BD cases under the "crimes against humanity" so that the crimes committed by the perpetrators do not remain unpunished. Though it appears that the Prosecution could not successfully prove a good number of genocide charges before the Tribunals, it should not be regarded that they could not prove the alleged crimes as a whole. For this reason, the Tribunal was also prone to change the legal characterization of the genocide charges considering the relevant evidences, statements of the witnesses, and arguments of the Prosecution to establish the "crimes against humanity" as an alternative to the "crime of genocide".

Bibliography

Books

- A. M. A. Muhith, *Bangladesh: Emergence of a Nation* (Dhaka: University Press Limited, 1978).

- A. Qayyum Khan, *Bittersweet Victory: A Freedom Fighter's Tale* (Dhaka: University Press Limited, 2013).

- A. S. M. Shamsul Arefin, *Associates of Pakistan Army* (Dhaka: Swaraj Prokashony (2nd ed.) 2009).

- Abdul Wahab, *One Man's Agony: A Sketch Book of Yahyan Oppression* (Dhaka: University Press Limited (2nd ed.) 1998).

- Ahmad Selim (ed.), *We Owe an Apology to Bangladesh* (Dhaka: Shahitya Prakash, 2012).

- Anthony Mascarenhas, *The Rape of Bangla-Desh* (Delhi: Vikas Publications, 1972).

- Archer K. Blood, *The Cruel Birth of Bangladesh: Memories of an AmericanDiplomat* (Dhaka: University Press Limited, 2002).

- Dan Stone, *The Historiography of Genocide* (New York: Palgrave Macmillan (1st ed.), 2008).

- Daniel Feierstein, *Genocide as Social Practice: Reorganizing Society under the Nazis and Argentina's Military Juntas* (New Brunswick, New Jersey and London: Rutgers University Press: (1st ed.), 2014).

- Faruq Aziz Khan, *Spring 1971: A Centre Stage Account of Bangladesh War of Liberation* (Dhaka: University Press Limited (2nd ed.) 1998).

- Frank Chalk & Kurt Jonassohn, *The History and Sociology of Genocide: Analysis and Case Studies* (New Haven and London: Yale University Press, 1990).

- Freda Utley, *The High Cost of Vengeance* (Chicago: Henry Regnery Company, 1949).

- G. W. Choudhury, *The Last Days of United Pakistan* (Dhaka: University Press Limited, 2011).

- Gul Hassan Khan, *Memoirs of Lt. Gen. Gul Hassan Khan* (Oxford University Press, 1993).

- Hasina Ahmed, *Media and the Liberation War of Bangladesh, Vol-III* (Dhaka: Centre for Bangladesh Studies, 2005).

- Humayun Kabir, Maulana Abul Kalam Azad: *India Wins Freedom* (Madras: Orient Longman, 1988).

- J. F. R. Jacob, Surrender at Dacca: Birth of A Nation (Dhaka: University Press Limited (3rd ed.), 2004).

- Kalim Bahadur, *The Jama'at-i-Islam of Pakistan: Political Thought and Political Action* (Lahore: Progressive Books, 1983).

- Kamal Hossain, *Bangladesh: Quest for Freedom and Justice* (Dhaka: University Press Limited, 2013).

- Khadim Hussain Raja, *A Stranger in My Own Country: East Pakistan, 1969-1971* (Dhaka: University Press Limited, 2012).

- Larry Collins & Dominique Lapierre, *Freedom at Midnight* (New Delhi: Tarang Paperbacks, 1978).

- M A Hasan and Tom Degan, *Beyond Denial: The Evidence of a Genocide* (London: New Millennium Publishing (1st ed.), 2013).

- M. A. Mannan & Chowdhury Sharifa Mannan (eds.), *International Documents of Great Liberation War in Bangladesh [1970-71] Vol-I* (Dhaka: Jatiyo Grontho Prokashan, 2008).

- M. A. Mannan & Chowdhury Sharifa Mannan (eds.), *International Documents of Great Liberation War in Bangladesh [1970-71] Vol-II* (Dhaka: Jatiyo Grontho Prokashan, 2008).

- M. Asghar Khan, *We've Learnt Nothing from History-Pakistan: Politics and Military Power* (Dhaka: University Press Limited, 2013).

- Mahmudul Islam, *Constitutional Law of Bangladesh* (Dhaka: Mullick Brothers (3rd ed.), 2012).

- Mohammad Ayub Khan, *Friends Not Masters: A Political Autobiography* (Dhaka: University Press Limited, 2008).

- Muhammad Nurul Quader, *Independence of Bangladesh in 266 Days: History and Documentary Evidence* (Dhaka: Mukto Publishers (4th ed.) 2012.

- Muntassir Mamoon, *Media and the Liberation War of Bangladesh, Vol-II* (Dhaka: Centre for Bangladesh Studies, 2002).

- Musa Kkhan Jalalzai, *Sectarianism in Pakistan* (Lahore: A. H. Publishers, 1992).

- Pervez Musharraf, *In the Line of Fire: A Memoir* (New York: Simon & Schuster, 2006).

- Rao Forman Ali Khan, *How Pakistan Got Divided* (Lahore: Jang Publishers, 1992).

- Raunaq Jahan, *Eyewitness Accounts: Genocide in Bangladesh* (New York: Garland Publishing, 1997).

- Reaz Ahmed, *Media and the Liberation War of Bangladesh, Vol-I* (Dhaka: Centre for Bangladesh Studies, 2002).

- Robert Gallately and Ben Kiernan, *The Specter of Genocide: Mass Murder in Historical Perspective* (New York: Cambridge University Press (1st ed.), 2003).

- Robert Payne, *Massacre: The Tragedy at Bangla-Desh and the Phenomenon of Mass Slaughter throughout History* (Macmillan Company (1st ed.), 1973).

- Rudolph J. Rummel, *Death by Government* (New Brunsweek, NJ: Transaction Publishers, 1994).

- Rudolph J. Rummel, *Statistics of Democide: Genocide and Mass Murder Since 1900* (Münster: LIT Verlag Minister, 1998).

- Seyyed Vali Reza Nasr, *The Vanguard of the Islamic Revolution: The Jama'at-i-Islami of Pakistan* (Los Angeles: University of California Press, 1994).

- Sheikh Mujibur Rahman, *The Unfinished Memoirs* (Dhaka: University Press Limited, 2013).

- Siddiq Salik, *Witness to Surrender* (Karachi: The University Press Limited, 1st ed., 1997).

- Sukumar Biswas, *Japan and the Emergence of Bangladesh* (Dhaka: Agami Prokashoni (1st ed.) 1998).

- Susan Brownmiller, *Against Our Will: Men, Women and Rape* (New York: Simon & Schuster, 1975).

- Tariq Ali, *The Duel: Pakistan on the Flight Path of American Power* (New York, Scribner, 2008).

- Tureen Afroz, *Genocide, War Crimes, & Crimes against Humanity in Bangladesh: Trial under International Crimes (Tribunals) Act, 1973* (Dhaka: Forum for Secular Bangladesh and Trials of War Criminals of 1971 (1st ed.), 2010).

- William A. Schabas, *Genocide in International Law: The Crime of* Crimes (New York: Cambridge University Press (2nd ed.), 2009).

- William B. Milam, *Bangladesh and Pakistan: Flirting with Failure in South Asia* (Dhaka: University Press Limited, 2010).

- Zahid Hossain (ed.), *Voice of Freedom* (Dhaka: Bangabandhu Parishad, 1999).

Journal Articles

- Adam Jones, "The Bangladesh Genocide Comparative Perspective," (2014) *Journal of the 1st Winter School* (Center for the Study of Genocide and Justice), Liberation War Museum.

- Ashfaque Hossain and Umme Wara, "The United Nations and the International Crimes (Tribunal) Act 1973 of Bangladesh," (2014) *Journal of the 1st Winter School* (Center for the Study of Genocide and Justice), Liberation War Museum.

- Hans W. Baade, "The Eichmann Trial: Some Legal Aspects," (1961) *Duke Law Journal*.

- Jean Galbraith, "New Facts' in ICTY and ICTR Review Proceedings," (2008) 21(1) *Leiden Journal of International Law*.

- Jonathan A Bush, "Lex Americana: Constitutional Due Process and the Nuremberg Defendants," (2001) 45 *Saint Louis University Law Journal*.

- M Rafiqul Islam, "Adoption of the *International Crimes (Tribunals) Act, 1973*: Its History and Application, Non-retroactivity and Amendments," (2014) *Journal of the 1st Winter School* (Center for the Study of Genocide and Justice), Liberation War Museum.

- Md. Sayedur Rahman, Md. Tanziul Islam, and Abu Reza Md. Towfiqul Islam, "Evaluation of Charismatic

Leader of Bangabandhu Sheikh Mujibur Rahman," 2014(4) *International Journal of Scientific and Research Publications.*

- Michael J. Bazyler and Julia Y. Scheppach, "The Strange and Curious History of the Law Used to Prosecute Adolf Eichmann," (2012) 34 *Loyola of Los Angeles International and Comparative Law Review.*

- Mirjan Damaska, "Structures of Authority and Comparative Criminal Procedure," (1975) 84 *Yale Law Journal.*

- Peter D Marshall, "A Comparative Analysis of the Right to Appeal," (2011) *Duke Journal of Comparative and International Law.*

- S.A. Karim, "Triumph and Tragedy," (2009) *The University Press Limited.*

- Tessa Mckeown, "Nuremberg: Procedural Due Process at the International Military Tribunal," (2013) *Victoria University of Wellington.*

- Wali-ur-Rahman, "A Brief History of the Farming of the *International Crimes (Tribunals) Act, 1973,*" (Dhaka, 2009).

- Wali-ur-Rahman, "Background Notes on Adoption of 1973 International Crimes (Tribunal) Act,1973," (2014) *Journal of the 1st Winter School* (Center for the Study of Genocide and Justice), Liberation War Museum.

- Wardatul Akman, "Atrocities against Humanity during the Liberation War in Bangladesh," (2002) 4*Journal of Genocide Research.*

209

- Yasmin Saika, "Beyond the Archive of Silence: Narratives of Violence of the 1971 Liberation War of Bangladesh," (2004) 58 *History Workshop Journal.*

Laws

- The *Bangladesh Collaborators (Special Tribunals) Order,*1972.

- The *Bangladesh Collaborators (Special Tribunals) (Repeal) Ordinance,* 1975.

- The *Constitution of the People's Republic of Bangladesh,* 1972.

- The *International Crimes (Tribunals) Act (No. XIX),*1973.

- The *Statute of theInternational Crimes Tribunal for Rwanda,* 1994.

- The *Statute of theInternational Crimes Tribunal for the Former Yugoslavia,* 1993.

- The*Rome Statute of the International Criminal Court,*1998.

- The *Statute of the Special Tribunal of Lebanon,* 2007.

Cases

Bangladesh

- *Abdul Quader Molla vs. The Government of the People's Republic of Bangladesh, represented by the*

Chief Prosecutor, International Crimes Tribunal, Dhaka, Bangladesh, Criminal Appeal Nos.24-25 of 2013.

• *Abdul Quader Mollah v. The Chief Prosecutor*, Criminal Review Petition Nos. 17-18 of 2013.

• *Bangladesh National Women Lawyers Association vs. Ministry of Home Affairs*, (2009) 61 DLR 371.

• *H.M. Ershad v. Bangladesh*, (2001) BLD (AD) 69.

• *Muhammad Kamaruzzaman vs. The Government of Bangladesh represented by the Chief Prosecutor*, International Crimes Tribunal, Dhaka, Criminal Review Petition No. 8 of 2015.

• *The Chief Prosecutor vs. Abdul Quader Molla*, ICT-BD Case No. 2 of 2012 [ICT-BD 2].

• *The Chief Prosecutor vs. Ashrafuzzaman Khan@ Naeb Ali Khan & Chowdhury Mueen Uddin,* ICT-BD Case No. 1 of 2013[ICT-BD 2].

• *The Chief Prosecutor vs. Delowar Hossain Sayeedi,* ICT-BD Case No. 1 of 2011[ICT-BD 1].

• *The Chief Prosecutor vs. Professor Ghulam Azam,* ICT-BD Case No. 6 of 2011[ICT-BD 1].

• *The Chief Prosecutor vs. A.T.M. Azharul Islam,* ICT-BD Case No. 5 of 2013[ICT-BD 1].

• *The Chief Prosecutor vs. Ali Ahsan Muhammad Mujahid,* ICT-BDCase No. 4 of 2012[ICT-BD 2].

- *The Chief Prosecutor vs. Md. Abdul Alim @ M.A. Alim*, ICT-BD Case No.1 of 2012 [ICT-BD 2].

- *The Chief Prosecutor vs. Md. Abdul Alim @ M.A. Alim*, ICT-BD Case No. 1 of 2012 [ICT-BD 2].

- *The Chief Prosecutor vs. Md. Abdul Jabbar Engineer*, ICT-BD Case No. 1 of 2014[ICT-BD 1].

- *The Chief Prosecutor vs. Md. Forkan Mallik @ Forkan*, ICT-BD Case No. 3 of 2014[ICT-BD 2].

- *The Chief Prosecutor vs. Md. Mahidur Rahman & Md. Afsar Hossain @ Chutu*, ICT-BD Case No. 2 of 2014[ICT-BD 2].

- *The Chief Prosecutor vs. Md. Mobarak Hossain @ Mobarak Ali*, ICT-BD Case No. 1 of 2013[ICT-BD 1].

- *The Chief Prosecutor vs. Mir Quasem Ali*, ICT-BDCase No. 3 of 2013[ICT-BD 2].

- *The Chief Prosecutor vs. Motiur Rahman Nizami*, ICT-BDCase No. 3 of 2011 [ICT-BD 1].

- *The Chief Prosecutor vs. Moulana Abdul Kalam Azad*, ICT-BDCase No. 5 of 2012[ICT-BD 2].

- *The Chief Prosecutor vs. Moulana Abdus Sobhan*, ICT-BDCase No. 1 of 2014 [ICT-BD 2].

- *The Chief Prosecutor vs. Muhammad Kamaruzzaman*, ICT-BDCase No. 3 of 2012[ICT-BD 2].

- *The Chief Prosecutor vs. Salauddin Quader Chowdhury*, ICT-BDCase No. 2 of 2011[ICT-BD 1].

- *The Chief Prosecutor vs. Sheikh Sirajul Haque alias Siraj Master, Khan Akram Hossain, and Abdul Latif Talukder,*ICT-BD Case No. 3 of 2014 [ICT-BD 1].

- *The Chief Prosecutor vs. Syed Md. Hachhan alias Syed Md. Hasan alias Hachhen Ali,* ICT-BDCase No. 2 of 2014[ICT-BD 1].

- *The Chief Prosecutor vs. Syed Md. Qaiser,* ICT-BDCase No. 4 of 2013[ICT-BD 2].

- *The Chief Prosecutor vs. Zahid Hossain Khokon @ M.A. Zahid @ Khokon Matubbar @ Khokon,* ICT-BD Case No. 4 of 2013[ICT-BD 1].

ICTR

- *The Prosecutor vs. Akayesu,* (ICTR Trial Chamber), September 2, 1998.

- *The Prosecutor vs. Bagilishema,* (ICTR Trial Chamber), June 7, 2001.

- *The Prosecutor vs. Bagosora, Kabiligi, Ntabakuze* and *Nsengiyumva,* (ICTR Trial Chamber), December 18, 2008.

- *The Prosecutor vs. Gacumbitsi,* (ICTR Trial Chamber), June 17, 2004.

- *TheProsecutor vs. Kajelijeli,* (ICTR Trial Chamber), December 1, 2003.

- *The Prosecutor vs. Kambanda,* (ICTR Appeal Chamber), 19 October, 2000.

- *The Prosecutor vs. Kamuhanda,* (ICTR Trial Chamber), January 22, 2004.

- *The Prosecutor vs. Karera,* (ICTR Trial Chamber), December 7, 2007.

- *The Prosecutor vs. Kayishema and Ruzindana,* (ICTR Trial Chamber), May 21, 1999.

- *The Prosecutor vs. Muhimana,* (ICTR Trial Chamber), April 28, 2005.

- *TheProsecutor vs. Musema,* (ICTR Trial Chamber), January 27, 2000.

- *The Prosecutor vs. Muvunyi,* (ICTR Trial Chamber), September 12, 2006.

- *The Prosecutor vs. Ntagerura, Bagambiki, and Imanishimwe,* (ICTR Trial Chamber), February 25, 2004.

- *The Prosecutor vs. Ntakirutimana,* (ICTR Appeals Chamber), December 13, 2004.

- *The Prosecutor vs. Rugambarara,* (ICTR Trial Chamber), November 16, 2007.

- *The Prosecutor vs. Rutaganda,* (ICTR Trial Chamber), December 6, 1999.

- *TheProsecutor vs. Semanza,* (ICTR Trial Chamber), May 15, 2003.

- *The Prosecutor vs. Seromba,* (ICTR Trial Chamber), December 13, 2006.

- *The Prosecutor vs. Simba,* (ICTR Trial Chamber), December 13, 2005.

ICTY

- *The Prosecutor vs. Blagojevic* and *Jokic,* (ICTY Trial Chamber), January 17, 2005.

- *The Prosecutor vs. Brdjanin,* (ICTY Trial Chamber), September 1, 2004.

- *The* Prosecutor vs. *Delalic et.al.,* (ICTY Trial Chamber), 16 November, 1998.

- *The Prosecutor vs. Krstic,* (ICTY Trial Chamber), August 2, 2001.

- *The Prosecutor vs. Stakic,* (ICTY Trial Chamber), July 31, 2003.

- *The Prosecutor vs. Vasiljevic,* (ICTY Trial Chamber), November 29, 2002.

INDIA

- *Adamji Umer Dolal vs. State of Bombay,* AIR (1952) SC 14.

- *Ambaram vs. State of M.P.,* AIR (1976) SC 2196.

- *Bachan Singh vs. State of Punjab* (1980) 2 SCC 684.

- *Delhi Gang Rape Case.*

- *Mahesh vs. State of M.P.,* AIR (1987) SC 1346.

- *Mangal Singh vs. State of U.P.*, AIR 1975 SC 76.

- *Mohammad Ajmal Amir Kasab vs. State of Moharastra*, Criminal Appeal No. 1899 – 1900 of 2011<http://indiankanoon.org/doc/193792759/>.

- *Registrar General, High Court of Karnataka vs. PrakashJadav*, 2006 CrLJ 3393 (3409).

- *Roghunath vs. Paria*, AIR 1967 Goa 95.

- *Satwant Singh vs. State of Punjab*, AIR 1960 SC 266.

- *Sham Sundar vs. Puran*, AIR 1991 SC 8.

- *Shashi Nayar vs. Union of India*, AIR 1992 SC 395.

- *State of Karnataka vs. Krishna alias Raju*, 1987 1 SCC 538.

ISRAEL

- *Attorney General v. Adolf Eichmann*, Criminal Case No. 40/61.

SCSL

- *The Prosecutor of the Special Court vs. Issa Sesay, Morris Kallon and Augustine Gbao*, (SCSL Trial Chamber), March 2, 2009.

UNITED KINGDOM

- *Connelly vs. Director of Public Prosecutions*[1964] A.C. 1254 at 1306 [H.L.(E.)].

Miscellaneous

- A Government gazette notification of 30 November 1973 shows that none of the war criminals had been pardoned; Suzannah Linton, "Completing the Circle: Accountability for the Crimes of the 1971 Bangladesh War of Liberation" (2010) 21 *Criminal Law Forum*.

- Bangabandhu's General Amnesty Declaration: Documentary Evidences and Relevant Stories, <http://www.ebangladesh.com/2010/07/24/bangabandhus-general-amnesty-declaration/>.

- Chintito, "Justice Delayed is Never Justice Denied," 9(12) *The Daily Star Weekend Magazine* (19 March 2010) <http://www.thedailystar.net/magazine/2010/03/03/chintito.htm>.

- Caitlin Reiger, "Fighting Past Impunity in Bangladesh: A National Tribunal for the Crimes of 1971" International Centre for Transnational Justice, Briefing Paper, July 2010.

- S Ahamed, "Trials and Error," *BD News* (5 June 2010) at page 13 <http://opinion.bdnews24.com/2010/06/05/trials-and-error/, 5 June 2010>.

- Justice Mohammad Gholam Rabbani, "The International Crimes (Tribunals) Act, 1973," Genocide, War Crimes & Crimes Against Humanity in Bangladesh, Trial under *International Crimes (Tribunals) Act*, 1973, Forum for Secular Bangladesh and Trial of War Criminal of 1971.

- *Figures from the Fall of Dacca byJagjit Singh Aurora in the Illustrated Weeklyof India*, 23 December, 1973.

- "Father of the Nation: Bangabandhu Sheikh Mujibur Rahman," High Commission for Bangladesh, London <http://www.bhclondon.org.uk/Father%20of%20the%20Nation.html>.

- Humayun Reza, 'War Crimes and Genocide in 1971: The Reality of the Trial' - a paper presented at the International Conference on Genocide, Truth and Justice, Dhaka, 1-2 March 2008; Conference Proceeding 2008.

- Nazrul Islam, "Pro-liberation Forces' Unity can Defeat War Criminals," *The Daily Star* (12 November 2007) <http://www.thedailystar.net/story.php?nid=11199>.

- M. A. Hasan, "War Crime Trials: Our Failure and Future," *The Daily Star* (14 December 2007) <http://archive.thedailystar.net/newDesign/news-details.php?nid=15341>.

- "Memory and Justice," *The Daily Star* (15 November 2013) <http://www.thedailystar.net/memory-and-justice-3100>.

- Tureen Afroz, "Trish Lokkho Shohider Shongkhya Totto," *The Bangladesh Protidin*(2 January 2016) <http://www.bd-pratidin.com/first-page/2016/01/02/118433>.

- Andreas Krieg, "The Nuremberg Trials: An Attempt of Bringing War Criminals to Justice," (2009) *The Pica Project*<www.thepicaproject.org>.

- Anne Klerks,Trials in Absentia in International (Criminal) Law, 18 <http://arno.uvt.nl/show.cgi?fid=81103>.

- Nazi Conspiracy and Aggression – Chapter IV, <http://www.yale.edu/lawweb/avalon/imt/document/nca_vol1/chap_04.htm>.

- Center on Law and Globalization <https://clg.portalxm.com/library/keytext.cfm?keytext_id=189>.

- Charter of the Nuremberg International Military Tribunal <http://www.yale.edu/lawweb/avalon/imt/proc/imtconst.htm#art12>.

- *Eichman's Case*, Matěj Jungwirth, The Aspirations and Shortcomings of Nazi Trials: Cases of the Nuremberg and Eichmann <http://postnito.cz/the-aspirations-and-shortcomings-of-nazi-trials-cases-of-the-nuremberg-and-eichmann/>.

- Extraordinary Chambers in the Courts of Cambodia, *Internal Rules* (Rev.1) as revised on 1 February 2008, Rule 8 <http://www.eccc.gov.kh/english/cabinet/fileUpload/27/Internal_Rules_Revision1_01-02->.

- **Human Rights Committee, General Comment 6, Article 6 (Sixteenth session, 1982), Compilation of General Comments and General Recommendations Adopted by Human Rights Treaty Bodies, U.N. Doc. HRI/GEN/1/Rev.1 at 6 (1994) <https://www1.umn.edu/humanrts/gencomm/hrcom6.htm>.**

- Kok-Thay Eng, Redefining Genocide <http://www.genocidewatch.org/images/AboutGen_Redefining_Genocide.pdf>.

- Law on the Establishment of the Extraordinary Chambers, with inclusion of amendments as promulgated on 27 October 2004 (NS/RKM/1004/006), article 33 <http://www.eccc.gov.kh/english/cabinet/law/4/ KR_Law_as_amended_27_Oct_2004_Eng.pd>.

- Report of the Secretary-General on the establishment of a special tribunal for Lebanon, UN Doc. S/2006/893, 15 November 2006, at paragraph 32.

- Ricky Gunawan, 'Death penalty does not deter drug traffickers,' *Jakarta (Online)*, December 10, 2014 <http://www.thejakartapost.com/news/2014/12/10/ death-penalty-does-not-deter-drug-traffickers.html>.

- 'Safeguards Guaranteeing Protection of the Rights of those Facing the Death Penalty, Approved by Economic and Social Council resolution 1984/50 of 25 May 1984'; <http://www.ohchr.org/EN/ProfessionalInterest/Pages/ DeathPenalty.aspx>.

- Special Court for Sierra Leone, *Rules of Procedure and Evidence* (amended on 19 November 2007), <http://www.sc-sl.org/Documents/rulesofprocedureand evidence.pdf>.

- Nuremberg Trials <http://www.history.com/topics/world-war-ii/nurem berg-trials>.

- United Nations-Treaty Series (No. 1021) <https://treaties.un.org/doc/publication/unts/volume% 2078/volume-78-i-1021-english.pdf>.

- Utkarsh Anand, How the Apex Court Defines 'Rarest of Rare', *The Indian Express* (Online), 12 February 2013

<http://archive.indianexpress.com/news/how-the-apex-court-defines-rarest-of-rare/1072728/>.

- *Bangladesh Documents Vol. II* (New Delhi: Ministry ofExternal Affairs, 1971).

- *Report of the Redress Trust* (London: Redress Trust, August 2004).

- *Shangshad BitorkoKhondo 2*, Shonkhya 37 (Bangladesh).

- International Criminal Law & Practice Training Materials, International Criminal Law Services <http://wcjp.unicri.it/deliverables/docs/Module 4 International war crimes courts.pdf>.

- Sarah Williams, *Hybrid International Criminal Tribunals* [2014] DOI: 10.1093/OBO/9780199796953-0069.

- Judgement of Bormann, <http://www.yale.edu/lawweb/avalon/imt/proc/judborma.htm>.

- *The Prosecutor vs. Sesay, Kallon and Gbao* (SCSL-04-15-T), 'Ruling on the issue of Refusal of the Third Accused, Augustine Gbao, to Attend Hearing of the Special Court for Sierra Leone on 7 July 2004 and succeeding days', 7 July 2004, <http://www.sc-sl.org/Transcripts/RUF-070704.pdf>.

- Nuremberg Trial Proceedings (Volume 2), 23 November 1945.

www.ingramcontent.com/pod-product-compliance
Lightning Source LLC
Chambersburg PA
CBHW030430290526
45786CB00001B/224